Australian Edition

Online Share Investing

FOR

DUMMIES®

by James Frost and Matt Krantz

WILEY

Wiley Publishing Australia Pty Ltd

Online Share Investing For Dummies®

Australian Edition published by
Wiley Publishing Australia Pty Ltd
42 McDougall Street
Milton, Qld 4064
www.dummies.com

Copyright © 2009 Wiley Publishing Australia Pty Ltd

Original English language edition text and art copyright © 2008 Wiley Publishing, Inc. This edition published by arrangement with the original publisher, Wiley Publishing, Inc., Indianapolis, Indiana, USA.

The moral rights of the authors have been asserted.

National Library of Australia

Cataloguing-in-Publication data

Author:	Frost, James.
Title:	Online Share Investing for Dummies / James Frost; Matt Krantz.
Edition:	Australian ed.
ISBN:	978 0 7314 0940 2 (pbk.)
Series:	For Dummies
Notes:	Includes index.
Subjects:	Stocks — Australia.
	Investment analysis.
	Investments — Computer network resources.
	Investments — Computer network resources — Directories.
	Electronic trading of securities.
	Portfolio management.
	Websites — Directories.
Other authors:	Krantz, Matt.
Dewey number:	332.602854678

All rights reserved. No part of this book, including interior design, cover design and icons, may be reproduced or transmitted in any form, by any means (electronic, photocopying, recording or otherwise) without the prior written permission of the Publisher. Requests to the Publisher for permission should be addressed to the Contracts & Licensing section of John Wiley & Sons Australia, Ltd, 42 McDougall Street, Milton, Qld 4064 or online at www.johnwiley.com.au/html/aboutwiley/permissions.html.

Printed in China by
Printplus Limited

10 9 8 7 6 5 4 3 2 1

About the Authors

James Frost is a finance journalist and online evangelist.

James joined *Eureka Report* in 2005 as a reporter; his writing has also appeared in *Smart Company* and the *Independent Weekly*. In 2007, he began producing podcasts for theage.com.au and smh.com.au. In 2008, he became the deputy commentary editor of *Business Spectator* and, later that year, he began writing the blog 'Everybody's Business' for *SBS World News Australia*.

James holds a degree in professional writing and undertook studies at both Deakin University, Victoria, and San Diego State University, California.

James also spent five years working for global internet measurement firm Hitwise in various roles before and after the first internet boom and the emergence of Web 1.0.

Matt Krantz is known across the United States as a financial journalist who specialises in investing topics. He has been a writer for *USA TODAY* since 1999, where he covers financial markets and Wall Street, concentrating on developments affecting individual investors and their portfolios. His stories routinely signal trends that investors can profit from, and that sound warnings about potential scams and issues investors should be aware of.

In addition to covering markets for the print edition of *USA TODAY*, Matt writes a daily online investing column called 'Ask Matt', which appears every trading day at USATODAY.com. He answers questions posed by the website's audience in an easy-to-understand manner. Readers often tell Matt he's the only one who has been able to finally solve investing questions they've sought answers to for years.

Matt has been investing since the 1980s and has studied dozens of investment techniques while forming his own. And, as a financial journalist, Matt has interviewed some of the most famous and infamous investment minds in modern history. Before joining *USA TODAY*, Matt worked as a business and technology reporter for *Investor's Business Daily* and was a consultant with Ernst & Young prior to that.

He earned a bachelor's degree in business administration at Miami University in Oxford, Ohio. Unlike other business majors who just focused on accounting, finance and investments, Matt took journalism classes in his own time. He was an editor of the campus newspaper and filed stories to several newspapers, including the *Cincinnati Enquirer*.

In addition to appearing in the print and online pages of *USA TODAY*, Matt's work has also been featured in *Men's Health* magazine. He has spoken for investing groups, including at the national convention of BetterInvesting and on *Nightly Business Report*, which airs on PBS.

Dedication

From James: This book would never have occurred without the encouragement of various people who convinced me that not only was writing a fun and interesting thing to do, but that it can also be a way to earn a living. Among them, thanks go to teachers such as Mrs Gemmill from St Augustine's Kyabram, as well as Clive O'Connell, Father Stan Hogan, Annie Rubira and Trish Thompson from Xavier College.

I would especially like to thank my mother and father, Carmel and Jeremy, who have supported any and all of my ill-advised attempts to become a writer. My mother, in particular, has been an invaluable sounding board for many chapters of this book. Mum, I couldn't have done it without you.

Finally, I would like to thank the lady in my life for whom the sun rises, the stars shine and the tide goes in and out. For your patience, encouragement and unconditional love, Michelle, I am eternally grateful.

From Matt: This book is dedicated to my wife Nancy, who has supported and carried me throughout the entire project from the very beginning. During the bleary-eyed writing sessions sitting in front of the computer at 1 am, Nancy was always there to suggest that perfect word I couldn't think of, bring in fresh-cut strawberries or read every single page. The book is also dedicated to my daughter, Leilani, who put up with a dad who was almost as nervous about being a first-time book author as he was being a first-time parent.

Author's Acknowledgements

From James: Thanks first to Charlotte Duff, who not only spearheaded the project but had the added pressure of having to talk me down from the ledge from time to time. A huge thanks to Kerry Davies, who is not only a talented and incredibly thorough editor, but clearly the most patient person on the planet. Thanks also to the efforts of Robi van Nooten of the Australian editorial team and John Wiley's US editors Carrie Burchfield and Jen Bingham, who kept me on the straight and narrow. And to Gabrielle Packman and Brigid Baker for their tireless efforts in tracking everything down and keeping things orderly.

I'd also like to thank various people at Australian Independent Business Media for their support, encouragement and ideas; in particular, *Business Spectator*'s editor-in-chief Alan Kohler, and *Eureka Report*'s editor James Kirby and sub-editor James Harrison. I'd also like to thank *Business Spectator*'s commentary editor Rob Burgess.

Thanks also go to the following people for their technical expertise and knowledge: Craig James and Matt Comyn at CommSec, Bruce Bramall at Stantins, Stephen Mayne of *The Mayne Report*, Tom Elliot at MM&E Capital, David Reid at Andex Charts, Pia Cooke at Macquarie, Ian Rogers at *The Sheet*, Alice Bennett at Merrill Lynch, Christine Winter at Morningstar, Tony Lewis of Lewis Securities, Louise Nealon at Callidus PR, John Daley at E*TRADE, Sandra Hanchard and Harley Giles of Hitwise, and Ben Silluzio of UBS, as well as everyone at Paritech, optionsXpress and Yahoo!7 Australia.

I'd also like to thank the writers of the US editions of *Investing Online For Dummies*, Kathleen Sindell and Matt Krantz, for writing such engaging and well-thought-out books.

A special thankyou goes to Trish Power, a great writer and an inspiration, without whom this book would never have come about.

From Matt: Staring at a flashing cursor on a blank Microsoft Word window, knowing I needed to fill hundreds of pages in a few months, was an intimidating task. That's why all the support I received kept me going. My editors at *USA TODAY* supported the book from its genesis and encouraged me along the way. My assignment editor, David Craig, as well as other *USA TODAY* editors, including Rodney Brooks, Ray Goldbacher, Jim Henderson, John Hillkirk, Ken Paulson, Geri Coleman Tucker and Kinsey Wilson, have supported this book or my development as a writer and reporter. Chris Woodyard, a fellow business reporter in *USA TODAY*'s Los Angeles bureau, has been a great source of ideas and daily encouragement. My wife, Nancy, continued her personal mission of stomping out every typo on the planet by reading every word in this book over my shoulder.

Wiley has been tremendous to work with as well, including Senior Acquisitions Editor Bob Woerner, Senior Project Editor Paul Levesque and Copy Editor Virginia Sanders. Julie Huynh, Technical Editor, made sure the book was free of 'dead links' by checking every URL. Big thanks to Matt Wagner, my literary agent, for thinking of me for the project and presenting it to me. Fane Lozman provided a hand by sharing his options expertise. Thanks to my mum and dad for instilling, at a very young age, a curiosity in investing, writing and computers (and for buying me my first computer well before having a PC was common). And thanks to my grandparents for teaching me the power of saving and investing.

Publisher's Acknowledgements

We're proud of this book; please send us your comments through our Dummies online registration form located at www.dummies.com/register/.

Some of the people who helped bring this book to market include the following:

Acquisitions, Editorial and Media Development

Project Editors: Kerry Davies, Paul Levesque

Acquisitions Editors: Charlotte Duff, Bob Woerner

Editorial Managers: Gabrielle Packman, Leah Cameron

Production

Layout and Graphics: Wiley Composition Services and Wiley Art Studio

Cartoons: Glenn Lumsden

Proofreader: Marguerite Thomas

Indexer: Don Jordan, Antipodes Indexing

The authors and publisher would like to thank the following copyright holders, organisations and individuals for their permission to reproduce copyright material in this book.

• IRESS Market Technology: page 30 IRESS, Colonial First State • Google Inc.: pages 39, 57 and 113 • Business Spectator: page 50 www.businessspectator.com.au • Newspix: page 52 • belldirect: pages 72 and 81 www.belldirect.com.au • Hubb Financial Group: page 74 optionsXpress Australia • CommSec: pages 77 and 301 www.commsec.com.au • Infochoice: pages 82 and 287 • Scripophily.com: page 93 Scripophily.com — The Gift of History • Ken Horton: pages 133 and 134 • SIMFA: page 148 Securities Industry and Financial Marketers Association, www.SIFMA.org • © Morningstar Australia: pages 152, 172 and 174 • Vanguard Investments Australia: pages 155 and 325 • ING Australia Ltd: page 157 ING DIRECT • © Fairfax Syndications: pages 179, 274 (lower)

and 302 • © Nuveen Investments Corp: page 197 • Barclays Global Investors: page 200 © Barclays Global Investors Australia Limited • Yahoo!7: pages 209, 211, 223, 308 and 322 Reproduced with permission of Yahoo!7 Pty Limited. Copyright © 2008 Yahoo!7 Pty Limited. YAHOO! and associated logos are trademarks of Yahoo! Inc. • ninemsn: pages 238 and 245 ninemsn Money http://money.ninemsn.com.au • Bloomberg L.P.: page 274 (top) © 2008 Bloomberg Finance L.P. All rights reserved. Used with permission.

Every effort has been made to trace the ownership of copyright material. Information that will enable the publisher to rectify any error or omission in subsequent editions will be welcome. In such cases, please contact the Permissions Section of John Wiley & Sons Australia, Ltd who will arrange for the payment of the usual fee.

Publishing and Editorial for Technology Dummies

Richard Swadley, Vice President and Executive Group Publisher

Andy Cummings, Vice President and Publisher

Mary Bednarek, Executive Acquisitions Director

Mary C. Corder, Editorial Director

Publishing for Consumer Dummies

Diane Graves Steele, Vice President and Publisher

Joyce Pepple, Acquisitions Director

Composition Services

Gerry Fahey, Vice President of Production Services

Debbie Stailey, Director of Composition Services

Contents at a Glance

Table of Contents

Introduction

· ·

You may be wondering why you need a book like this one to help you invest online. After all, if you're looking for information about investing online, you can certainly type **investing online** into a search engine and get thousands of search results.

But that's the problem. You get thousands of search results. Some of the sites you find using a search engine may have secret agendas and push financial products hazardous to your goals. Other sites offered up by a search engine may be filled with bad information that isn't correct, causing you to unknowingly make poor investment decisions. Worse yet, you may stumble on fraudulent websites determined to steal your identity or money. Sure, you can find some good websites through a web search, but how can you tell the good from the bad when you get hundreds, if not thousands, of results?

Along comes *Online Share Investing For Dummies*, Australian Edition. This book is here to act as a down-to-Earth guide for getting started with online investing. We steer you clear of unnecessary investing gobbledygook and point you to resources that you can trust. We've already done all the mucking through the thousands of investing websites to find good ones — there's no reason you should have to do so as well!

About This Book

Online Share Investing For Dummies has been completely rewritten in this Australian edition to be your intelligent guide through this often confusing and constantly changing world of investing online. As the authors, we can share the tricks, tips and secrets we've learned from years of writing about online investing for readers just like you. This book saves you the trouble of fumbling through the internet looking for the best online resources. Combined, our experience places us at the forefront of the online investing frontier. As finance reporters with extensive online backgrounds, we know exactly what kind of information you're looking for. Because of the immediacy of the internet, we're both in contact with thousands of investors like you. That puts us in the position of knowing not only the big questions that most investors ask, but the answers too.

Don't worry, *Online Share Investing For Dummies* isn't just a directory of websites that robotically lists hundreds of web addresses and leaves it up to you to look everything up. Those directory-type books, we've found, tend to be frustrating for investors looking for a road map and some handholding to get started investing online. Instead, we've taken special care to bake in principles about investing first and then show you how to use the internet and your computer to boost your success.

This book doesn't attempt to highlight every single investing website, but instead, it focuses on the best ones. Most of the sites we've selected have been around long enough to prove to be reliable and accurate. And, because this book's purpose is to help you make and save money, not spend it, it sticks mainly to websites that are free. When a site requires a subscription, we let you know so you can decide whether the fee is worthwhile.

We have one big caveat. Keep in mind, as you follow our directions to access some of the web pages within a site, that the internet is so fast-changing, you may find a page or two has shifted or a feature is no longer offered. So you may have to ditch our instructions and play around to find what's different. Occasionally even the web address for a homepage may not work. Don't assume the site has gone to internet heaven. Try entering the name of the site into a search engine using techniques described in the first part of the book. More times than not, the site is still online but has just changed its address slightly.

Who Invests Online?

Online investing isn't just an interesting niche for techies and daytraders. As of December 2007, 7.1 million Australians were internet subscribers. More than 4.5 million of them use online transaction facilities provided by their banks. Roughly the same number of people book travel arrangements online and around 3.5 million Australians book event tickets online. But the number of Australians who use the internet to invest is only 1.5 million. Maybe because the rest are too busy booking holidays and going to concerts!

Research conducted by Hitwise Australia shows that online investors are among the most affluent in our society, and data from Nielsen Net Ratings shows that 46 per cent of Australians who fit the online trading category are aged 50-plus. This is interesting for two reasons. First, because it shows the smart money — that's money invested by the wealthy — is being invested or at least tracked online. These are people who know how to make money and keep it, so we should probably pay attention to them! Second, it shows that almost half the people who use the internet for investing purposes are over 50, so if you're not using online tools to manage your investments you're running out of excuses.

Foolish Assumptions

No matter your skill or experience level with investing, you can get something out of *Online Share Investing For Dummies*. We assume some readers haven't invested in anything apart from their wardrobe and have no clue of where to even start. If that describes you, the first part of the book is custom-made for you and takes extra care to step through all the key points, keeping the language in plain English as much as possible. (When we have no choice but to use investing jargon, we'll tell you what it means.) But we also assume more advanced investors may pick this book up too, looking to discover a few things. The book takes on more advanced topics as you progress through it and select online resources that will add new tools to your investing toolbox.

Conventions Used in This Book

We want to help you get the information you need as fast as possible. To help you, we use several conventions:

- ✔ `Monofont` is used to signal a web address. This convention is important because there are so many web addresses in the book. It's also used for spreadsheet functions.

  When this book was printed, some web addresses may have needed to break across two lines of text. If that happened, rest assured that there aren't any extra characters (such as hyphens or spaces) to indicate the break. So, when using one of these web addresses, just type in exactly what you see in this book, pretending that the line break doesn't exist.

- ✔ *Italics* signal that a word is a unique and important term for online investors.

- ✔ **Bold** words make the key terms and phrases in bulleted and numbered lists jump out and grab your attention, or they're words you need to type into a search field.

- ✔ Sidebars, text separated from the rest of the type in grey boxes, are interesting but slightly tangential to the subject at hand. Sidebars are generally fun and optional reading. You won't miss anything critical if you skip the sidebars. If you choose to read the sidebars, though, we think you'll be glad you did.

How the Book Is Organised

All the chapters in this book are self-contained and can be read by themselves. That means you don't need to read *Online Share Investing For Dummies* like you would *Lord of the Rings*, and hopefully you won't fall asleep as much as you might if you were reading *Lord of the Rings* either. Jump around. Flip through. Scan the index and find topics you've been dying to read about for years. And don't fear that you'll get in over your head if you read the back of the book first. If you need to know specific concepts at any point, we carefully add references to those pages in the book so you can jump around. This book is a reference, and you shouldn't feel as if you need to suffer through topics you already know or don't care to know. With that said, though, the book is assembled in a logical order. Our goal is to start simple and then ramp things up as the book goes on.

The book is divided into five parts.

Part I: Getting Started Investing Online

If you like the idea of investing online but haven't the foggiest on where to start, this part is for you. You find everything you need to know to get up and running with online investing, ranging from mastering the terminology to getting your computer set up for online trading. We help you decide what kind of account to open and explain how to pick an online broker. After reading the chapters in this part, you should have a good idea of what's entailed in investing online and what kinds of returns you can expect.

Part II: Using Online Investment Resources

Have you ever seen any of the *Terminator* movies? Apart from featuring Arnold Schwarzenegger alternately destroying and saving the world, the plot involves some sort of computer system that ends up enslaving the human race. If you've ever seen people struggling with and cursing their computers, that sci-fi nightmare isn't all that far-fetched. This part lets you turn the tables on the home computer and put the internet to work for you, rather than getting worked over by the internet. We show you how to get your computer to help you design the perfect portfolio for you.

Part III: Finding the Right Investments

If you've ever wondered why financial advisers get paid the big bucks and what they do all day, you can find out in this part. Here we explore investment products like managed funds and listed managed investments, including exchange-traded funds, and how to find the product that's right for you. Part III also delves into some advanced topics, such as how to pick investments and study a company's financials. What's unique about this part, however, is that it shows you how to do these advanced analyses using your computer and the internet.

Part IV: Expanding Your Investment Opportunities

Investing is a little like going to a restaurant. Some dishes on the menu are tried and true, but the offerings also include options for the more adventurous. This part deals with some of the specialty dishes that the more confident investors choose from time to time. We look at derivatives like going short and buying options. We also show you the different ways people interpret charts and how to buy stocks in companies from other countries.

Part V: The Part of Tens

These final and short chapters wrap up many of the basic lessons illustrated throughout the book in easy-to-digest nuggets. You find ways to avoid making the ten most common online investment mistakes, as well as ten ways to protect your money and identity online.

Icons Used In This Book

When you're flipping through this book, you may notice some icons that catch your attention. That's done on purpose. We use several distinct icons to alert you to sections of the book that stand out.

These icons highlight info that you should etch on the top of your brain and never forget, even when you're getting caught up in the excitement of investing online.

Read these sections to quickly pick up insider secrets that can boost your success when investing online.

Some of the things covered in the book get a bit hairy and complicated. This icon flags such sections for two reasons. First, you may decide to avoid the headache and skip over them — the info isn't vital. Second, the icon is a heads-up that the paragraph is probably loaded with investment jargon. Don't be embarrassed if you need to read the section a second or third time. Hey, you didn't want this book to be too easy, did you?

Avoid the landmines scattered throughout the sharemarket that can decimate your good intentions at building wealth with these sections.

Where to Go from Here

If you're a new investor or just getting started investing online, you may consider starting from the beginning of this book. That way, you're ready for some of the more advanced topics introduced later in the book. If you've already been investing online, have a strategy you think is working for you and are pleased with your online broker, you can skip to Part II. And, if you're dying to know about a specific topic, nothing's wrong with looking up those terms in the index and flipping to the appropriate pages.

Part I
Getting Started Investing Online

Glenn Lumsden

'Could your computer match me up with my ideal online broker?'

In this part ...

The idea of investing online is irresistible to most investors. Low trading commissions, cutting out high-price brokers and gaining tremendous financial control are all possible with online investing. What's not to like, right?

The trouble though, for many investors, is just how to get started. Investing online is laden with enough jargon and websites to send some beginners running. Consider this part to be your user's manual on how to get started investing online. You discover everything you need to know to get yourself and your computer ready to pick, buy and sell investments online. We go over all the key terms you need to know to set up investment accounts, pick a broker and get started. Even more importantly, you discover the main ways to invest online and quickly gain the wisdom of more experienced investors. You also find the answers to two of the most common questions investors ask: 'How do I get started investing online?' and 'How much money do I need to invest online?'

Chapter 1

Getting Yourself Ready for Online Investing

*1*f you've ever watched a baby learn to walk, you've seen how cautious humans are by nature. Babies hold themselves against a wall and scoot along before actually going toe-to-toe with gravity and trying to walk. That anxiety stays with most people as they get older. Before doing something risky, you probably think good and hard about what you stand to gain and what you may lose. Surprisingly, many online investors, especially those just starting out, lose that innate sense of risk and reward. They chase after the biggest possible returns without considering the sleepless nights they'll suffer as those investments swing up and down. Some start buying investments they've heard others made money on without considering whether those investments are appropriate for them. Worst of all, some fall prey to fraudsters who promise huge returns in get-rich-quick schemes.

So, we've decided to take it from the top and make sure the basics are covered. In this chapter, you discover what you can expect to gain from investing online — and at what risk — so you can decide whether this is for you. You also find out how to analyse your monthly budget so you have cash to invest in the first place. And you find what kind of investor you are by using online tools that measure your taste for risk. After you get to know your inner investor better, you can start thinking about forming an online investment plan that won't give you an ulcer.

Why Investing Online Is Worth Your While

Investing used to be easy. Your friend would recommend a broker. You'd give your money to the broker and hope for the best. But today, thanks to the explosion of web-based investment information and low-cost online trading, you get to work a lot harder by taking charge of your investments. Lucky you! So, is the additional work worth it? In our opinion, taking the time to figure out how to invest online *is* worthwhile because

- ✔ **Investing online saves you money.** Online trading is much less expensive than dealing with a broker. You save heaps on commissions and fees, which you can then invest.

- ✔ **Investing online gives you more control.** Instead of entrusting someone else to reach your financial goals, you're personally involved. It's up to you to find out about all the investments at your disposal, but you're also free to make decisions.

- ✔ **Investing online eliminates conflicts of interest.** By figuring out how to invest and doing it yourself, you don't have to worry about being given advice that may be in your adviser's best interest and not yours.

Some of you reading this book may be anxious about events you've seen on TV or read in the papers. Between 30 June 2007 and 30 June 2008, the Australian stock market lost around 16.9 per cent (and the world market's swan dive continues at the time of writing, in October 2008). Investors were understandably upset, especially those with significant sums of superannuation invested in shares.

But what you may not be aware of is that for the previous four years the Australian stock market produced returns of roughly 20 per cent a year. Investors had already produced outstanding profits (in some cases doubling their money) but were unhappy at having to hand some of those profits back. That's understandable . . . but that's investing.

The good thing about investing is that, over time, history has shown that the market continues to reach new highs. To remind you of that fact, the Australian Securities Exchange (the ASX, what used to be called the Australian Stock Exchange) produces a great resource showing the ups and downs of the market from 1900 onwards. Check it out in Figure 1-1. To get the full benefit, though, go to the ASX homepage (www.asx.com.au) and follow these steps:

1. **Click on About ASX Ltd on the left of the page and choose ASX at a Glance.**

2. **Scroll down to History of the Market.**

3. **Click on the link for the Australian market and choose Performance of the All Ordinaries, where you find the document *Australian Share Price Movements*.**

4. **Print it out and keep it somewhere you can see and refer back to.**

   You don't want to go through that search again, do you?

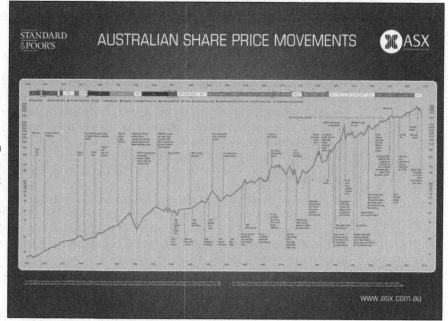

Figure 1-1: This chart of the All Ordinaries since 1900 reminds you that investing is about the long term.

Getting Started

If you don't have a background in finance, investing online can seem like a daunting task. In fact, studies show that people who defer making any decisions about financial topics do so to their detriment. No matter who you are or where you're from, investors looking to take control all ask the same question: 'I want to invest but where do I start?'

Getting started in investing seems so overwhelming that some people get confused and wind up giving up and doing nothing. Others get taken in by promises of gigantic returns and enrol in seminars, subscribe to stock-picking newsletters or agree to invest in odd assets like payphones, only to be disappointed. Others assume that all they need to do is open a brokerage account and start madly buying stocks. But, as you'll notice if you look at the Table of Contents or flip ahead in this book, we don't talk about picking a broker and opening an account until Chapter 3. We have just a few things to cover first.

But don't let that intimidate you. Check out our easy-to-follow list of things you need to do to get started. Follow these directions, and you'll be ready to open an online brokerage account and start trading:

1. **Decide how much you can save and invest.**

   You can't invest if you don't have any money, and you won't have any money if you don't save. No matter how much you earn, you need to set aside some money to start investing. (Think saving is impossible? We show you computer and online tools later in this chapter, in the section 'Measuring How Much You Can Afford to Invest', that can help you build up savings that you can invest.)

2. **Master the terms.**

   The world of investing has its own language. We help you to understand the lingo now so you don't get confused in the middle of a trade when you're asked to make a decision about something you've never heard of. (See 'Mastering the lingo' later in this chapter, and Chapter 2 has more on the language of online investing.)

3. **Familiarise yourself with the risks and returns of investing.**

   You wouldn't jump out of a plane without knowing the risks, right? Don't jump into investing without knowing what to expect, either. Luckily, online resources we show you later in this chapter and in

Chapter 6 can help you get a feel for how markets have performed over the past 100 years. By understanding how stocks, bonds and other investments have done, you'll know what is a reasonable return and set your goals appropriately.

We can't stress how important this step is. Investors who know how investments move don't panic — they keep their cool. Panic is your worst enemy because it has a way of talking you into doing things you'll regret later.

4. **Get a feel for how much risk you can take.**

   People all have different goals for their money. You may already have a home and a car, in which case you're probably interested in saving for retirement. On the other hand, you may be starting a family and hope to buy a house within a year. These two scenarios call for very different tastes for risk and *time horizons* (how long you're comfortable investing money before you need it). You need to know what your taste for risk is before you can invest. We show you how to measure your taste for risk in the section 'Gut-Check Time: How Much Risk Can You Take?' later in this chapter.

5. **Understand the difference between being an active and passive investor.**

   Some investors want to outsmart the market by darting in and out of stocks at just the right times. Others think doing that is impossible and don't want the hassle of trying. At the end of this chapter, you find out how to distinguish between these two types of investors, active and passive, so that you're in a better position to choose which one you are.

6. **Find out how to turn your computer into a trading station.**

   If you have a computer on your desk and a connection to the internet, you have all you need to turn it into a source of constant market information. You just need to know where to look, which you find out in Chapter 2.

7. **Take a dry run.**

   It's not as silly as it sounds. Matt says that many professional money managers got their starts by pretending to pick stocks and tracking how they would have done. It's a great way to see whether your strategy might work, before potentially losing your shirt. You can even do this online, which we cover in Chapter 2.

8. **Choose the type of account you'll use.**

   You can do your investing from all sorts of accounts, all with different advantages and disadvantages. We cover them a little in Chapter 2 and go into more detail in Chapter 3.

9. **Set up an online brokerage account.**

   At last, the moment you've been waiting for: Opening an online account. After you've tackled the preceding steps, you're ready to get going. This important step is covered in Chapter 3.

10. **Understand the different ways to place trades and enter orders.**

    We explain in Chapter 4 the many different ways to buy and sell stocks, each with very different end results.

11. **Boost your knowledge.**

    After you have the basics down, you're ready to tackle the later parts of the book, where we cover advanced investing topics. This involves picking an asset allocation (covered in Chapter 7), researching stocks to buy and knowing when to sell (covered in Chapter 11), and evaluating more exotic investments (the stuff you find in Chapters 15, 17 and 18).

The danger of doing nothing

After reading through the 11 steps for getting started, you might be wondering whether you've taken on more than you bargained for. Stick with it. The worst thing you can do now is put this book down, tell yourself you'll worry about investing later, and do nothing.

Doing nothing is extremely costly because you lose money if you don't invest. Seriously. Even if you stuffed your cash under a mattress and didn't spend a cent, each year that money becomes worth, on average, 3 per cent less due to inflation. Suppose you win $1 million in the lottery and stuff it in a hole in your backyard with the plan of taking it out in 30 years to pay for your retirement. In 30 years, all of your $1 million will still be there, but it will buy only $400,000 worth of goods.

Even if you put your extra cash in a savings account, you're not doing much better. Because savings accounts usually let you get the money anytime, they pay low levels of interest, most less than the inflation rate. Term deposits and high-yield savings accounts are better but you're still not getting ahead by much. To be successful, you need to move money you don't need for a while out of savings and into investments. Investments have the potential to generate much higher returns.

Measuring How Much You Can Afford to Invest

Online investing can help you accomplish some great things. It can help you pay for school fees, buy the house you've been eyeing, retire or travel to the moon. Okay, maybe not the last one . . . yet. But you get the idea. Investing helps your money grow faster than inflation. And, by investing online, you can profit even more by reducing the commissions and fees you must pay to different advisers and brokers.

One thing online investing can't do is make something out of nothing. To make money investing online, you have to save money first. Don't get frustrated, though, because you don't need as much to get started as you might fear. If you have a job or source of income, building up ample seed money isn't too hard.

Turning yourself into a big saver

If you want to be an investor, you must find ways to spend less money now so you can save the excess. That means you must retrain yourself from being a consumer to being an investor. Many investors just starting out have trouble getting past this point because being a consumer is so easy. Consumers buy assets that they can use and enjoy, but almost all of those assets lose value over time. Cars, electronic gadgets and clothing are all examples of things consumers 'invest' their money in. You don't even need money to spend — plenty of credit-card companies gladly lend it to you. Consumers fall into this spending pattern vortex and end up living from payday to payday with nothing left to invest.

Investors, on the other hand, find ways to put off current consumption. Instead of spending money, they invest it in building businesses or goods and services that earn money, rather than deplete it. The three main types of investments are stocks, fixed-interest securities and real estate, although others do exist, which we cover in later chapters.

Here are a few things you can do now to help you change from being a consumer to an investor:

- **Start with what you can manage by putting aside a little each month.** Cutting back on that takeaway café latte you treat yourself to each day could save you $90 a month. That's more than $1,000 per year!

- **Keep increasing what you put aside.** If you do it gradually, you won't feel the sting of a suddenly pinched pocket.

- **Hunt for deals and use coupons and discounts.** Put aside the saved money.

- **Buy only what you need.** Don't be fooled into buying things you don't need because they're on sale.

Scouring the web for savings help

Even fastidious savers have unavoidable basic expenses. Investors, though, find ways to be smart about even these routine costs. These sites can help:

- **Understanding Money** (www.understandingmoney.gov.au): This website, produced by the federal government, recognises the fact that lots of Australians have trouble controlling their finances. It contains a great budget planner, and a financial health check helps you understand more about your own money-management skills. You may be surprised at the results!

- **Youth Central** (www.youthcentral.vic.gov.au): Click on Managing Money from the list at the left for another website aimed at raising awareness of money-management skills, this one for the young, or just the young at heart.

- **Choice** (www.choice.com.au): *Choice* magazine has long been the stalwart of Australia's most thrifty. Now available online, the site features content that empowers consumers to make sure they're getting the most out of every dollar.

- **Squanderlust** (http://blogs.news.com.au/squanderlust): This blog from News.com.au contains some great tips on how to save money without becoming a social pariah. (See Chapter 2 for more on blogs.) A practical approach to saving that should strike a chord with female readers.

- **Feed The Pig** (www.feedthepig.org): This US site urges you to stop wasting money and offers tips to help you get out of debt by cutting excess spending. The site can calculate how to get out of debt and even how much you can save by packing a lunch instead of buying one.

Using personal finance software

The word *budget* is a real turn-off. It conjures up images of sitting at the kitchen table with stacks of crumpled-up receipts, trying to figure out where all your money went. As an investor who prefers to do things online, this image probably isn't too appealing.

Finding other ways to see how much money is coming in and how much is going out is worth your while. Fortunately, you have a painless option available — *personal finance software*, which helps you track your spending and investments.

In the past, it was a two-horse race between Microsoft Money and Intuit's Quicken. But Microsoft hasn't released an update for the Australian version of Money since 2005 — and doesn't plan to in the near future — so, unless you're already familiar with the software, it's hard to recommend. You can still download or buy the US edition (www.microsoft.com/money); however, many of its automated features, designed to work in conjunction with your account, won't work.

In terms of off-the-shelf solutions, try Quicken. Quicken, like Money before it, is an outstanding piece of software for tracking where all your money goes. You have a choice of two versions, Quicken Personal for tracking your spending and Quicken Personal Plus for tracking both your spending and investing.

Quicken Personal Plus offers the advantage of having all your data in the one place, but many of the investment-tracking tools are available elsewhere for free. In fact, you could probably do everything the software does in a spreadsheet but it would require a great deal of maintenance. Quicken is occasionally criticised for its sunset clause, which requires you to renew for a fee every two years. (See Figure 1-2.)

Quicken Personal can be bought from the store without the bulky manual for about $45 or from the site for $95, whereas Quicken Personal Plus starts at $180, with versions for both Windows and Mac users. Visit www.quicken.com.au to download the free three-month trial before you make up your mind. Select Products and click on Personal Finance to view the details and download the trial.

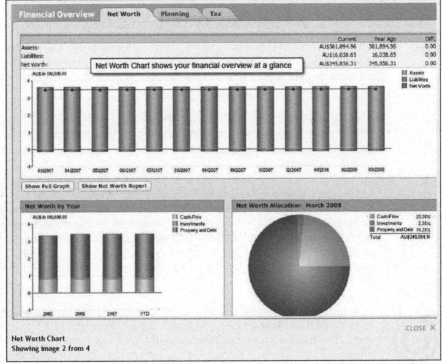

Figure 1-2:
Quicken offers a great selection of programs that can assist you with saving.

Money and Quicken may be the big kids on the block, but they aren't alone. Be sure to check out these other options:

- ✔ **Home Budget** (www.cnet.com.au) is great if you're already using Money or Quicken — Home Budget can work with your existing files. Best of all it's free, which means you're already saving money. Type **Home Budget** into the search field and Version 4.02 or later should appear in the list.

- ✔ **Buddi** (http://buddi.thecave.homeunix.org) is another free option. But, unlike other personal finance software, Buddi is designed to track budgets and spending, not investment portfolios.

- ✔ **PearBudget** (www.pearbudget.com) is almost-free budgeting software (it's $3 per month) that works in Microsoft Excel or other popular spreadsheet programs. The software tracks your costs and tells you whether you're sticking with the plan.

Microsoft also provides several helpful budgeting spreadsheets, which you can find by entering the word **budget** in the search field of the Microsoft Office Templates page (go to `http://office.microsoft.com` and click on Templates).

Perusing personal finance websites

Before you can put personal finance software to work, you often need to download and install it on your computer. You then need to spend some time figuring out how to actually use it. If that's exactly the kind of thing that scared you away from making a budget in the first place, you may want to consider personal finance websites. The main benefits of personal finance websites include the fact they let you see your information from any computer connected to the internet, and you generally don't have to install software to make them work. Here are a few to check out:

- **FIDO** (`www.fido.gov.au`) is ASIC's consumer website. Go to the homepage, select Publications & Resources, choose Calculators from the dropdown menu and scroll down to Manage Your Money to access its three different versions of a budget planner — online, spreadsheet and PDF. So there's no excuse for not getting started straightaway! It's comprehensive but well worth the effort.

- **Wesabe** (`www.wesabe.com`) lets you enter your budget and track it, after you've registered. But it has a twist: Other Wesabe users can see where your money is going and offer suggestions on ways to save more. Even though it's based in the US, the site has a strong Australian presence. It's free, too, which saves you some money right away.

- **ninemsn Money** (`http://money.ninemsn.com.au`) also has an excellent tool that allows you to identify areas in your budget for improvement. Click on Managing Money from the list at the left, choose Managing Money Tools and click on Budget Planner. It's another free site but you have to register with ninemsn for access.

Many financial websites are designed for older investors. If you're a parent hoping your kids will be more responsible with money, check out Youth Central (`www.youthcentral.vic.gov.au`). Click on Managing Money from the list to find a lot of good advice on everyday money matters like mobile phone plans and credit cards. You'll be soon saving more money than you ever thought possible. Now that's what we call cool.

Saving with web-based savings calculators

If personal finance software or sites seem too much like a chore or too Big Brotherish, you may consider web-based tools that measure how much you could save, in theory, based on a few parameters that you enter. Here are a few sites that have web-based calculators:

- ✔ **ANZ (**www.anz.com**):** Click on Use a Calculator from the Quicklinks at the right of the page, scroll down to Everyday Banking and Saving, and select Saving Over Time. This calculator asks you to input what you think you can put aside on a regular basis and tells you how much this amounts to over different periods ranging from months to years.

- ✔ **AMP (**http://amp.com.au**):** Click on the Banking tab, choose Everyday and Savings Accounts, and then click on Calculators. This site also includes a budget planner to help you work out realistically how much you save, based on your current spending habits.

Relying on the residual method

Are you the kind of person who has no idea how much money you have until you take out a wad of fifties from the ATM and check the balance on the receipt? If so, you're probably not the budgeting type and, for you, the best option may be to open a savings account with your bank or open a high-yield online savings account and transfer in money you know you won't need. Watch the savings account over the months to see how much it grows. That can give you a good idea of how much you could save without even feeling it. You can find out where you can get a high rate of interest on your savings from Infochoice.com (www.infochoice.com.au).

Being prepared for emergencies

When creating your budget and moving money from savings to an investment account, be sure to keep an emergency fund. This is money that's readily available in case of an emergency, stored in an account you can access immediately, such as a bank savings account. A decent guideline is to always have enough cash handy that you could pay two months of living expenses. Add up how much you spend each month on necessities such as housing (rent or mortgage and rates), food, utilities and transport. Multiply by two to get a general idea how much you should have for emergencies.

Using web-based savings goal calculators

All the preceding methods help you determine how much you can save. But the following sites have calculators that help you determine how much you *should* save to reach specific goals:

- ✔ **NAB** (www.nab.com.au): Under Online Tools, click on Calculators & Financial Tools and choose Savings Calculator from the list of Personal Budgeting and Savings Tools. This web-based calculator asks you what you're saving for, whether it's a car, holiday or investing, and provides a selection of inputs to ensure that you know how best to reach your goal.

- ✔ **ING DIRECT** (www.ingdirect.com.au): Choose Savings from the navigation bar, then Calculators from the list at the right and select the Savings Goal Calculator. This calculator is like ANZ's, but it works in the opposite order. First, create your goal, expected rate of interest, how much you've already saved and the timeframe for reaching your goal, and it tells you how much you need to add to succeed.

Understanding retirement calculators

Investors nearing retirement age have different needs, and these calculators are formulated with key considerations in mind. FIDO's calculator was created by Australians *for* Australians, whereas Vanguard's site is US-oriented but still contains excellent insights.

- ✔ **FIDO** (www.fido.gov.au): Select Retirement Planner from the Calculators dropdown menu at the right and click Go. It's never too early to start thinking about your retirement! To get the most out of this you'll need an up-to-date statement from your super fund.

- ✔ **Vanguard** (https://personal.vanguard.com/us): Click on the Planning & Education tab, select Retirement Planning, click on I'm Already Saving for Retirement, then Set Your Retirement Goals, and then hang on to your hat. This website from Vanguard may just blow some retirement myths right out of the water. The site prompts you to enter how much you make, how long you have until retirement and how much you want to live off when you're retired. Don't say we didn't warn you!

Preparing Yourself for Successful Investing

Becoming a successful investor is like becoming a professional athlete — it doesn't just happen by accident. Fortunately for you, it doesn't involve getting up at 5 am and going for a five-kilometre run either, although discipline will play a role, but mostly applied to your wallet.

The great thing about investing is that the sooner you get started, the better. An investor's time in the market is her greatest asset. Being able to talk the talk is important too, because you can't begin to use information to your advantage until you can understand the shorthand used in financial circles.

Deciding how you plan to save

After you've determined how much you need to save and how much you can save, you need to put your plan into action. The way you do this really depends on how good you are at handling your money and saving. The different methods include:

- **Automatic withdrawals:** Ever hear the cliché, 'pay yourself first'? It's a bit corny but it actually makes sense. The idea is that before you go shopping for a pair of shoes or head to the pub on payday with a fistful of cash, you should set money aside for savings. Some people have the discipline to do this themselves, but many don't. For those people, the best option is to set up *direct debits*, which is a way of giving a brokerage firm or bank permission to automatically extract money once a month. When the money is out of your hands, you won't be tempted to spend it.

- **Retirement plans:** If your goal is investing for retirement, you want to find out what options you have for adding to your superannuation. Superannuation is one of the great investment initiatives, like your home, where investing escapes the heavy hand of the tax man. Depending on your situation, you may choose to *salary sacrifice*; that is, put more money into superannuation than your employer is required to, before it's taxed.

- **On your own:** If you have money left over after paying all your bills, don't let it sit in a savings account. Leaving cash in a low-interest-bearing account is like giving a bank a cheap loan. Put your money to work for you. Brokers make it easy for you to get money to them via electronic transfers.

Want to be a successful investor? Start now!

The greatest force all investors have is time. Don't waste it. The sooner you start to save and invest, the more likely you'll be successful. To explain, take the example of five people, each of whom wants to have $1 million in the bank by the time they retire at age 65. The first investor starts when she's 20, followed by a 30-year-old, 40-year-old, 50-year-old and 60-year-old. Assuming each investor starts with nothing and averages 10 per cent returns each year (more on this later), Table 1-1 describes how much each must save per month to reach his or her goals.

Table 1-1 How Much Each Must Save to Get $1 Million, Part I	
An Investor Who Is	*Must Invest This Much Each Month to Have $1 Million at 65*
20 years old	$95.40
30 years old	$263.40
40 years old	$753.67
50 years old	$2,412.72
60 years old	$12,913.71

See, youth has its advantages. A 20-year-old who saves less than $100 a month will end up with the same amount of money as a 60-year-old who squirrels away $12,914 a month or $154,968 a year! That's largely due to the fact that money that's invested early has more time to brew. And, over time, the money snowballs and *compounds*, which is a concept we cover in the section 'The power of compounding' later in this chapter.

Mastering the lingo

Just about any profession, hobby or pursuit has its own lingo. Car fanatics, cricket tragics and music fans have terms that they seem to learn through osmosis. Online investing is no different. Many terms, like stocks and bonds, you may have heard but not completely understood. As you read through this book and browse the websites we mention, you may periodically stumble on unfamiliar words.

Don't expect a standard dictionary to help much. Investing terms can be so specialised and precise that the old Macquarie may not be a big help. Fortunately, a number of excellent online investing glossaries explain in detail what investing terms mean. Here are a few for you to check out:

- ✔ **Investopedia** (www.investopedia.com) has one of the most comprehensive databases of investing terms out there, with more than 5,000 entries. The site not only covers the basics, but explains advanced terms in great detail as well. It's also fully searchable so you don't waste time getting the answer.
- ✔ **Yahoo! Financial Glossary** (http://biz.yahoo.com/f/g) is all about quick answers. The database, written by Campbell Harvey, a US professor of finance, explains most basic investment terms in one or two sentences.
- ✔ **Virgin Money** (http://virginmoney.com.au) is a good source for terms specific to the Australian investment market, all done in the typical irreverent Virgin fashion of course. Click on the Super tab, choose FAQs, Forms and Help from the list at the left and select Jargon Unplugged.
- ✔ **Business Spectator Glossary** (www.businessspectator.com.au) contains a good selection of terms commonly used in market reports. Type **Business Spectator Glossary** into the search window.

Setting Your Expectations

Have you ever talked to a professional investor or financial adviser? One of the first things they tell you is how much experience they have. We couldn't tell you how many times we've been told, 'I've been in finance for 30 years. I've seen it all.'

Some of that is certainly old-fashioned bragging. But these claims are common because, in investing, experience does count. It's easy to say you could endure a bear market until you're watching, white-knuckled and sweating bullets, as your nest egg shrivels from $100,000 to $80,000 or $70,000. Experience brings perspective, which is very important.

But, if you're new to investing, don't despair. Online tools can help you acquire the brain of a grizzled Wall Street veteran. And don't forget that we're here to set you straight as well. In fact, we're set to start talking about how much you can expect to make from investing. And you'll be hearing a great deal about a little something called the *rate of return*.

Keeping up with the rate of return

Don't let the term *rate of return* scare you. It's the most basic concept in investing, and the most important. Just remember that it's the amount, measured as a percentage, that your investment increases in value over a certain period. If you have a savings account, you may understand the concept already. If you put $100 in a bank account paying 4.5 per cent interest, you know that by the end of the year you'll receive $4.50 in interest. You earn a 4.5 per cent annual rate of return. Rates of return are useful in investing because they work as a report card to tell investors how well an investment is doing, no matter how much they have invested.

You can calculate rates of return yourself with the following:

- ✔ **A formula:** Subtract an asset's previous value from its current value, divide the difference by the asset's previous value and multiply by 100. If a stock rises from $15 a share to $32, you would calculate the rate of return by first subtracting 15 from 32 to get 17. Next, divide 17 by 15 and multiply by 100. The rate of return is 113.3 per cent.

- ✔ **Microsoft's Excel spreadsheet software:** This software, which is available on most computers, calculates rates of return fairly easily. You can find out how with the instructions at www.office.microsoft.com. Click on the Products tab, select Excel from the Desktop Programs list at the left and then enter **CAGR** in the search window, using Excel 2003 for your search option.

- ✔ **Financial websites:** Many handy sites can calculate rates of return for you, including www.moneychimp.com. Click the Calculators tab and choose Return Rate/CAGR from the options at the top right.

When you calculate the rate of return for a portfolio you've added money to or taken money from, you must take an extra step. We explain how to calculate your portfolio's performance in that scenario in Chapter 6.

The power of compounding

Famous physicist Albert Einstein once called compounding the most powerful force in the universe. *Compounding* is when money you invest earns a return and then that return also earns a return. (Dizzy yet?) When you leave money invested for a long time, the power of compounding kicks in.

Imagine you've deposited $100 in an account that pays 4.5 per cent in interest a year. In the first year, you'd earn $4.50 in interest, which brings your balance to $104.50. But, in the second year, you'd earn interest of $4.70. Why? Because you've earned 4.5 per cent on the $4.50 in interest you earned. The longer you're invested, the more time your money has to compound.

Compounding works on your side to fight against inflation and taxes. Financial data and news provider Bloomberg (www.bloomberg.com) has a web-based calculator that tells you whether your rate of return is putting you ahead. Select Calculators from the Investment Tools dropdown menu, scroll down to Investment and click on Investment Returns.

Determining How Much You Can Expect to Profit

Why bother investing online? To make money, of course. But how much do you want to make? Understanding what you can expect to earn is where you need to start. Whenever you hear about an investment and what kind of returns it promises, you should be able to mentally compare it with the kind of returns you can expect from stocks, bonds and other investments. That way you know whether the returns you're being promised are too good to be true.

How do you do this? By relying on the hard work of academics who've done some heavy lifting. Academics and market research firms have ranked investments by how well they've done over the years. And we're not just talking a few years, but for decades — in many cases going back to the 1920s and earlier. The amount of work that's gone into measuring historical rates of return is staggering, but, if you're using online resources, you're just a click away from finding out how most types of assets have done.

What you expect to earn is a number that will affect most of your investment decisions, usually rather dramatically. The next table is a revised version of Table 1-1 — the one that showed how five different people could expect to save $1 million by the time they reached 65 years of age. Table 1-2 looks at how much they must save to make their goal changes, based on how much they think they will earn from their investments.

Table 1-2   How Much Each Must Save to Get $1 Million, Part II

An Investor Who Is	Must Invest This Much Each Month If Earning 5%	Must Invest This Much Each Month If Earning 10%	Must Invest This Much Each Month If Earning 15%
20 years old	$493.48	$95.40	$15.28
30 years old	$880.21	$263.40	$68.13
40 years old	$1,679.00	$753.67	$308.31
50 years old	$3,741.00	$2,412.72	$1,495.87
60 years old	$14,704.57	$12,913.71	$11,289.93

The 20-year-old must save nearly $500 a month extra if she thinks she'll earn only 5 per cent a year from her investments instead of 15 per cent. But, even scarier, if she saves $15.28 thinking she'll earn 15 per cent a year, but earns only 5 per cent, she'll have just $30,963 instead of the $1 million she was counting on.

Taxing your capital gains

Since 1999, investors who make a profit on the sale of shares are required to pay *capital gains tax (CGT)*. The tax is not a separate tax, but actually a component of income tax. When you complete your income tax return you need to include any realised profits or losses from investing activities and they'll be taxed accordingly.

Of course, if your losses exceed your profits, then you don't have to pay any tax (hardly a cause for celebration, but that's life!). If the shares have been held for less than 12 months, then your total capital gains are taxed at your marginal tax rate; that is, the highest band of income tax that your income is currently subjected to. But, if you hold them for 12 months or more, then you're only charged CGT on half of your profit, which is a big incentive to hang on to your investments for at least 12 months!

Studying the past

If someone asks you how stocks are doing, he often means how much they went up or down that day. Cable TV stations reinforce this preoccupation with the here-and-now by scrolling second-by-second moves in stock prices across the bottom of the screen.

But second-by-second moves in stocks don't really tell you much. If a stock goes down a bit, and a company didn't report news, did anything really change during that second? Watching short-term movements of stock prices doesn't mean much in the overall scheme of things.

To understand how investments behave, analysing their movements over as many years as you can is more helpful. That way, recessions are blended with boom times to get you to a real, smooth average. Doing this requires the painstaking method of processing dozens of annual returns of stocks and analysing the data. Luckily, some academics and industry pioneers have done much of the work for you, and you can access their findings if you know where to look. And we just happen to know a few places where you can start your search:

- **Bogle Financial Markets Research Center** is maintained by the founder of Vanguard, John C. Bogle. Bogle revolutionised the investment industry by creating the world's largest managed fund, the Vanguard 500, which is designed to mirror the performance of the US stock market index. Stock market indices, such as the S&P/ASX 200 and the Dow Jones Industrial index are benchmarks that let you track how the market is doing. Visit the Vanguard homepage (www.vanguard.com), click on Other Sites at the bottom right-hand corner of the screen and then click on the top link on the page to get there.

  Bogle's site is invaluable because he explains that the market, on average, returns about 10 per cent a year. That benchmark will be very important later as you evaluate different stocks. Indices (the plural used in the US is indexes) are covered in more detail in Chapter 6.

- **Russell Investments** (www.russell.com) lets you look up how all types of stocks, ranging from small to large, in addition to bonds, have done over the years. There's also a handy sheet that shows you how they've all done every year since 1997. Click on Indexes in the top menu bar, select the Performance tab and click on Russell US Indexes.

- ✔ **Index Funds Advisors** (www.ifa.com) compiles much of the research done by academics and helps explain it in plain language. You can order a colourful book from the site, called *Index Funds: The 12-Step Program for Active Investors*, by Mark T. Hebner (IFA). The book explains how different types of stocks perform long term and how much you can expect to gain. It also shows long-term returns of bonds. You can download the book for free if you take the site's Risk Capacity Survey, explained in the section 'Gut-Check Time: How Much Risk Can You Take?' later in this chapter.

- ✔ **Robert Shiller's website** (www.econ.yale.edu/~shiller) contains exhaustive data on how markets have done over the long term. You can view the data and draw your own conclusions. Shiller is a well-known economics professor at Yale University.

- ✔ **ASX** (www.asx.com.au) produces the chart we recommended you print out at the very beginning of this chapter, in the section 'Why Investing Online Is Worth Your While'. You can also see it in Figure 1-1, though without its full-colour glory. The chart shows the returns produced by the Australian stock market since 1900, in this case using the All Ordinaries, which was the default measure up until 2000. Yes, there are significant dips and troughs over the years but, overall, sticking with the market has been very profitable.

  If you didn't print it out earlier, here are the directions: Go to the homepage (www.asx.com.au), click on About ASX Ltd on the left of the page and choose ASX at a Glance. Scroll down to History of the Market, click on the link for the Australian market and choose Performance of the All Ordinaries, where you find the document *Australian Share Price Movements*. Now you know why we recommend you print it out!

Don't get too hung up if you don't understand everything on these sites. Several get pretty sophisticated, especially Shiller's — after all he does have an index named after him (no, not Schindler's List). Just scan through the annual returns so you can get a general feel for how markets behave over time — the idea here is for you to gain perspective, not cram for an economics exam.

What the past tells you about the future

Exhaustive studies of markets have shown us that Australian stocks, if we go back to 1900, return about 12 per cent a year. Through the years, 12 per cent returns have been the benchmark for long-term performance, making it a good measuring stick for you and something to help you keep your bearings. But long-term studies of securities also show that, to get higher returns, you usually must also accept more risk.

Why knowing the past is valuable

By studying how investments have done, you get an idea, on average, of what to expect. This gives you a perspective that lets you not only decide whether an investment is worthwhile but also gives you a BS meter. If you get a flyer in the mail talking up a 'promising new company' that's expected to generate 10 per cent returns, walk away. Why would you take a chance on a shaky company if you can expect the same return by investing in a lower risk, diversified index fund? Similarly, a return that's much higher than 10 per cent must be much riskier, no matter what the flyer says.

Don't make the mistake of thinking that investing in stocks guarantees you a 10 per cent return every year, like a savings account. That's not the case. Stocks are risky and tend to move in erratic patterns, and they test your confidence with sudden drops and surges.

Research from Colonial First State has shown that these surges can add up to quite a lot over time. Over a period of 10 years leading up to 31 March 2008, the annualised rate of return from the All Ordinaries was 11.52 per cent. If you missed the 10 best days over that 10 years, your annualised performance dropped to 7.6 per cent. If you missed 20 days, it dropped to 5.03 per cent and, if you missed 30 days, it dropped to 2.89 per cent. Table 1-3 illustrates the point.

Table 1-3   Wild Days for the All Ordinaries, to 31 March 2008

Period of investment	Annualised Rate of Return
10-year performance	11.52%
10-year performance less 5 best days	9.23%
10-year performance less 10 best days	7.60%
10-year performance less 20 best days	5.03%
10-year performance less 30 best days	2.89%

Source: Compiled from IRESS, Colonial First State.

Gut-Check Time: How Much Risk Can You Take?

It's time to get a grip — a grip on how much you can invest, that is. Most beginning investors are so interested in finding stocks that make them rich overnight that they lose sight of risk. But academic studies show that risk and return go hand in hand. That's why you need to know how much risk you can stomach before you start looking for investments and buying them online.

Several excellent online tools can help you get a handle on how much of a financial thrillseeker you are. Most are structured like interviews, by asking you a number of questions to help you decide what kind of investor you are. These are like personality tests for your investment taste. We cover several of these in more detail in Chapter 7, where we discuss how to create an investing road map, called an *asset allocation*. For now, these questionnaires are worthwhile to take right away so you can understand what kind of investor you are.

- **Colonial First State's Risk Profiler Calculator (**www.colonialfirst state.com.au**):** This calculator examines your risk profile in relation to your investment horizon, goals and how much volatility you're prepared to tolerate. Click on Calculators at the top and select What Investments Suit Your Risk Profile? At the end of the questionnaire you're given a summary of your risk profile and the proportion of different asset types — the asset allocation — that suits your tolerance to risk.

- **AXA Investor Profile Calculator (**www.axa.com.au**):** Click the Calculators tab on the right to select this profiler. It looks at your best superannuation options, taking into account your timeframe for investment, your investment experience and your attitude to risk, as well as your own view of how long you expect to rely on your super. A worthy exercise for anyone interested in superannuation — and that should be everyone!

- **Vanguard's Investor Questionnaire (**https://personal.vanguard. com.us/home**):** Choose Planning & Education from the menu bar, click on Create Your Investment Plan and choose Complete the Investor Questionnaire. It asks you ten salient questions to determine how much of a risk taker you are with your money. It determines what your ideal asset allocation is. Take note of the breakdown. The closer to 100 per cent that Vanguard recommends you put in stocks, the more risk-tolerant you are, and the closer to 100 per cent in bonds, the less risk-tolerant you are.

Passive or Active? Deciding What Kind of Investor You Plan to Be

Investing may not seem controversial, but the fact is that, any time you talk about money, people have some strong opinions about the right way to do things. The first way investors categorise themselves is by whether they're passive or active. Because these two approaches are so different, the following sections help you think about what they are and which camp you see yourself in. Where you stand won't only affect which broker is best for you, which we discuss in Chapter 3, but also which chapters in this book appeal to you most.

How to know if you're a passive investor

Passive investors don't try to beat the stock market. They merely try to keep up with it by owning all the stocks in an index. An *index* is a basket of stocks that mirrors the market. Passive investors are happy matching the market's performance, knowing they can boost their real returns with a few techniques we discuss in Chapter 7.

You know you're a passive investor if you like the following ideas:

- **Not picking individual stocks:** These investors buy large baskets of stocks that mirror the performance of popular stock indices like the S&P/ASX 200 or the S&P 500, so they don't worry about whether a small upstart company they invest in will release its new product on time or whether it will be well received.

- **Owning managed and exchange-traded funds:** Because passive investors aren't looking for the next Microsoft, they buy managed and exchange-traded funds that buy hundreds of stocks. (We cover managed and exchange-traded funds in more detail in Chapters 8 and 9, respectively.)

- **Reducing taxes:** Passive investors tend to buy investments and forget about them until many years later when they need the money. This can be lucrative because, by holding on to diversified investments for a long time and not selling them, passive investors can postpone when they have to pay capital gains tax.

✔ **Not stressing about stocks' daily, monthly or even annual movements:** Passive investors tend to buy index managed funds and forget about them. They don't need to sit in front of finance TV shows, read magazines or worry about where stocks are moving. They're invested for the long term, and everything else is just noise to them.

Sites for passive investors to start with

One of the toughest things about being a passive investor is sitting still during a bull market when everyone else seems to be making more than you. Yes, you may be able to turn off the TV, but inevitably you'll bump into someone who brags about her giant gains and laughs at you for being satisfied with 10 per cent market returns.

When that happens, sticking with your philosophy is even more important. Following the crowd at this moment will undermine the value of your strategy. That's why even passive investors are well served going to websites where other passive investors congregate:

✔ **Bogleheads** (www.bogleheads.org) is an electronic water cooler for fans of Vanguard index funds and passive investors to meet, encourage and advise each other. They call themselves Bogleheads in honour of the founder of Vanguard, John (Jack) Bogle.

✔ **Indextown** (www.indextown.com) is a blog written for investors who believe in the long-term success of buying managed funds tied to indices.

✔ **The Arithmetic of Active Management** (www.stanford.edu/~wfsharpe/art/active/active.htm) is a reprint of an article by an early proponent of passive investing, William Sharpe, who explains why active investing will never win.

✔ **Vanguard's website** (www.vanguard.com.au) contains many helpful stories about the power of index investing and offers them for free, even if you don't have an account. Check under the Fund Performance and Tools and Education tabs.

✔ **Mad Money Machine** (http://madmoneymachine.com) is an internet radio show, or podcast (we explain these in more detail in Chapter 2), that tries to make the seemingly boring world of passive investing more exciting. The host, Paul Douglas Boyer, weaves jokes, music and facts in a way to keep you investing passively.

How to know if you're an active investor

Active investors almost feel sorry for passive investors. Why would anyone be satisfied just matching the stock market and not even try to do better? Active investors feel that, if you're smart enough and willing to spend time doing homework, you can exceed 10 per cent annual returns. Active investors also find investing to be thrilling, almost like a hobby. Some active investors try to find undervalued stocks and hold them until they're discovered by other investors. Another class of active investors are short-term traders, who bounce in and out of stocks trying to get quick gains.

You're an active investor if you

- ✔ **Think long-term averages of stocks are meaningless.** Active investors believe they can spot winning companies before everyone knows about them, buy their shares at just the right time and sell them for a profit.

- ✔ **Are willing to spend large amounts of time searching for stocks.** These are the investors who sit in front of finance TV shows, analyse stocks that look undervalued and do all sorts of prospecting trying to find gems.

- ✔ **Believe they can hire managed-fund managers who can beat the market.** Some active investors think that certain talented managed-fund managers are out there and that if they just give their money to those managers, they'll win.

- ✔ **Suspect certain types of stocks aren't priced correctly and that many investors make bad decisions.** Active investors believe they can outsmart the masses and routinely capitalise on the mistakes of the great unwashed.

- ✔ **Understand the risks.** Most active traders under-perform index funds, some without even realising it. Before deciding to be an active trader, be sure to test out your skills with online simulations, as described in Chapter 2, or make sure you're measuring your performance correctly, as described in Chapter 6. If you're losing money picking stocks, stop doing it immediately.

Many investors try, but very few are able to consistently beat the market. Consider Bill Miller, portfolio manager for the Legg Mason Value Trust managed fund. Miller had beaten the market for 15 years and turned into a poster child for active investors, and proof that beating the market was possible if you were smart enough. But even Miller's streak came to an end in 2006. That's when his Legg Mason Value Trust fund didn't just trail the market, it lagged by a mile, returning just 5.9 per cent while the market gained 15.8 per cent. Active investors lost their hero, but there will certainly be another hot manager to take his place.

Sites for the active investor to start with

Ever hear of someone trying to learn a foreign language by moving to the country and picking it up through 'immersion'? The idea is that, by just being around the language, and through the necessity of buying food or finding the restrooms, they eventually get proficient.

If you're interested in active investing, you can do the same thing by hitting websites that are common hangouts for active investors. By lurking on these sites, you can pick up how these investors find stocks that interest them and trade on them. These sites will show you the great pains active investors go through in their attempt to beat the market. A few to start looking at include the following:

- ✔ **Google Business News** (http://news.google.com.au): Active investors have to have access to the very latest in business and finance news, and Google scours the world for it. Just click the Business tab on the left. Thanks to Google's renowned search abilities this page brings you the news as it happens.

- ✔ **Deal Journal** (http://blogs.wsj.com/deals): A blog site (see Chapter 2 for more on blogs) for the *Wall Street Journal* and a regular destination for active investors trying to keep up-to-date with that most fortuitous of events, the takeover.

- ✔ **FT Alphaville** (http://ftalphaville.ft.com): Another hot web destination for the dedicated active investor. It may seem a little chaotic at first, but often that's the way things are for the active investor.

Chapter 2

Getting Your PC Ready for Online Investing

*Y*ou live in a do-it-yourself world. You're expected to fill your own petrol tank at the service station, pour your own soft drink at the cinema, and book, and even print, your own airline tickets. It's the same story with investing. If you want to reach your financial goals and retire comfortably, it's up to you to make it happen. Thanks to the introduction of compulsory superannuation, you're now expected to fund your retirement yourself, with some investors going one step further and investing in it themselves with DIY super.

If you ask for help, you're almost always pointed to the internet and told to look it up or do your own research. That sounds reasonable, except that the internet is a massive collection of web pages, and you can find dozens, if not hundreds, of sources for investing advice, much of which is conflicting or, worse, wrong. No wonder many investors throw their hands up in utter frustration.

That's where this chapter comes in. In Chapter 1, we fill you in on what it takes to prepare yourself to be an online investor. Here, in Chapter 2, it's time to prepare your computer for online investing and make it a tool that quickly provides you with the answers you need. This chapter helps you tweak your computer until it's like your personal investing workstation. It'll feel as comfortable to you as an old leather chair. And, by using mostly free online resources, you'll save yourself some money in the process.

We escort you through the morass of financial websites and show you which ones you need to know. You find out what types of investing information are available online and how to access what you need from your computer. You also find out how to use online simulation sites that let you take a dry run, investing with fake money to make sure you know what you're doing before using real money.

Turning Your PC into a Trading Station

When you think of a stock trading floor, you probably picture a room full of traders wearing brightly coloured jackets throwing papers around and yelling out market orders. Some of that drama still exists on the New York Stock Exchange floor and the London Metals Exchange, but it's largely a throwback from the old days.

Today, trading floors look more like insurance offices. They have rows of desks with computers not unlike the one that's probably sitting on your desk. Professional traders do have an advantage: Many have high-end trading systems and software that costs thousands of dollars a month. That might be beyond your price range, but you may be amazed at how much market information you can get for free or for little money, if you know where to go.

Using favourites to put data at your fingertips

The easiest way to turn your computer into a market monitoring station is by bookmarking, or creating favourites, to key sites with data you need. *Favourites* (also sometimes called *bookmarks*) are links in your internet browser that let you quickly reach a web page when you need it, without typing a long website address. Most internet browsers have this capability, and they all work slightly differently. But, just so you have an idea, if you're using Microsoft's Internet Explorer 7 or 8, you can create favourites by following these steps:

1. **Navigate to the website you're interested in saving.**

2. **Click the Favorites icon (the little gold star) in the middle of the toolbar.**

   You can see the star in Figure 2-1.

3. **Choose Add to Favorites.**

   An Add a Favorite dialog box pops up.

4. **Give the site a name you can remember.**

   Most sites will do this for you.

5. **In the Create In space, choose the folder you want to put the favourite into.**

   If you want to put this favourite in a separate folder, you can create a folder by clicking the New Folder button. If you're not sure, just use the default Favorites folder.

6. **Click the Add button.**

   If you want to access that address again, click the Favorites icon (the gold star) and scroll down until you see the title of the page you're interested in.

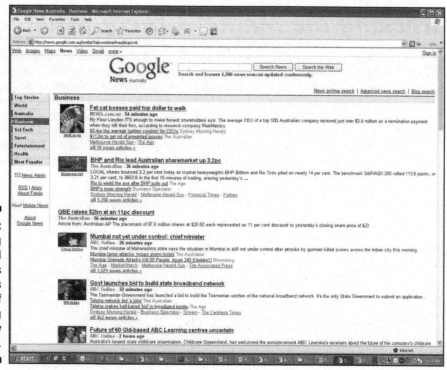

Figure 2-1: Setting financial websites as favourites is a matter of just clicking a few buttons.

Compiling a list of must-watch sites

So you know how to create favourites. But what sites are worth creating *as* favourites? Our suggestion is to take a page from the professionals and try to replicate the data they're most interested in. Most professional trading workstations are set up so that they can take on five distinct tasks:

- Tracking the market's every move
- Monitoring news that has the potential to affect stock prices
- Checking in on market gossip
- Accessing company financial statements and company announcements through ASIC and the ASX
- Executing trades

Create separate favourites folders for all five functions and then fill them up with the sites we recommend in the rest of this chapter. To execute trades you need to log on to the website of your broker, but don't worry about this just yet — we go over the dizzying number of choices you have for online brokers in Chapter 3.

Tracking the Market's Every Move

You're probably hoping to study the market and find ways to score big and fast. Hey, everyone wants to get rich quick. Just remember that making money by darting in and out of stocks is extremely tough to do, and most investors, online or not, will be better off forming a long-term investment strategy and sticking with it. The difference between long-term investing (the in-it-for-the-long-haul approach, called *passive* investing) and short-term trading (the darting-in-and-out way of doing things, called *active* investing) is discussed in Chapter 1, where we also give you the tools necessary for figuring out how to decide which approach is best for you.

No matter what kind of investor you plan to be, watching real-time stock movements is fascinating. Watching rapid price moves, with stock prices dancing around and flashing on the computer screen, is a guilty pleasure and a source of entertainment for some investors.

You can find a great deal of overlap among online investing resources. Many of the following sites do more than what we highlight here. Explore the different sites and see if certain ones suit you best.

There's no shortage of places where you can get stock quotes and see the value of popular market indices such as the All Ordinaries, the S&P/ASX 200, the Dow Jones Industrial Average and the S&P 500. That's why you can afford to demand more from websites if they're going to earn a position as one of your favourites. In Chapter 6, we list multiple sites best suited for tracking specific parts of the market. But the next section has a quick list that can help you get started creating general-purpose online-investing favourites. The sites listed here make the cut because they not only provide stock quotes, but also go a step further by being the best at a certain aspect of tracking the market.

When you look up a stock quote, on many sites you'll usually see three quotes:

- ✔ **The last sale:** The last sale is what you probably think of as the quote and is what runs in newspaper listings and on websites. That's the price at which a buyer and seller agreed to a transaction.
- ✔ **The bid:** The bid, though, is the highest price other investors are willing to pay for the stock.
- ✔ **The ask:** The ask is the lowest price investors who own the stock are willing to sell it for.

Getting price quotes on markets and stocks

Nearly any site gives you stock quotes for the day, including the financial news websites discussed in the section 'Monitoring Market-Moving News' later in this chapter. But a few sites deserve special mention because they make it easy to get stock quotes for days in the past. Importantly, however, none of them are perfect, which is why we list three of them instead of one. Whether you choose to use one, two or a combination of all three is up to you.

✔ **Trading Room** (www.tradingroom.com.au) is a good source of information for investors, not only because it's free but because it's live. For looking up prices of stocks and market indices, Trading Room is hard to beat because it's fast and gives you everything you need, from the movement over the day, the volume of shares traded, the dividend (cash payments) and when the dividend was last paid. This type of information is common among similar websites; however, it's almost always delayed by 15 to 20 minutes. If you register your details (and we recommend that you do), Trading Room's data is live.

Another great aspect of Trading Room is that, when you look up a company's vital statistics, it also shows you official company announcements that are lodged with the ASX, which may have a bearing on how that stock is performing today. These are available from the ASX site but it's convenient to have them all on the same page. The site also offers links to recent news stories, but you'll have to pay to access them. These exact same stories are free elsewhere, so we suggest that you keep your credit card in your wallet at this point in time.

✔ **Yahoo!7 Finance** (http://au.finance.yahoo.com) is one of the most popular destinations on the web, and with good reason. It's comprehensive, it's intuitive and you're only ever one or two clicks away from all the information you need. If you want to check your portfolio or keep up-to-date with a prospect, then Yahoo!7 Finance tells you everything you need to know. When you enter a stock code into Yahoo!7 Finance, the summary gives prices (delayed by 20 minutes), 12-month high and low prices, news headlines and a chart of how the stock has performed over the course of the day. Pretty neat don't you think? And all for free.

✔ **Business Spectator** (http://asx.businessspectator.com.au/summary) is primarily a news and commentary site but it also provides well-laid-out markets and stock information. Business Spectator's market summary is the perfect place to go if you're busy and want to get the 'big picture' quickly. Although, like Yahoo!7 Finance, the data is delayed by 20 minutes, you can tell at a glance what the markets in Australia, the US and Asia are doing. You can also see how the biggest companies on the ASX are faring, as well as the ten biggest rises and falls of the day. Definitely worth considering adding to your favourites. If you're more interested in the performance of specific stocks, then just enter the ASX code in the box in the top-left corner for all the usual vital statistics and ASX announcements.

Knowing your exchanges

When you get a stock quote from most websites, you also need to see what exchange the stock trades on. This is important information. For Australian investors, the most important exchange is the ASX — the Australian Securities Exchange. This is going to be your home turf, the place where all your favourite companies (teams) are listed (playing).

The next group of exchanges you hear about regularly are the overseas exchanges. James recommends starting in your own neighbourhood first, but eventually your curiosity may get the better of you, which is why we've covered international stocks in Chapter 18.

In the US, the most important and reputable exchanges are the New York Stock Exchange and the NASDAQ Stock Market. These exchanges are home to some of the biggest companies in the world. The NASDAQ (the National Association of Securities Dealers Automated Quotation system) tends to attract newer growth and technology companies.

Other important exchanges around the world include the London Stock Exchange and the London Metals Exchange, where — you guessed it — base metals like copper are traded. Rounding out the list are the Asian 'tigers' — the Hong Kong Stock Market, the Tokyo Stock Exchange and the Shanghai Stock Exchange.

These aren't the only exchanges in the world, but they are the most reputable and have the most stringent regulators, which levels the playing field for all investors.

You may also come across Australia's other two exchanges, the Bendigo Stock Exchange (BSX) and the National Stock Exchange of Australia (NSX). These are smaller operations that deal with smaller companies. James suggests that you avoid these exchanges for the most part — they're like your local amateur football club compared with the AFL.

Slicing and dicing the markets

Although quite a few market indices exist — we discuss many of them in Chapter 6 — there are some major market benchmarks *all* online investors need to be familiar with. These are the ones so commonly discussed that they need to be part of your investor vocabulary. Table 2-1 presents them in all their market-dominating glory.

Table 2-1	Key Market Indices
Index Name	*What It Measures*
S&P/ASX 200	Maintained by Standard & Poor's, this contains the 200 largest companies on the ASX and is the index of choice for most investors and professionals.
All Ordinaries	The All Ordinaries is made up of the 500 largest companies listed on the ASX. It's a broad market indicator.
Dow Jones Industrial Average	Thirty big industrial companies. When investors hear about 'the market', more often than not they think of the Dow.
S&P 500	Big companies, including 500 of the most well known stocks in the US. Moves very similarly to the Dow, even though it includes more stocks.
NASDAQ Composite Index	Stocks that trade on the NASDAQ Stock Market. It tends to closely track technology stocks.
FTSE 100	The Financial Times Stock Exchange index includes the 100 biggest companies on the London Stock Exchange.
Nikkei 225	Japan's closely watched index of the 225 biggest stocks on the Tokyo Stock Exchange.
Hang Seng	The 45 biggest companies on the Hong Kong Stock Market.
Shanghai Composite	Comprises all 50 stocks that trade on the Shanghai Stock Exchange.

How the S&P/ASX 200's value is calculated

Market indices, such as the S&P/ASX 200, are priced not by traders, but by calculators. Mathematical formulas analyse the stock movements inside an index to arrive at the value of the index. The S&P/ASX 200 is a *weighted* index, which means that the size of a company informs its contribution to the index.

At any point in time, the value of the index is the sum of the total market capitalisation divided by the *divisor*. The divisor is used to smooth out interruptions, such as when a company issues new stock, which is not an event that moves the index, but rather its weighting.

Nearly all financial news websites let you monitor the indices we list in Table 2-1. But sometimes you want to go deeper and examine individual sectors. Yahoo!7 Finance (http://au.finance.yahoo.com) is a good starting point for this information. To view the major Australian indices click on ASX Indices under the Investing tab in the left-hand column.

This brings up a table of the most popular Australian indices, including the All Ordinaries and the S&P/ASX 200. Above that table is a link titled ASX 200 GICS Sectors, which breaks the index down into industry components. This breakdown allows you to compare whether financial stocks on the ASX, such as banks, are out-performing energy stocks, such as oil producers.

Yahoo!7 Finance makes tracking market indices easy, so you don't have to memorise or look up cryptic codes for indices. You can find more tips about researching different industries in Chapter 13.

Don't confuse stocks with indices. Stocks are shares in individual companies, such as BHP Billiton or NAB. The prices of stocks reflect how much you need to pay for a share of the stock. Indices, on the other hand, are mathematical formulas that tell you how much a collection of stocks has changed in value. When the S&P/ASX 200, which contains 200 stocks, hits 7,000, that doesn't mean you can buy it for $7,000. It's just a number that represents relative value in the same way that temperature represents weather conditions.

Getting company descriptions

Professional investors like to bone up on what a company does, who's in charge and how profitable it is, without poring over dozens of industry reports. You can get the same kind of quick snapshot information with online company descriptions. All the main investing sites we discuss have sections that describe the business a company is in. Here are a couple more sites worth bookmarking:

✔ **ASX** (www.asx.com.au): The homepage of the Australian Securities Exchange (ASX) is one of the most valuable resources available to investors. Companies are required to keep the information they provide to the ASX up-to-date, so this is one of the first places to look for company information. In the top right-hand corner of the ASX website is a search field marked Codes. Directly underneath that is a link titled Find a Code. To find the code of a company you're looking for, click on Find a Code. Another window will pop up asking you to enter the first few letters of the company you're looking for. If you're looking for

Telstra's code you would type in **Tel**. Among the companies it returns are the Telecom Corporation of New Zealand and Telstra Corporation. Next to the company names are the ASX codes (TEL is actually NZ Telecom and TLS is Telstra, the one you're looking for). Remember that code!

Now go back to the homepage, type that code into the Codes search window and click Go. The site takes you to a page that records the company's movement for that day. Under the heading Shares, click on the code one more time to go to the ASX company factsheet for Telstra. This lists the company's main areas of operations, board of directors, closing prices for the previous five days, price history for the year and dividends. More often than not, the company page also provides a link to the company's corporate website, where you can find out even more details about the company's operations.

✔ **Yahoo!7 Finance** (`http://au.finance.yahoo.com`): Yahoo! has been around for a long time, primarily because of the strength of its finance portal. The homepage provides you with a good mixture of news and market information, but the real power of this site lies in the company profiles. Below the title Finance Homepage is a text box that asks you to Enter Symbol/s. Entering the same symbol as you did in the previous example, TLS, and clicking on Go takes you to a company summary.

This summary contains a lot more information than the ASX site and the column on the left-hand side headed More on TLS.AX offers you even more options. Towards the bottom of that list, under the heading Company, are the links Profile and Key Statistics. These two pages deliver you all the information most people want about a company, including its key people, its business and, of course, its profitability. Further down the column is the heading Financials, which provides an even more detailed look at the company's bottom line, but more on that in Chapter 10.

Your crystal ball: Predicting how the day will begin

Investors can get an idea of which way the stock market is likely to move over the course of the day in a number of ways. The big US indices, the Dow Jones Industrial Average and the S&P 500, are the strongest indicators. The US market closes just a few hours before the Australian market opens (between 6 am and 8 am AEDT, depending on what time of the year it is) and, in the absence of any significant events on the domestic front, will set the tone of ASX trading for at least part of the day.

If you're a patriotic Australian, you may think that slavishly following the US market is a bit unseemly. Fortunately you can choose another way to predict the day's direction and that's with the *futures market.* The futures market is used heavily by commodity traders to lock in prices for things like oil, wheat and copper months and years into the future. You can also see what the futures market is saying about stocks.

By looking at the ASX website before the market opens, you get the jump on other investors by visiting its futures page. Follow these steps:

1. **Load the ASX website (**www.asx.com.au**).**

2. **Click on Prices, Research & Announcements in the left-hand menu and click on the last option, Market Statistics.**

   From here, look for the heading SFE Trading Statistics and click on the Futures Summary link.

3. **Follow the left-hand column down to the letters AP and click on them.**

   That will take you to the SPI 200 futures page, which is like the sister version of the S&P/ASX 200. The figure you're looking for is at the top of the column titled Change. This indicates how much up or down the market is expected to open.

If you're the type of person who doesn't like surprises, then a combination of these two methods — checking the US market and checking the futures market — will make sure you're always up to speed.

Keeping tabs on commodities

We have more on how to research the exciting world of commodities — such as the oil, timber and coal that companies use to make their products — in Chapter 13, but, if you can't wait until then, check out the following websites:

- ✔ **Bloomberg** (www.bloomberg.com) has a professional-grade site that lets you watch movements in just about any commodity you can imagine, including gold, silver and platinum. Under Market Data in the menu bar choose Commodities from the dropdown menu and then select Commodities Futures. Interested in soybean futures? Yes, you can see the price. This data is necessary if you want to invest in commodities directly. Still, even if you don't buy or sell commodities, they're good to watch. For example, if you own shares in any of Australia's big resource companies, you want to know which way metal prices are moving.

- ✔ **Chicago Board of Trade** (www.cbot.com) lists prices on many of the major commodities such as corn, soybeans, wheat and ethanol.

Tracking bonds and US treasuries

A *bond* is an IOU issued by a government (typically the US government, where they're also called *treasuries*), a company or another borrower. If you own a bond, you're entitled to receive the borrowed funds back by a certain date at a predetermined interest rate. Even if you're not interested in investing in bonds, you still should know what their rates are doing, because bond prices are one of the best indicators of sentiment in the world economy. We go into more detail on bonds in Chapter 14.

Bonds don't deliver the same kind of returns that stocks are expected to deliver in good times. But, in economic downturns, companies rarely deliver the same kind of performance as bonds do. This causes sections of the market to move away from the stock market and head for the safety of the bond market, where investors are guaranteed returns, albeit at a lower rate. So, when you see the bond market making significant moves, this is a signal that the market isn't so optimistic about the future performance of the stock market and is instead being funnelled into the bond market.

This is especially true of the US, where a strong bond market has much broader implications. If US bonds are rising, then the outlook for the equity market, and therefore the overall US economy, is bleak. As the US is one of the biggest consumers of products and services worldwide, this has implications for the producers of those products; that is, other economies such as China and Mexico. When the outlook of those economies is affected by circumstances in the US, their forecasts are revised and their own activities modified as a result. This is the basis for the much-repeated phrase, 'When the US sneezes, the whole world gets a cold.'

You can check the pulse of the US economy and the performance of the bond market on Bloomberg, at www.bloomberg.com (choose Rates & Bonds from the Market Data dropdown menu and select Government Bonds) or read the commentary available on Business Spectator (www.businessspectator.com.au). The regular SCOREBOARD column is listed on the right-hand side of the page each work day from 8 am.

Monitoring Market-Moving News

Ever see a mining stock skyrocket after the company announced good surveying results? Or a biotech stock jump in price after making an announcement regarding a breakthrough treatment? That's the power of news — called *market-moving news* in these particular cases. Markets are constantly taking in and digesting all sorts of developments and changes, both good and bad. And, to stay on top of these developments, you want to set a few leading financial news sites as favourites. The following sections explore the different kinds of financial news sites in greater detail.

Financial websites

Many of the financial sites mentioned earlier in this chapter are also great places to get market-moving news. Yahoo!7 Finance (http://au.finance.yahoo.com) picks up stories written by wire services on the markets and on individual stocks, making it a helpful resource but not entirely unique. Bloomberg (www.bloomberg.com) is another helpful resource that covers finance news globally, but is usually best at covering its home turf, the US. Other excellent sources of market-moving news include:

- **Google News Australia** (http://news.google.com.au): The Business section (choose from the list on the left-hand side) is a must-read for any serious investor trying to keep on top of the daily flow of information. Google doesn't produce any unique content itself, it collates news from a range of sources and presents it all in one place. It's not the prettiest website, but Google's power comes from its functionality. If a single story is covered by a number of outlets, it groups them all together, allowing you to choose which source you prefer. Of course you can also use Google's famed search features based on keywords like company names, locations and dates.

- **Business Spectator** (www.businessspectator.com.au): A round-the-clock news and commentary website dedicated to the world of business and finance, the site is essentially divided into three sections. The middle section contains breaking news stories, with an emphasis on news featuring listed companies or market-moving news. The column on the right contains commentary and analysis, where experienced commentators interpret the news and what it may mean for companies and sectors. On the left are industry categories that you can click on to see the latest news and commentary on a particular sector, whether it's mining or IT. The strength of Business Spectator is that not only is the news in real-time, which we expect in this day and age, but the commentary is real-time as well, so you don't have to wait for the following day's newspaper to read analysis of events. Best of all, it's completely free. (See Figure 2-2.)

- **MarketWatch** (www.marketwatch.com): A comprehensive site for all the US business news you need. Like Business Spectator, it has columns from various financial writers who opine about everything from companies' accounting practices to technology. It also features lots of nifty applications that can email you stories on companies you're interested in.

Figure 2-2: Business Spectator is a free round-the-clock news and commentary website.

Many financial websites and news stories use the terms *bullish* and *bearish*. When investors are bullish, they think the stock market is going to go up. And, when investors are bearish, they think stocks will go down.

Do you speak company code?

Nearly every financial website is centred on the company code. These are the three- or five-letter abbreviations used to symbolise stocks or investments. But the code has taken on a new use in the online era, so much so that most sites have an empty text box at the top where you enter the code first, click a button and then get sent to another part of the site, where you're handed all the information pertaining to that stock on a silver platter.

Company codes have become so popular that investors sometimes use them instead of a company's name. For example, Commonwealth Bank is often referred to as CBA, its company code. National Australia Bank was referred to as NAB by just about everyone except the bank itself before taking to using the abbreviation in its marketing in 2007. Although some company codes are easy to remember (AMP, AXA, CSL, CSR are all the same as their company names), others are not as obvious as you may think. Telstra Corporation, for example, is TLS. You can check a company's code on most finance websites, including the ASX site.

Traditional financial news sites

Many of the financial news providers you may already be familiar with from newspapers, magazines and TV also provide data useful to investors online, including the following:

- **News.com.au Business (**www.news.com.au/business**):** One of the latest entrants on the online business news scene, News.com.au Business is a well-laid-out website that draws its content from the *Australian*, the *Daily Telegraph*, *Herald-Sun* and other content partners, including US business news giant Dow Jones, which owns the *Wall Street Journal*. Its rich selection of content and market information, as well as its crisp, clean layout make it another worthy addition to your bookmarked news sites. (See Figure 2-3.)

- **Business Day (**www.businessday.com.au**):** This site pools the resources of two big Australian newspapers, the *Sydney Morning Herald* and the *Age*, in one convenient online destination. In addition to the content from the newspapers, it updates breaking news and commentary throughout the day. It also includes a business news wire and the kind of market information that you'd expect from a big business news website.

- **AFR (**www.afr.com**):** The online offering of Australia's leading business newspaper, the *Australian Financial Review*, contains a mix of free and subscriber-only content. The top news items and videos are free, but to access most of the site requires a subscription. There's no question that this is one of the most comprehensive sources of business news in Australia, but subscriptions aren't cheap. If you're curious, take advantage of the 14-day trial to see if it suits your needs.

- **Wall Street Journal Online (**www.wsj.com**):** You might be familiar with the print edition of the *Wall Street Journal*; this is the online version, a source of breaking financial news. This site charges for much of its content, but top news stories and opinion are free.

- **Financial Times (**www.FT.com**):** A London-based business publication, it provides a unique spin on business events here in Australia. It's a good source of merger announcements.

- **BusinessWeek.com (**www.businessweek.com**):** A stand-out site for investors, largely due to the fact that it's owned by McGraw-Hill, which also owns Standard & Poor's. The site offers some truly professional-level tools that are worth your while, as well as excellent insights into the direction of the economy, individual sectors and specific companies.

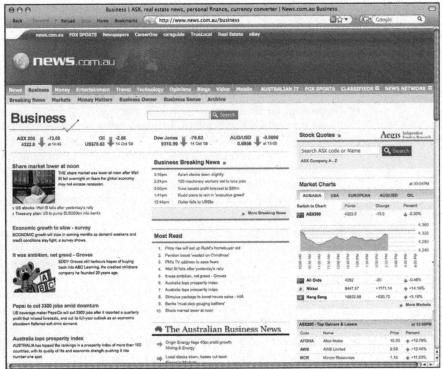

Figure 2-3:
News.com.
au Business
is a rich
source of
business
news and
market data.

Checking In on Market Gossip

Rumour and innuendo are key parts to traders' lives. Because stock prices
are highly sensitive in the short term to what other traders and investors
are saying about a stock, traders make it their business to follow any
murmur. As an individual investor, you're somewhat at a disadvantage in
this department because you don't have portfolio managers of giant funds
calling you to tell you what they're hearing. But you can use chat rooms,
which we cover in more detail in Chapter 5, or online blogs and podcasts
(we cover these next), if you're interested in the scuttlebutt.

If you're a passive investor, you probably couldn't care less about rumours.
Even so, you can take advantage of blogs and chat rooms that are dedicated
to index investing. Just remember that these are casual and sometimes
unreliable ways to keep up with the market chatter on various topics.

Beware of rumours

Investors can't help themselves when it comes to rumours. And sometimes certain blogs and podcasts only feed your innate desire to get the inside scoop on an investment about to explode in value. Investment rumours are kind of like celebrity gossip: You're probably better off ignoring them, but sometimes it's impossible to resist. Just remember that making investment decisions based on rumours is usually a very bad idea.

Even giant stocks can get swept up in rumours and result in pain for gullible investors. Here's a recent example: On 8 June 2007, U.S. Steel, one of the world's largest producers of steel, saw its stock price soar 8 per cent to US$125.05. The move created more than US$1 billion in shareholder wealth overnight. And it was all because of rumours and speculation that the company was going to be bought. But investors who piled in were sorry when it turned out the rumour wasn't true. In the following two trading days, the stock crumbled more than 9 per cent, erasing the entire gain, and then some.

Everyone's an expert: Checking in with blogs

Thanks to low-cost computers and internet connections, just about anyone with an opinion and a keyboard can profess their view of investments to the world. Some of these opinions are worth listening to, but many aren't. One popular vehicle for sharing opinions is a *blog* (short for web log), which is a sort of online journal. Blogs can vary greatly in quality. Some are the modern-day equivalent of a crazy person on the street corner wearing a sandwich-board and yelling at anyone who walks by with a bullhorn, whereas other blogs are thoughtful and well informed. It's *buyer beware* with blogs, and you have to decide whether the person is worth listening to. Ask yourself what the blogger's track record is and how the blogger makes money.

With so many blogs out there, sometimes the toughest part can be finding them. Here are several ways you can locate them:

✔ **General search engines:** All the leading search engines, including Yahoo!7 and Google, let you search much of the blogging world. If it's a major blog, you're likely to find it just by searching this way: Enter the name of the company in the search window of any search engine and add the word **blog** to it to find blogs and blog entries about your chosen company. Different search engines are likely to deliver different results, so make sure you try a few out.

- ✔ **Blog search tools:** Technorati (`www.technorati.com`) was the original, and some say the best, blog search engine, tracking 112 million blogs as of June 2008. Blogs are organised under topic, which makes browsing much easier! Another popular option is Google's Blog Search (`http://blogsearch.google.com`). Just enter investment terms you're interested in and you get a list of the sites that meet your criteria.

- ✔ **Community sites:** Sites such as MySpace (`www.myspace.com`) and Facebook (`www.facebook.com`) are best known as places for musicians to promote their latest albums and for families to share photos with each other. But some financial blogs are also lurking on these community sites. To find them, just log on to the site and search for the words *financial*, *money*, *investing* or *stocks*.

- ✔ **Mainstream media:** Almost all of the news sites have some of their writers penning blogs as well. Many blogs are available via Really Simple Syndication (RSS), which we explain in the section 'Getting your computer to do the work: RSS feeds' later in this chapter.

Getting in tune with podcasts

Next time you see someone listening to an iPod or iRiver with earphone cords dangling from his ears, don't assume he's rocking out. He may be researching stocks or learning about investing. A *podcast* is an audio broadcast that's transferred electronically over the internet to your computer or MP3 player — they're like radio shows for the internet age but they're available any time you like. Like blogs, podcasts are often done by amateurs, so the same need for caution applies. But, also like blogs, some podcasts are produced by major media.

Podcasts haven't really taken off by storm, partly because the methods of delivery are still evolving. As podcasts become available to download to handheld devices wirelessly, another surge of interest can be reasonably expected from listeners and creators alike.

So, if you're still *desperate* to get started with podcasts, you can have a play with Apple's iTunes podcasting software. Apple is widely known for its easy-to-use products and its iTunes store is no exception. iTunes is free software that was used to launch Apple's popular iPod, but you don't need an iPod to take advantage of it. It's a reasonably large download though — about 60 MB — so it might take a while, depending on the speed of your internet connection. To get started, follow these steps:

1. **Visit** www.apple.com/itunes **and click the big blue button that says Download iTunes.**

   You need to enter your email address before clicking the same button again. Now might be a good time to make yourself a cup of tea! When it's finished downloading, double-click the file to install and then follow the prompts.

2. **After it's installed, open the program by clicking on iTunes Store on the far left.**

   This will reveal the much-lauded iTunes Store and will most likely be advertising whatever music it is young people are listening to these days. But it also has an excellent podcast search function, which you can access from the Store link.

3. **Click on the Podcasts link and, from the categories below that, select Business.**

   Here you can scroll through heaps of available podcasts with an emphasis on Australian podcasts.

You can listen to most podcasts in three ways:

✔ **Listen on the site.** You can listen to most podcasts by clicking a link, usually labelled Listen, directly on the site.

✔ **Download.** Some podcasts let you click a Download button or, with Windows PCs, right-click the Listen link and download them.

✔ **Subscribe.** You can install special software that will search your favourite podcasts and automatically download new episodes when they're available.

   Specialised podcasting software programs are also available. If you're running Windows on your computer, you can download and install Doppler (www.dopplerradio.net) or Juice (juicereceiver.sourceforge.net), which is also available for Mac.

Some podcasts let you download episodes using Really Simple Syndication, (RSS) links. We explain how to do this in the next section.

Getting your computer to do the work: RSS feeds

If you want to read investing news, read blogs or listen to podcasts, you can use the Favorites or Bookmark feature of your web browser to keep a bunch of sites in your Favorites list and then methodically make your way through them at your leisure. But some savvy online investors don't have time for that, so they use something called Really Simple Syndication, or *RSS feeds*. RSS feeds are kind of like notices sent out by some blogs, podcasts and news sites to let the world know that something new is available. If you use RSS feeds, you subscribe to a news website, blog or podcast, and the news comes to you.

It's easy to get started. First you need to have a way to receive the RSS feeds, through one of three main methods:

- **Install an RSS reader.** An RSS reader lets you tell the computer what websites you'd like to subscribe to. The RSS reader software then pulls the feeds containing articles from the different news sites you've chosen and presents them all to you in one page. Because RSS readers are software, the RSS articles the reader downloads are stored on your hard drive so you can read them later, even if you're not connected to the internet.

  FeedDemon is one example of an RSS reader for Windows, available from NewsGator (www.newsgator.com). Click on Products, choose RSS Readers and scroll down to FeedDemon. You can also find specialised RSS reader software programs, such as Investor Vista (www.investorvista.com), designed with the needs of online investors in mind. When they first came out, these types of readers weren't free; now you should be able to find something without having to pay for it.

- **Subscribe to a web-based RSS aggregator.** An *aggregator* creates a tailor-made page with all the RSS feeds you've requested. So, rather than logging on to individual sites, you log on to this one site that has dutifully pulled in all the RSS feeds you've subscribed to. A popular RSS aggregator is Google Reader (www.google.com/reader). If you use Google's Gmail and Google News, this can be another powerful addition to your web armoury.

  Some aggregators require you to be connected to the internet to read your RSS feeds. Google Reader (www.google.com/reader), however, allows you to download some of the RSS content if you install the separate Google Gears plug-in (http://gears.google.com).

- **Use your web browser.** If you're like us, you like to install as little software on your computer as you can get away with, and you don't like signing up for all kinds of web services. If that describes you, you may consider checking to see whether your internet browser supports RSS. The latest version of Internet Explorer, version 8, makes it pretty easy. Go to the website you'd like to subscribe to and click the orange

RSS feed icon, usually located to the right of the home icon on the menu bar. You see a list of all the available RSS feeds from the site, like the one in Figure 2-4. Click the Subscribe to This Feed icon, which looks like a gold star with a green plus sign. A dialog box pops up, letting you name the feed and click on Subscribe. After you subscribe, just click the Favorites icon (a gold star without a green plus sign) and select the Feeds tab, and you see a list of all the updates that were pulled down for you. You can download Internet Explorer here: www.microsoft.com (select from the Highlights or Popular Downloads list).

For more options, check the Yahoo! list of RSS readers and aggregators at http://dir.yahoo.com. (Click on Computers & Internet, select Data Formats, then XML and finally RSS. Then just click on RSS Readers and Aggregators.)

After you get your RSS software, web-based reader or browser set up, it's easy to start getting RSS feeds. Just navigate to your favourite investing sites and look for links that say RSS Feed or XML and click on them. Your reader, aggregator or browser then gives you instructions on how to subscribe.

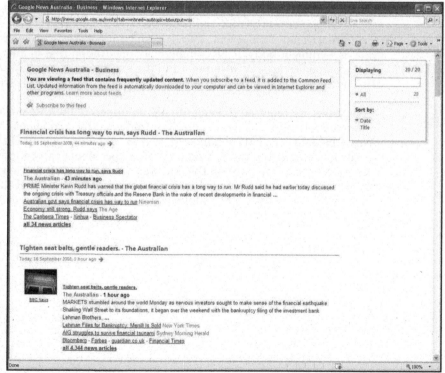

Figure 2-4:
Internet Explorer 8 makes it easy to subscribe to RSS feeds.

Understanding the Umpires: ASIC and the ASX

As an investor, it's important to pay attention to those bodies that make the rules, the regulators. In Australia, a number of regulators have important roles, but the most important role is the regulation of the market. That role is divided between two groups, a government body and the exchange operator — the Australian Securities and Investments Commission (ASIC) and Australian Securities Exchange (ASX). When comparing their roles it's easy to think of ASIC as the letter-of-the-law body and the ASX as the spirit-of-the-law body.

✔ **ASIC** (www.asic.gov.au) regulates the activity of companies, financial services and financial markets. If an individual or company is thought to be doing something misleading, deceptive or illegal, ASIC will pursue a course of action. ASIC's role is to protect consumers, investors and creditors. ASIC is also responsible for monitoring and ensuring compliance on behalf of the ASX.

✔ **ASX** (www.asx.com.au) is responsible for the regulation of listed companies on the ASX and is obliged to run a market that is fair, orderly and transparent. The ASX isn't a regulator in the sense of a government body; it's a commercial organisation that monitors the way companies are run with regard to the exchange, as a condition of its government licence.

Companies are required to keep the ASX informed of their financial position and material events, as well as director trades in the companies they direct. This reporting is called *continuous disclosure* and hefty penalties apply to companies that fail to do so. Company announcements can be found on a company's summary page on the ASX website. If you want to view company announcements as they're filed over the course of the day, visit the website, click on Prices, Research & Announcements and select Announcements (see Figure 2-5).

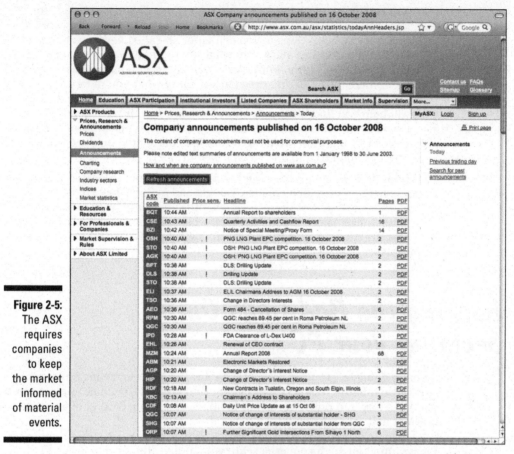

Figure 2-5:
The ASX
requires
companies
to keep
the market
informed
of material
events.

Searching the Internet High and Low

If you're not able to find what you're looking for by using the tips and
techniques in the preceding sections, hit the main web search engines. Some
of the most popular search engines include:

- **Google (**www.google.com**):** Definitely the biggest and most popular
  web search engine; so much so that investors often say they'll *Google*
  a stock. Because the site is so clean and Zen-like, it has the benefit of
  being very easy to use.

✔ **Yahoo!7** (http://au.dir.yahoo.com): Yahoo!7 is a good place for investors to search because it has two types of searches, keyword and directory. As with Google, you can enter so-called *keywords* to search for. But if you're not quite sure what the right keywords are, use the link above. The entire World Wide Web is put into categories for you. From there, you can drill down in search of what you're looking for. For example, click on the Business & Economy category and the directory will help you find blogs and other business resources. There's also a Finance and Investment sub-category that pinpoints sites on precise topics ranging from brokerages to bonds and initial public offerings. Another good tool to add to your favourites.

✔ **Dogpile** (www.dogpile.com): Dogpile isn't so much a search engine but a collection of search engines. Google and Yahoo!7 have most of the market sewn up but there are a few other minor players in the search market, like Ask.com and Microsoft's Live Search. Dogpile will run your search terms through these search engines and a few more for good measure.

Keeping the Bad Guys Out: Securing Your PC

If you're going to use your computer to process your investing and banking tasks, you'd better lock it down. Cyber criminals have become sophisticated and have targeted online investors in hopes of gaining control of a person's account and stealing money.

Please, don't let such concerns scare you off investing online. After all, cars get broken into and you still drive. It's just that you must take certain precautions to make it harder for the bad guys to get into your PC. These precautions include:

✔ **Installing antivirus software:** If a sinister code designed to wreak havoc on your computer gets on your machine, it can be a real hassle. Viruses can corrupt system files and make your computer unreliable or unusable. Antivirus software is the easy solution. It runs in the background, looking at any program that tries to run on your computer and stopping the program if it tries to do something improper. Many antivirus software programs are available, including:

• **Commercial:** Antivirus programs from McAfee (www.mcafee.com), Symantec (www.symantec.com) and TrendMicro (http://us.trendmicro.com) are popular. But these will cost you.

- **Free versions:** Another option is to download and install a free antivirus software program, such as AVG Free (http://free.avg.com), for Windows only.

✔ **Installing antispyware software:** Spyware is software that attaches itself to your computer without your permission and runs behind the scenes. It's especially sinister because it might forward personal information to a third party, usually for marketing purposes. AVG (http://free.avg.com) offers free Anti-Spyware software as does Avira (www.avira.com — click on Downloads), but countless others are available. Just search for the word *spyware* at Download.com (www.download.com) and see which ones work for you. Many are free.

✔ **Using firewalls:** A firewall is an electronic barrier that (selectively) separates you from the internet at large. A proper firewall is like a moat around a castle — only traffic that you lower the drawbridge for can get in.

- **Built-in:** If you have Microsoft Vista, you have a firewall turned on by default. Windows XP has a built-in firewall, too, but you have to make the extra effort and turn it on. Just call up the Run dialog box (choose Start⇨Run), type **Firewall.cpl**, click OK, click the General tab in the dialog box that appears, and then select the On (recommended) option.

- **Router:** Another way to protect your computer with a firewall is to install a router. A router is a small box that sits between your computer and the wall jack that connects you to the internet. Many routers work like a software firewall and can even make your computer invisible to other computers. Depending on your router, you may need to enable the firewall (refer to the preceding point). Check the router's instructions to find out how.

- **Third-party software:** A number of companies make firewall software, some of which is free. ZoneAlarm Pro (www.zonealarm.com.au) is one option, which costs $45. Comodo Free Firewall (www.personalfirewall.comodo.com), you guessed it, is free.

✔ **Installing all-in-one security:** If the idea of installing three different levels of security (antivirus, antispyware, firewall) seems complicated, check out the available all-in-one answers. Microsoft offers Windows Live OneCare (http://onecare.live.com), and Symantec has Norton 360 (www.symantec.com — click on Norton 360 under the For Home options).

For the time being, the malicious creators of such terrors as viruses and spyware have ignored Mac users but that's no reason to get complacent. SecureMac, McAfee, Norton and Alsoft all make at least one product for Mac users.

Mastering the Basics with Online Tutorials and Simulations

Online investing is like life; there are no second chances. If you invest all your money in a speculative company that goes belly up, you lose your money. Don't expect the government to bail you out and don't think you can sue the company to get your money back. It's gone. That's why, if you're new to investing, you may want to try the tutorials and simulations we suggest in the following sections, before using real money.

Online tutorials

Before you jump into any risky activity, take a deep breath, relax and make absolutely sure you understand how the process works. Several excellent online tutorials can step you through the process to make sure you know what to expect before you start investing for real. If you're just starting out, run through one of the following first:

- **ASX audio-visual presentations** are an excellent way to brush up on the basics of investing. Go to the homepage (www.asx.com.au), click on Education & Resources from the list at the left, select Education and scroll down to Online Education Resources. Running for just a few minutes each and covering topics such as 'What is the stockmarket?' and 'The language of trading' (see Figure 2-6), this is yet another must-visit destination for any aspiring investor. The presentations require sound, so get out your headphones or plug in your speakers, pour yourself a cup of tea and sit back and enjoy.

- **CommSec's online seminars** are geared toward CommSec members, but that doesn't mean that you can't sit in on their presentations for free! Go to the homepage (www.commsec.com.au), click on Tools & Support from the menu bar and click the More button next to Education at the bottom right. These bright multimedia presentations are clear and concise. The presentations range from introductory topics to the more advanced techniques of trading. To get the full benefit, you need sound on your computer to follow the presentations in their entirety.

✔ **Eureka Report** is a subscription website that also contains a free beginner's section. Go to the homepage (www.eurekareport.com.au) and click on How To in the menu bar. If fancy multimedia presentations aren't your thing, then this collection of web pages is a good place for any budding investor looking for a grounding in the essentials.

✔ **ASX's Getting Started in Shares** is a great alternative if you're tired of spending time in front of the computer. Looking to rest your eyes? Then look no further. Just go to the ASX homepage (www.asx.com.au), click on ASX Products, choose Shares and scroll down to Simple Ways to Get Started. Getting Started in Shares is an excellent guide from the ASX designed for printing, so you can investigate the basics of the sharemarket from the comfort of your armchair. Enjoy!

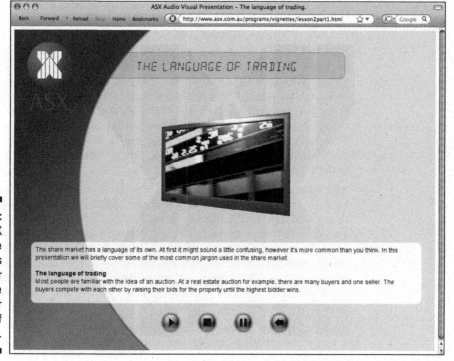

Figure 2-6:
The ASX website contains a number of online tutorials for all types of investors.

Be careful about which online tutorials you read and pay attention to. Many so-called tutorials are thinly guised pitches for investment professionals trying to get you to hire them. Some also promote specialised trading techniques with the purpose of getting you to buy books, videos and other materials.

Simulations

Online games, or simulations, let you buy and sell real stocks using only funny money. Online simulations are a good idea for investors because they let you get a taste for investing before you commit to a strategy. Making your first few trades can be a nerve-wracking experience, and these simulators will help make you more confident when you're ready to trade.

A few simulators you can try out include:

✔ **ASX Trading Simulation** is a nifty little application that's a cross between a tutorial and a simulator. Go to the homepage (www.asx.com.au), choose Education & Resources and then Education, and scroll down to New Online Shares Courses. The simulator is number 5b. It takes you through the process of buying a stock from motivation to research to execution using the familiar layout of the ASX website as a basis for the transaction (see Figure 2-7). Straightforward and to the point, James wishes he knew about this simulator when he was first getting started!

✔ **ASX Sharemarket Game** is a virtual stock market where you can hone your trading skills with a pretend $50,000, which makes sense in a world where all kinds of virtual entertainment is the norm. Again, go to the ASX homepage (www.asx.com.au), choose Education from the Education & Resources list and scroll down to Games. The ASX operates two sharemarket games, one for students and one for the general public. The games are run twice a year so don't despair if registrations are closed at the time you visit the site. Just put a note in your diary to check back soon.

✔ **Sydney Futures Exchange Trading Simulator** is the game for you if you know what you're doing in the sharemarket and are after something a bit more exotic — like the futures market, which we cover in Chapter 15. Follow the instructions for the ASX Sharemarket Game and choose from the Games list. In this simulator, you start with $250,000 but, be warned, futures are a highly volatile trading instrument. That $250,000 may disappear sooner than you think!

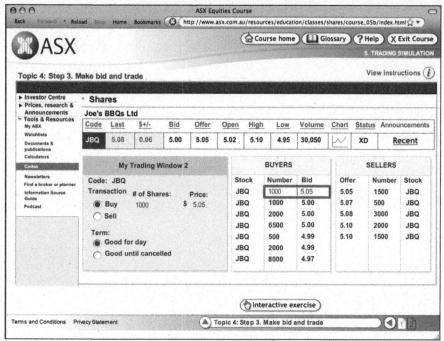

Figure 2-7:
The ASX trading simulator is excellent preparation for the real thing.

Chapter 3

Connecting with an Online Broker

- -

In This Chapter

▶ Deciding what you need from a broker

▶ Knowing the differences between self-service and full-service brokerage

▶ Protecting yourself against hidden fees

▶ Checking out broker report cards

▶ Making sure your money is safe with your broker

▶ Accessing your account with your broker

▶ Keeping track of where your funds are

▶ Flying solo without a broker

▶ Setting up your account and getting started

- -

*I*n this chapter, we dive through the offers from all the major online brokerages to pinpoint which ones fit your needs. Why can't we save you the trouble and just tell you which broker is the best? It's not that easy. Choosing 'the best' brokerage is like choosing the most beautiful painting in an art museum. Everyone has an opinion based on what's most important to them. When choosing a broker, if you're most interested in dirt-cheap commissions and don't care much for service, you have one set of brokers to pick from. On the other hand, you may be interested in accessing broker research or making complicated trades, in which case you have an entirely different set of candidates.

You may think you don't need this chapter because you like a certain broker's ads on TV or have a friend who swears by his online broker. But don't underestimate the benefits that can accrue for you if you thoroughly research your broker options — face it, your broker is the gatekeeper of your money, and picking the right one partially determines how successful you are as an investor.

Finding the Best Broker for You

People are constantly looking for the 'best' of everything. Photography buffs pore through magazines and websites looking for the best camera, commuters seek the best car, and parents search for the best stroller. Similarly, investors are on a constant quest for the best online broker. But, just as different cameras, cars and strollers fit different people's needs, the same is true with brokerages. As we explain in the previous two chapters, investors have different goals, taste for risk and resources. And that's why one person's broker can be perfect for her, but completely wrong for you.

 Not thoroughly researching your broker is a mistake. The fact that people often rush to pick an online broker may explain why many aren't happy with their choice. Many investors find it difficult to change after they've made their choice.

Main factors to consider

Brokers differ from one another in eight main ways. If you're aware of these eight things and understand what you're looking for, you can quickly eliminate brokers that don't fit your needs. The factors to consider are:

- **Commissions:** Perhaps the most important consideration for many investors is the price charged for executing trades, known as the *commission*. We discuss fees at length in the section 'Avoiding Hidden Fees' later in this chapter.

- **Availability of advice:** One way brokers separate themselves is whether or not they give you any help picking investments. On one end of the spectrum are the *full-service traditional brokers* that are all about giving you personalised attention. Not only will they pick stocks for you, but they'll also pour you coffee and serve you petit fours when you visit them in their fancy offices. If you're not interested in paying for such niceties, the *self-service brokers* are happy to oblige. Self-service brokers give you the tools you need, and then you're pretty much on your own. A few brokers fit somewhere between full-service and self-service brokerage.

- **Other banking services:** A brokerage account doesn't have to be a financial island. Some brokerage firms let you move money from your trading account into other types of accounts, such as high-interest savings or cheque accounts.

✔ **Speed of execution:** When you click Buy or Sell on your broker's website, it doesn't mean the trade is done. Your order snakes its way from your computer to other traders on the Australian Securities Exchange (ASX), where it's filled. Some brokerages spend a great deal of effort giving you the fastest path to other traders. This speedy track means you get a price that reflects the true value of the stock you're buying or selling, which is generally beneficial. Depending on your strategy, you may not want your orders piling up in a bin, waiting to be filled. Speed of execution is tracked by broker-rating services, discussed later in this chapter in the section 'Finding Out What Reviewers Think'.

✔ **Customer service:** Do you have a question about your account or about making a trade? When you do, you'll need to reach the broker and ask it. The levels of service vary wildly. Some brokers have customer service reps available at your beck and call either in offices or on the phone. Others let you email a question and wait for an answer.

✔ **Site reliability:** You don't want to be in the position of finding a promising investment only to discover that your online brokerage is down for repair. Some brokerages focus on limiting system downtime, which may be important to you if you trade many times a day. Again, this is something broker-rating services measure.

✔ **Access to advanced stock-buying tools:** Some brokerage sites are pretty bare-bones because they assume the investors already have the software and tools they need. Other brokerages, though, provide comprehensive tools that track your performance, help you go prospecting for stocks, or monitor market movements or breaking news.

✔ **Ease of use:** Online brokers geared for people new to online investing or who plan to trade very infrequently are minimalist and have as few buttons as possible. But those aimed for hyperactive traders who click Buy and Sell so many times they have calluses on their fingers tend to give investors dozens of options, allowing them to do some advanced stuff. You place a buy order when you want to own a stock and a sell order when you want to unload it.

'Gotchas' to watch out for

Brokerage firms often have confusing commission structures to fool you into thinking you'll pay less than you ultimately do. Make sure you check to see if the firm charges extra for certain types of orders, such as limit orders (we discuss limit orders in Chapter 4) or managed funds. Some brokers sting you with fees or inflate commissions if you don't keep a balance of a certain size.

Some brokers also charge you for switching to another broker. Always check for covert fees before signing up. The section 'Avoiding Hidden Fees' later in this chapter will help you spot things to watch out for.

Separating the Types of Brokerages

Choosing a brokerage firm might seem intimidating, but it's really no different from picking a restaurant. There are fast-food restaurants, where you have to walk up to the counter, place your order and find a place to sit. Then there are full-service restaurants where you're seated and pampered by dressed-up waiters who bring everything at your command and even clean the breadcrumbs away when you're done.

The same goes for brokerages. Self-service brokers give you everything you need to get the job done and let you go for it. Because you're doing much of the work yourself, unless you ask for help, self-service brokers tend to have the lowest commissions. Self-service brokers are commonly grouped into three baskets — *deep discounters*, *discounters* and *premium services*. Then there are the full-service traditional brokerages, which hold your hand through the whole process, down to suggesting investments, analysing your portfolio and offering estate-planning services. Remember that these are general brokerage types, and sometimes the lines blur a bit because some self-service brokers let you buy advice from them if you ask.

If you can't find a page on the broker's site that lists all its fees, commissions and other charges in less than three mouse clicks from the homepage, look elsewhere. Brokers that bury fees do so for a reason.

How do you decide what you need? It's really a matter of deciding ahead of time how often you intend to trade, what types of investments you plan to buy and how long you'll hold them. Knowing this in advance is difficult, but methods of figuring it out exist. For example, did you perform the trading simulations we mention in Chapter 2? If so, how often did you trade? Next, familiarise yourself with the four types of online brokers — deep discounters, discount brokers, premium services and traditional brokers. The following descriptions show you what to expect at each level. Decide whether the extra whistles and bells are worth the extra cost. To make things easy, the key stats are summarised in charts after each section. We include the standard commissions to give you the most realistic scenario for each broker.

Double-check brokers' fees before signing up — they change frequently. Also remember some brokers may charge lower commissions if you pay a monthly subscription fee, meet certain balance thresholds or hold other types of accounts in addition to the brokerage account.

Deep discounters

These brokers are the Kmarts and Big Ws of the brokerage world. When you sign up with a deep discounter, you're on your own. But, if you know what you're doing, that's a good thing because you don't have to worry about getting pestered by a financial adviser trying to pitch stocks you have no interest in. And you'll get all the basics that you truly need, such as year-end tax statements, company information mailed to your door (if you choose paper delivery), basic access to stock quotes and research, and the ability to buy and sell stocks and other investments. But the real beauty of these brokers is their sweet, low price: Because they usually don't offer niceties like branches, they can have the lowest commissions, starting from $6 a trade. Leaders include:

- ✔ **Interactive Brokers:** A US-based brokerage firm with operations in over 70 markets worldwide. In terms of commissions, it is the cheapest of the brokers covered here, offering trades from just $6. To open an account with Interactive Brokers you need to start with $5,000. Interactive Brokers offers a healthy headline interest rate for your cash, but it only applies to sums over $10,000. The company also charges a minimum monthly commission of $10, so, unless you're trading more than two parcels of shares a month, it's not for you. Interactive Brokers is pitched at the active or professional trader.

- ✔ **Amscot Discount Broking:** Offers three different services. 'One-Off Sales' are for those looking to buy or sell shares without opening an account. 'Phone Trading' is for investors who want to deal with someone over the phone. 'Online Trading' is, you guessed it, its online service. Trades start at $14.85 and, as a standard account holder, you have access to HTMLIRESS, an entry-level market data tool that provides market information on a 20-minute delay.

- ✔ **Bell Direct:** The online brokerage arm of Bell Potter Securities. The new kid on the block, Bell plans to shake up the industry with rock-bottom prices and a full product suite. Bell Direct offers trading from $15 a parcel and includes either live or 20-minute-delayed trading data with its accounts. Bell's all-new trading platform is very easy to use and navigate both online or via a hand-held device like an iPhone. Bell also offers account holders the choice of trading online or by SMS at no extra charge. Cash sitting in your account with Bell will receive an adequate rate of interest, with no minimum deposit. (See Figure 3-1.)

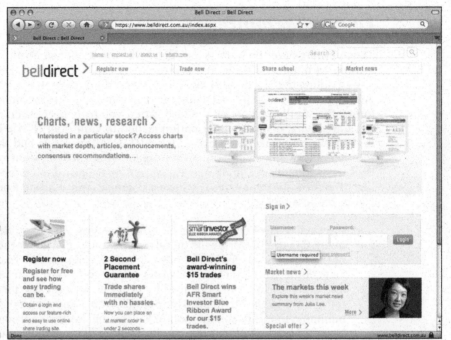

Table 3-1 sums up the main differences between the deep discounters.

Table 3-1	Deep Discounters		
Broker	**Website**	**Fee**	**Bracket**
Interactive Brokers	www.interactivebrokers.com.au	$6 0.08%	$500–$7,500 $7,501–$100,000,000
Amscot Discount Broking	www.amscot.com.au	$14.85 $19.80 0.088%	$500–$5,000 $5,001–$22,500 $22,501+
Bell Direct	www.belldirect.com.au	$15 0.1%	$500–$15,000 $15,001–$250,000

Beginning investors always want to know how much money they need to start and where they can get started investing online. The ASX requires trades to be no smaller than $500 so, if you choose a broker like Bell Direct, with no minimum deposit requirement, you can get started really quickly. Most people prefer to trade in multiples of $2,000 because of the relative cost of commissions.

Discount brokers

If the thought of being completely on your own makes you nervous, but you're not willing to give up low-cost commissions, then discount brokers sit in the sweet spot for you. These brokers suit most investors, ranging from beginners to the more advanced, and offer trading in small parcels of shares from $17.95 to $20. Some of them offer real-time stock information, some provide research and some offer automated *stop-loss trading orders* (which sell your shares automatically when they reach a certain price — we explain these orders in detail in Chapter 4). But what they won't do is provide you with everything. Here's a selection of some of the best discount brokers:

- ✔ **OneTrade Stockbroking:** Offers trades from $17.95 but, overall, it offers significantly fewer features than those provided by its competitors. It doesn't provide updates on the state of the market or access to analyst research. And it doesn't provide access to managed funds, so investors looking to diversify their portfolios should look elsewhere. It does, however, offer a stop-loss feature. Overall, this type of account is hard to recommend to anyone seeking more than just a broker through which to buy shares.

- ✔ **netwealth:** Product offerings here are a little more sophisticated than OneTrade's. It offers research, market reports and an online demonstration. Sophisticated investors will also be pleased to know netwealth offers access to managed funds and initial public offerings (or IPOs — see Chapter 17 for more information). However, it doesn't provide anywhere near the level of features that you can expect from some of the bigger brokers. It doesn't offer access to international shares or options, or provide a forum for investor discussion. It doesn't offer a stop-loss feature either.

- ✔ **optionsXpress Australia:** The Australian arm of this long-established Chicago-based operation specialises in options. We explain options in more detail in Chapter 15, but essentially *options* are financial instruments that let investors either reduce risk or turbo-charge their returns. But optionsXpress Australia also offers access to stocks on the ASX and international markets for the flat fee of $23.95 per trade without charging a monthly account fee (see Figure 3-2). It also provides real-time stock information, simulators and reports.

Figure 3-2:
optionsXpress isn't the cheapest online broker but it does offer real-time stock data.

Table 3-2 sums up the main differences between the discount brokers.

Table 3-2	Discount Brokers		
Broker	**Website**	**Fee**	**Bracket**
OneTrade	www.stockbroking.onetrade.net.au	$17.95 $24.75 $27.50 0.077%	$500–$5,000 $5,001–$15,000 $15,001–$30,000 $30,001+
netwealth	www.netwealth.com.au	$17.99 $19.95 $26.99 0.11%	$500–$5,000 $5,001–$10,000 $10,001–$25,000 $25,001+
optionsXpress	www.optionsxpress.com.au	$23.95	$500+

Are free trades really free?

When anything claims to be 'free' in online investing, your defences should go up instantly. CommSec, E*TRADE and others promise free trades to investors. Be on guard and evaluate all the stipulations, though, before assuming these free offers are best for you. (See the section 'Avoiding Hidden Fees' later in this chapter.) The first thing to remember when looking at free brokerages is, if they require you to open a specially linked account, don't overlook what interest rate they pay. Not paying attention to interest rates could wipe out any savings you think you're getting from free trades.

Here's what we mean. Say you trade five times a year and normally leave about $10,000 of uninvested cash in your account. If trades are free, it's true, your commission costs would be zero. But you still could be overpaying if you're not getting a high rate of return on your uninvested cash. In fact, you'd be $500 better off paying $30 a trade if you get 6.5 per cent interest on cash sitting in your account.

Matt's come up with a formula that takes the guesswork out of 'free' trades:

1. **Multiply the number of trades you do each year by the commission. Save this number.**

2. **Multiply the amount of uninvested cash you expect to keep in your account by the interest rate you will collect. Divide this number by 100 and save the result.**

3. **Subtract the result of Step 2 from the result of Step 1.**

This formula shows you how much the commissions are costing you: The lower the number, the better. If you're choosing between a couple of brokers, crunch this formula and choose the broker with the lowest (or negative) number.

Premium services

Premium services aren't trying to win your business by tempting you with dirt-cheap commissions. You can generally expect to pay around $30 or more per trade unless you're a frequent trader or open a special linked account with the service provider. These brokerages attempt to justify their costs by providing a better service. They aim to provide a full suite of research tools but, in some cases, they fall short. You may feel more secure knowing that you're dealing with an established brand, in many cases one of Australia's 'big four' banks — ANZ, Commonwealth Bank, NAB and Westpac. Some of the premium-service providers are listed next.

- **CommSec:** Australia's largest online broker is operated by Australia's second-largest bank, Commonwealth Bank, but it isn't exactly cheap. Trades in parcels under $10,000 can fall to $19.95 if you open a Direct Investment Account. For regular investors, parcels of shares between $500 and $25,000 will cost you $29.95; and parcels above $25,000 attract a commission of 0.31 per cent, which is by far the most expensive. The CommSec trading platform is easy to use and easy on the eye (see Figure 3-3). CommSec's service provides all clients with real-time trading data, market reports and access to international markets, managed funds and margin lending. (We explain margin lending in Chapter 15.)

- **E*TRADE:** A flat fee of $32.95 per trade applies to transactions up to $30,000 and the service provides investors with real-time sharemarket data. With the higher price point, investors are drawn to E*TRADE by the extra features, which include research and analysis from a wide range of sources. Active traders are also catered for with E*TRADE's frequent-trader discount. After making ten trades in a month, trades 11–20 cost you only $27.45 each and trades 21+ cost $21.95 each. E*TRADE is backed by Australia's third-largest bank, ANZ.

- **Westpac Broking:** Another service from one of Australia's big banks, although it comes a distant third in terms of market share to CommSec and E*TRADE. It offers little in the way of technical analysis tools and only garden-variety research. As far as premium-service online brokers go, Westpac is relatively cheap compared with the competition, offering trades for $29.95 for parcels up to $25,000. However, unlike CommSec, you can't access international markets. Many of the services are handled by Westpac's wealth and funds-management division, BT. All Australia's big banks now have online broking services, but that doesn't mean they were all made equally.

- **Macquarie Prime:** The online trading platform from Australia's leading investment bank, Macquarie Bank. It charges a flat fee of $20 or 0.12 per cent (whichever is greater) on trades up to half a million dollars After that, it drops down to 0.10 per cent. This product has all the bells and whistles that you expect from an investment bank. You can borrow money to invest, trade derivatives and take *short positions* (sell shares you don't own with the intention of buying them back later at a profit, but more on that in Chapter 15). Account holders can also access Macquarie's highly regarded research. This type of account is not so much aimed at the active trader as the high-net-worth trader.

Figure 3-3:
Australia's largest broker appeals to investors looking for a mix of functionality and reliability.

Table 3-3 shows you how the pricier outfits differ from one another.

Table 3-3	Premium Services		
Broker	**Website**	**Fee**	**Bracket**
CommSec	www.commsec.com.au	$29.95 0.31%	$500–$25,000 $25,001+
E*TRADE	www.etrade.com.au	$32.95 0.11%	$500–$30,000 $30,001–$999,999
Westpac Broking	http://broking.westpac. com.au	$29.95 0.15%	$500–$25,000 $25,001–$999,999
Macquarie (MQ) Prime	www.macquarie.com.au/ prime	$20 or 0.12% 0.1%	$500–$499,999 $500,000–$1,999,999

The dreaded AMSLA

The year 2008 was a big year for investors in Australia for a number of reasons. The five-year bull market came to an end, the US downturn continued and prime broker Opes Prime collapsed. Opes Prime catered to the very top end of the market, active traders of high net worth. In English, this means wealthy people who trade a lot.

Opes charged a flat $33 per trade for parcels up to $200,000. But clients who traded much larger parcels of shares did so at a rate far cheaper than its competitors. For example, if you sell a $2 million parcel of shares through CommSec, it charges you $6,200, Macquarie Prime charges $2,000 and Amscot Discount Broking charges $1,760. Opes charged $750 for the same parcel. Quite a saving.

Opes also offered a lot of exotic features that this type of investor tends to favour, such as *margin lending*, where you borrow money to invest in shares. However, when these investors joined Opes Prime, they signed an agreement that effectively transferred ownership of their shares into the hands of the broker. This agreement was called an *AMSLA*, or *Australian Master Securities Lending Agreement*. As a result, when the broker collapsed, its creditors seized its assets, which included the share portfolios of its clients. We strongly advise you to avoid any broker that asks you to sign one of these agreements.

Traditional brokers

Because you're reading *Online Share Investing For Dummies*, chances are that you're a do-it-yourself kind of investor or one looking for minimal handholding. But maybe, after reading the preceding descriptions, you're looking for even more help. That's when you may want to consider a full-service traditional broker.

Traditional brokers pride themselves on being part of your team — 'people' who you call on routinely for advice, like your real estate agent, housekeeper and mechanic. The top full-service traditional brokerages are the big Wall Street firms you've probably heard of, such as Goldman Sachs JBWere, Morgan Stanley and UBS, and their Australian counterparts, Macquarie Private Wealth and Colonial First State. Most can now legitimately call themselves online brokerages because they have websites that let you view your accounts. Services that these firms provide include the following:

- ✔ **Constant stock recommendations:** Most big broking firms have famous strategists and analysts who think big thoughts and come up with stock tips. The brokers then pass those tips on to you.

- ✔ **Access to initial public offerings:** When companies go public, they first sell their shares to large investment banks. Those shares, especially if the initial public offering is expected to be popular, are often a sought-after commodity because they have the chance to pop in value the first day. If you're an active customer with these firms' brokerage divisions, you may get a shot at buying these shares at the IPO price. (You find more on IPOs in Chapter 17.)

- ✔ **Availability of other financial services:** If you're a customer with a full-service traditional brokerage, you may get extra financial services, such as help with your taxes or estate planning.

But, before you get too excited about the extra services that traditional full-service brokers may provide, consider the downsides:

- ✔ **High cost:** Investment banks have to somehow pay for those plush offices you're enjoying. The fees tend to be higher, and you may pay a lofty commission for each trade or pay a percentage of your assets.

- ✔ **Uneven treatment:** Remember that you becoming Goldman Sachs JBWere's best customer is unlikely, so don't expect to get the real goods. For instance, when shares of the next truly promising IPO are doled out, if you're not a top customer or famous, you probably won't get shares anyway. (Fees and rates can vary, too, which is why we didn't produce a table comparing fee structures for the full-service traditional brokerage crowd. As a rule, it starts at a minimum of $200.)

- ✔ **Potential for conflicts:** Because brokers are often paid by commission, they may have an incentive to urge you to trade more frequently than you want to.

Be sceptical if a friend or family member recommends a broker to you. Many brokerage firms give customers cash rebates or free trades as rewards if someone they refer signs up. We're not telling you that you can't trust your friends. Just know that people recommending their broker may have a motive other than telling you which broker is best for you.

Avoiding Hidden Fees

The stock trade commission is likely to be the fee you'll pay the most often, so it's wise to pay the most attention to it. But don't think it's the only fee. Brokers often charge a host of other fees, which, depending on your circumstances, can add up fast. You should look for a web page that discloses these fees, like the one shown in Figure 3-4. Here are some common hidden fees you should be aware of:

- **Duplicate CHESS statements** carry a fee you don't need to incur. Avoid the need to ask for a reprint for your records by keeping a comprehensive filing system of all your important documents! Alternatively, expect to be charged $16.50 for a reprint.

- **Fail fees** occur when you don't have enough money in your nominated account to settle with your broker. *Settlement* occurs three working days after the purchase (also called *T+3*). Fail fees or fines can vary wildly; however, you won't need to pay these at all if you're careful.

- **Maintenance fees** are monthly, quarterly or annual fees some brokers charge you just to have an account with them. Don't pay maintenance fees. Period. If you're paying them, you're probably at the wrong broker. Most brokers exempt you from paying maintenance fees if you meet certain requirements. If you can't meet them, switch to a different broker.

- **Margin fees** are interest charges resulting from borrowing money from the broker to buy investments. Buying on margin is only for the most risk-ready investors, and we explain why in Chapter 15.

- **Off-market transfer fees** are charged when you want to part ways with your broker. Expect to get slugged with a fee of $55 or higher, which brokers charge supposedly to cover their cost of shipping all your stock holdings and transferring cash to your new broker. The only way to avoid this charge is to sell all the stocks in the old account and then write a cheque to the new broker drawn on your old account. But this may not work. Keep in mind that you'll incur commissions for every stock you sell, and tax considerations might cost you well over $55.

- **Special orders** are added fees if you trade more than a set number of shares. Some brokers also charge extra for placing so-called *at-limit orders* — trades in which you set the price you're willing to accept. Limit orders are covered in more detail in Chapter 4.

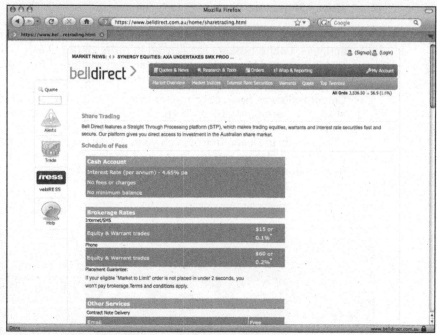

Figure 3-4:
Bell Direct
discloses all
its miscel-
laneous
fees on a
Schedule of
Fees page.

Finding Out What Reviewers Think

Analysing all the brokers' commissions can be overwhelming — there appear to be more moving parts than in a Swiss watch. Minimum requirements and fees vary, and it's hard to know how fast a broker's website will be until you actually sign up and try it. Luckily, some professional reviewers have kicked the tyres for you. Different rating services and publications that evaluate brokers each year include the following:

✔ **InfoChoice** (www.infochoice.com.au): A leading source of comparison-based information for a range of financial products, from home loans to insurance. The website, shown in Figure 3-5, also contains a comprehensive section dedicated to online brokers.

✔ **Choice** (www.choice.com.au): A website and a magazine run by the Australian Consumers Association. Not only do they provide consumers with the information needed to make good choices but they also lobby for change when they feel consumers are being ripped off. Click on Money to access information about how to choose an online broker.

✔ ***Money Magazine*** (http://money.ninemsn.com.au): This magazine also has an online presence. It holds annual readers' choice awards in December, when credit cards, super funds, frequent-flyer programs and, yes, online brokers are ranked in order of popularity. The readers and writers at *Money Magazine* are all very switched on about financial matters so expect only the best services to be listed here.

✔ **CompareShares** (www.compareshares.com.au): A new website pitched at sophisticated investors who trade derivatives. But there's plenty here that's relevant if you're just getting started. Like *Money Magazine*, it also runs awards in December of each year. It runs separate awards for Best Broker, Best Margin Lender, Best Forex Broker, Best Futures Broker and Best Options Broker. Another good source to compare your findings.

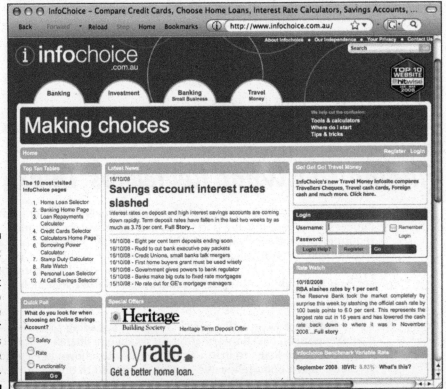

Figure 3-5: InfoChoice is a great site to compare all broker offerings in the one place.

Is Your Money Safe? Checking Out Your Broker

When you're about to hand over your life's savings to a broker, especially one with no offices, you want to make sure it's a reputable outfit. In response to the credit crisis of 2008, the Australian government moved to guarantee all deposits with authorised deposit-taking institutions on 12 October 2008. This was later refined on 25 October to include only those deposits that contained $1 million or less. It is expected that the government will continue to refine this guarantee as required.

You can find a list of these institutions on the Australian Prudential Regulation Authority website at www.apra.gov.au. Load up the homepage, place the cursor over Authorised Deposit-taking Institutions in the top navigation bar and then click on List of ADIs. For more information about the guarantee itself, visit Treasury's homepage at www.treasury.gov.au and, under Business, click on Financial Services. Under the heading General, click on Australian Government's 2008 Deposit and Wholesale Funding Guarantees.

Not all brokers are covered by this guarantee and it pays to check that your broker is covered. However, all brokers operating in Australia, both online and offline, must be licensed by ASIC with an Australian Financial Services Licence (AFSL). You can check to see that your broker is licensed at www.fido.gov.au/checkfirst. ASIC ensures that AFSL holders have the appropriate qualifications, comply with financial services laws and have appropriate dispute-resolution systems in place.

By dealing with an AFSL-registered entity, you're provided a financial services guide that outlines the services offered and fees charged by the group you're dealing with. You're also guaranteed access to an independent complaints-resolution scheme if something goes wrong. This includes the new Financial Ombudsman Service (www.fos.org.au).

Cutting the Cord: Wireless Trading

If the idea of checking up on your portfolio and placing trades while sipping margaritas by the pool appeals to you, get a hobby! Well, okay, sometimes you *do* need to check up on your account, even when you're not sitting behind a computer at your desk. To help, plenty of brokers provide wireless access to account information so customers can access their portfolios at any time, be it from a BlackBerry, iPhone or other wireless device. You have several ways to accomplish this, including:

- ✔ **From a laptop:** Most laptops are equipped with wireless capabilities. If your laptop is set up for wireless access, using popular Wi-Fi technology you can go online at thousands of locations that offer wireless internet connections, called Wi-Fi hotspots. Many hotspots available across the country are free to use, and the number of places offering free wireless internet is growing all the time. McDonald's has announced that it plans to offer free wireless in more than 720 restaurants across Australia. You can also connect using Wi-Fi services that charge access fees. If you try to go online in many of these places, you'll be prompted by a sign-up screen to give a credit card number and pay.

- ✔ **From a mobile phone or PDA:** Several online brokers reformat their web pages so they appear on the small screen of mobile phones and BlackBerries. Just open the wireless browser in your web-enabled BlackBerry, iPhone or Windows Mobile device and type the address of the broker. Some brokers, such as Bell Direct and CommSec, detect you're accessing them from a phone and reformat the pages automatically. Others require you to go to a special website from your phone.

Pay Attention to Where Your Cash Is Parked: Cash-Management Funds

You're an online investor, right? So why would you care about money you haven't invested? It turns out that one of the biggest secrets in the brokerage world is what happens to cash sitting in your account that's not invested. Don't underestimate how important this concept is. If you have $10,000 in cash in your account waiting to be invested, that's worth $650 a year at a 6.5 per cent interest rate. Which is our way of telling you that, before choosing an online broker, you want to be absolutely sure what rate of interest your uninvested cash gets and how it's handled.

Ideally, you want a *sweep* account. With a sweep account, idle cash is automatically scooped up and put into a cash-management account. You don't have to do anything, and you're certain your money is working for you. Just make sure your money is being swept into a cash-management account that pays an interest rate that is competitive with the going market rate. Bell Direct (www.belldirect.com.au) and MQ Prime (www.macquarie.com.au/prime) are two brokers that offer this service.

A word about wireless security

Security is a serious concern when dealing with your money, and we discuss how to keep your money safe in more detail in Chapters 2 and 20. But, when you access your stock data wirelessly, especially from a public area, you need to pay special attention to security. Here are two ways to do just that:

✔ Make sure your data is encrypted. Most internet browsers let you know whether the data is being *encrypted*, or scrambled. If you're using Microsoft's Internet Explorer, you can check by looking for the icon of a gold padlock. The gold padlock icon usually appears to the right of the address bar when a website asks for potentially sensitive information, such as account numbers, or when the website address begins with https (*s* stands for secure) rather than the usual http. When you see a gold padlock icon, that's a signal to you that the data is being scrambled to make it harder for the guy sitting next to you at McDonald's to read your information. Your computer and operating system scramble your data, which is then *decrypted*, or unscrambled, by the website.

You can click the gold padlock icon to get more information about the security of the website. Be sure to select the check box that pops up to confirm that the site's certificate, or identification, lists the name of your brokerage firm. If the gold padlock doesn't appear, that may mean the site uses a different method of securing data, which is something you should ask your broker about.

The padlock safeguard is a big help, but even scrambling isn't 100 per cent secure. To be extra safe, wait for Internet Explorer's address bar to turn green, which validates the connection is safe, although not all online brokers support this yet.

✔ **Use virtual private network (VPN) software.** VPN is a technology used to protect your data from snoops over the internet. Some internet service providers (ISPs) offer this service to customers, or, if you're using your work laptop, a VPN may be installed already, as corporations are keen to protect sensitive data.

Investing without a Broker

Australians have one of the highest rates of share ownership in the world. One of the reasons for this is the process of *demutualisation*, when companies that are owned by their customers list on the ASX. This happened quite a bit in the 1990s, the rationale being that it would help those companies expand, and it did.

The companies involved included AMP, AXA Asia Pacific (then National Mutual) and IAG (then NRMA). As a result, the policy owners in these mutually owned companies received stock in the mail. This has produced a peculiar situation where many Australians own shares without ever having gone near a broker.

Shares: Getting a slice of the action

Although acquiring stocks is possible without a broker, selling them is just about impossible. In order to sell shares, you need access to the market, and your broker is the gatekeeper.

The 'market' isn't a physical space, where you can trade goods with other interested parties, but more like a heavily regulated computer network called ITS (we go into more detail about ITS in Chapter 4). If you want to trade shares you must go through ITS, and if you want access to ITS then you must have an account with a licensed broker.

Shares can also be acquired as a gift, through a property settlement or by inheriting them. To put these shares in your name you need an Australian Standard Transfer Form. To get one of these forms, contact the share registry of the company whose shares you've been given.

Ultimately, developing an investment strategy based on shares without a broker isn't possible.

Managed funds: Straight from the source

Buying managed funds without a broker is not only possible, but also an excellent way to save money. *Managed funds* gather money from many investors and use the cash to invest in a basket of assets. When you buy a managed fund, you're joining a pool of other investors who own assets, rather than owning the assets yourself. You can read more about managed funds in Chapter 8.

One of the best things about managed funds is that you can buy them with no transaction fee if you deal directly with the fund. This can be a tremendous advantage, especially if you're making frequent and regular investments into a fund. In many cases, you can arrange for regular automated payments to be made via direct debit from a savings account. After you figure out what fund you want to buy, log on to the company's website, open an account and buy in. You'll save yourself some cash.

Opening and Setting Up Your Account

When you've made the decision about which broker to go with, the hard work is done. All you need to do to get started is open an account and get your cash to the broker, either online or through the mail. If you're comfortable signing up and transferring money online, which we imagine you are because you're reading *Online Share Investing For Dummies*, the online route is definitely the way to go because you can be up and running in a few hours or days. Signing up by mailing in a cheque and application, on the other hand, could take weeks.

Checklist: What you need to know

The biggest button on most brokers' websites is the Open an Account or Start Now button, so you won't have trouble finding it. Typically, that's all you need to launch the area of the website that will set up your account. (If you want to sign up through the mail, click on a link to download the necessary forms.)

Typically, you need to know two things to complete the application:

✔ **The kind of account you want to create:** This is usually a cash account or margin account. We cover margin accounts in more detail in Chapter 15.

✔ **The number of people associated with this account:** Is this just for you or for you and your spouse? This will determine whether you create an individual or joint account.

Checklist: What you need to have

You need these bits of info if you want to set up an account:

- ✔ **A photocopy of your driver's licence, passport or proof-of-age card:** If you're signing up online you'll need to scan it in.

- ✔ **Your tax file number (TFN):** If you're creating a joint account, you'll also need the TFN of the person you're setting up the account with. This is used for reporting purposes.

- ✔ **The account and BSB numbers of the account from which you'll transfer money:** Keep in mind some brokers won't let you open an account with electronically transferred money if you're depositing less than $500. In those cases, you need to mail a cheque.

- ✔ **The address of your employer:** You'll need to give this if you're a director of a publicly traded company.

See, that wasn't hard. And here's the best part: Now that you've entered all your information and funded your account, you're all set to start investing.

Chapter 4

Getting It Done: How to Enter and Execute Trades

. . . .

In This Chapter

▶ Understanding the trading process

▶ Placing orders and tailoring your trades

. . . .

All the theory in the world about online investing won't do you a bit of good if you can't seal the deal and *execute* your trades. Trade execution is the process of logging on to your online broker and buying or selling investments. You may be wondering what's so hard about buying a stock: Just log on to the online broker's website and click the Buy button. And in some cases, you're right. But sometimes you want to be a little more exacting. You can tailor your buys and sells so your broker carries out the transaction precisely how you want it handled. For example, you may want to buy a stock only if it falls below $25, or you may want your broker to automatically sell shares if they fall below a certain price.

In this chapter, we start at the beginning and go over all the ways you can hold your stock and how that decision affects how your trades are executed. Then we go over the main ways to enter orders — ranging from market orders to limit orders — and talk about the advantages and costs of each.

Understanding How Stock Trades and Shares Are Handled

When you buy or sell a share of stock online, you click a few buttons and everything is done. In a few seconds, if even that long, you'll often have a confirmation sitting in the messages section of your online broker's website or in your email inbox. The *confirmation* is a memo showing you what stock you bought or sold, the number of shares involved and the price at which the trade was executed.

But, perhaps unbeknown to you, after you clicked the Buy button, your trade wriggled its way through countless computer networks where buyers and sellers competed for your order to buy stock until it was ultimately *executed*, or filled. You may never need to know how this works, much like you may never need to know what's going on under the bonnet of your car, but it's an important part of investing online. So, the following sections describe a day in the life of a trade that's on its way from being an order on your computer screen to a done deal.

Ways you can hold your investments

Holding paper stock certificates as a means of record keeping was phased out in Australia by 1998 and, today, ownership of shares is recorded electronically. The register records your name, postal address and the size of your shareholding, so the companies can keep you updated and know who's on the register. You can hold stock in Australia in two ways.

CHESS

The Clearing House Electronic Sub-register System, or CHESS, was rolled out in 1993 as an alternative to paper stock certificates, and is by far the most popular way to hold shares among retail investors (individuals, as opposed to, for example, superannuation funds). To use CHESS you need a holder identification number (HIN), and to get a HIN you must be sponsored by a broker. Many online brokers register you with CHESS as part of the registration process. The Australian Securities Exchange (ASX) then provides you with a HIN.

All the shares you buy from this broker are then held under the one HIN, which makes it easy to keep track of. When you add to your holdings, CHESS sends you a statement at the end of each month (see Figure 4-1). The number of CHESS sponsors or HINs you can have is unrestricted, but shares bought through one CHESS sponsor must be sold through the same sponsor. You can transfer them to another CHESS sponsor and another HIN, but this defeats the purpose of using CHESS to begin with.

Apart from making paperwork easier, CHESS is also the system that transfers ownership of shares for payment. It performs the transaction when funds are moved between the participants' respective banks, called *settlement*, but we go into more detail on settling transactions in the section 'A second in the life of a trade' later in this chapter.

Issuer-sponsored trades

You can also hold your trades through the issuer-sponsored sub-register, in which case you'll be given a shareholder registration number (SRN). Every company on the ASX has an issuer-sponsored sub-register and, when you buy shares in a company, they will, by default, be registered there unless you've asked your CHESS sponsor to register them on the CHESS sub-register.

An SRN registers an investor's shareholding in a single listed company. If you choose to be issuer sponsored and hold shares in more than one company, you'll have a different SRN for each shareholding. As your portfolio grows, so too will your list of SRNs.

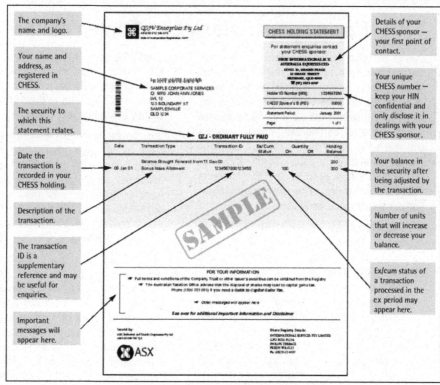

Figure 4-1: The CHESS system was designed to reduce paperwork for investors.

So, what's the difference between CHESS and issuer-sponsored trades?

Some investors like to retain more than one broker. In this case, holding shares in an issuer-sponsored sub-register under multiple SRNs is easier than using CHESS. When those investors want to sell, they aren't tied to a particular broker, and simply transfer the stock into their preferred broker's CHESS account. The downside is, if you move or need to amend your personal details, you'll need to contact all of the companies you hold stock in individually to inform them of the change.

CHESS, on the other hand, was developed to make it easier for investors to keep track of their shareholdings and eliminate the need for multiple SRNs. In this case, investors who move simply inform their broker, who in turn informs all the companies in which they hold stock. CHESS issues monthly holding statements for each security when the holding balance changes.

Buying paper stock certificates online

Due to the disadvantages listed elsewhere in this chapter, holding paper stock certificates for the shares in your portfolio doesn't make much sense. But some investors still like to buy paper stock certificates as gifts. Some people collect old stock certificates (mainly from the US) much like you'd collect stamps or coins. And the art of collecting stock certificates even has its own title — *scripophily*. If this interests you, check out these online services, which let you buy paper stock certificates:

✔ **OneShare.com** (www.oneshare.com) **and Frame-A-Stock** (www.frameastock.com): These single-share sales sites understand the lost art and beauty of many stock certificates. Both are US sites that let you buy a share of stock in companies that have certificates popular with individual investors. Both of these services even frame the certificates for you. The sites make it easy to find the perfect stock for the need. You can sort through the available certificates based on the occasion, recipient or interest. For men,

OneShare recommends Harley Davidson and Boston Beer, and for women it suggests Tiffany and Coach. Some certificates are also popular due to their artwork, with Disney being the best example.

Just be forewarned that you'll pay much more to acquire stock this way than through an online broker. In addition to the share price and framing fees, a US$39 transfer fee to acquire the stock is also applicable. A US$38-a-share stock may easily cost nearly US$130 by the time all the fees are added.

✔ **eBay** (www.ebay.com): Not surprisingly, eBay is a source for paper certificates. But, because eBay isn't licensed to sell securities like stocks, it has to be careful about what kinds of certificates its members sell; otherwise, eBay risks running foul of securities law. Only two types of stock certificates may be sold on eBay. The first type concerns old or collectible certificates of defunct companies, such as old railroads or internet companies. The other type that may be sold on eBay are single-share stock certificates packaged as gifts and marked as being non-transferable. eBay requires that these certificates sell for at least twice the current market value of the stock as evidence they're priced based on their keepsake value.

✔ **Scripophily.net** (www.scripophily. net): Certificate-collection sites such as Scripophily.net provide prices on some hard-to-find certificates. Even if you're not a collector, it's interesting to see what some of the certificates go for when they're popular with collectors. Some Standard Oil stock certificates, personally signed by John D. Rockefeller, for instance, sell for US$3,000 or more. Pixar stock certificates,

decorated with characters from *Toy Story* like Buzz Lightyear, were a hot commodity when the company was bought by Disney. Old shares of *Playboy* were popular for their, um, artwork, because the company's certificates used to display certain, let's say, assets. The old certificates have become even more sought-after since *Playboy*'s new certificates were changed to be more family friendly. The old shares sell for US$300 or more, which is greater than the share price of the company.

And some infamous companies, like Enron, as shown in the figure below, also have collectible value, even though the companies themselves have largely vanished.

A second in the life of a trade

When you buy or sell a stock on your online broker's site, your order is usually filled in seconds. But, before that transaction is completed, in milliseconds your order snakes its way through an advanced security trading system that has taken decades to build. Instead of making a call to your broker and then your broker making a call to a floor trader at the ASX, the transaction is now done through your online broker at the click of a button. Here's what happens in the split second it takes to execute an online trade:

1. **You enter your order with your online broker.**

2. **The order is reviewed by your online broker and placed into the ASX database known as ITS (see 'From SEATS to ITS' later in this chapter).**

3. **The database checks your order against all the different *bids* (buy requests) and *offers* (sell quotes) giving priority to the highest bid and lowest offer in a system called *price time priority*.**

    If two orders with the same price are received, then the order placed first gets priority.

4. **ITS matches a buyer with a seller and sends a confirmation to both parties' brokers.**

5. **The order and the price are reported to the ASX so they can be displayed to all investors.**

After that process is completed, the brokers have three days, called *T+3*, to actually exchange the cash and shares. This period is called *settlement*. When you buy a house you usually settle in 30, 60 or 90 days. When you trade stocks, you have just 3 days, so make sure your affairs are in order!

How things used to be

When you think of the stock market, sometimes you can easily conjure up an image of traders shouting and throwing complicated hand signals at the 'chalkies' who scribble away furiously at a blackboard before taking their next instruction. This system, known as *open outcry*, was once considered the most efficient way to discover the value of a stock. The difference computers have made is amazing. Today, the old system operates in only a few commodity exchanges like the London Metals Exchange, and hasn't been used in Australia for almost 20 years.

From SEATS to ITS

Open outcry was superseded by the Stock Exchange Automated Trading System (SEATS) in 1987. SEATS was a computer-based automated matching system that removed human error and was capable of recording and presenting information many, many times faster than even the most agile chalkie.

Importantly, SEATS allowed traders to not only sell for the going price but also to place an order in the system with an instruction to buy or sell only at a predetermined level (a sort of set-and-forget instruction with a nominated expiry date). SEATS started covering just a few stocks but, by 1990, it covered all listed securities on the ASX.

Although the SEATS system was a vast improvement on open outcry, it was still flawed. In 2004, the ASX began trialling the Integrated Trading System (ITS). ITS has the advantage of being more reliable, faster and able to handle more-complicated trades. However, even though you can 'see' the market through your online broker, you don't have access to ITS. You never have direct access to the market. Only online licensed brokers have access to ITS. Your online broker collects your instructions and routes your trades through ITS, often in less than a blink of an eye.

When compared with the days of open outcry, today the ASX is a much more sedate place. You can still visit the state offices of the ASX in Sydney, Melbourne, Brisbane, Adelaide and Perth but in place of open outcry you'll find an oversized electronic scoreboard displaying the day's movements of the 200 biggest stocks on the ASX (the S&P/ASX 200).

Getting It Done: Executing Your Trades

If you're buying something from a regular shop, like a new jacket, you can either buy it or not. End of story. But in marketplaces, where prices are fluid and change according to supply and demand, buying and selling is done strategically. It might surprise you that buying stock is more like a market than shopping at your local shopping centre, where prices are set. Because investments are priced in real-time through active bidding between buyers and sellers, traders employ certain techniques to buy and sell.

Types of orders

When dealing with investments, you have four main ways to buy or sell them online:

- **At-market orders** are the most common. By placing an at-market order, you inform your broker that you want to buy or sell shares now at the best possible price offered. This doesn't necessarily mean that the deal is transacted at the same price as the last sale. If you want to buy stock in XYZ and the last sale price was $10, an at-market order secures the stock for the best possible price available at the time — that may be $10.12.

  Conversely, if you're looking to sell shares in XYZ and the last sale price was $10, you may only get $9.92. An *at-market order* simply means that your broker is obliged to execute your order as quickly as possible at the best available price at that time. At-market orders have the advantage of being executed quickly, which can make a difference if a stock is rising or falling. They're also unlikely to attract any additional commissions, which makes them cheaper for the investor. At-market orders are only accepted inside market hours (10 am to 4 pm).

- **At-limit orders** are when you specify a price that you're willing to pay for shares or willing to sell shares at. With an *at-limit order*, your order is only filled if your broker can find a party to transact with at your price or better. This can become slightly more complicated if you're looking to sell at limit.

  For example, imagine you own 100 shares of XYZ, which are trading for $50 a share. The stock has been on a tear, but you're convinced it will soon fall dramatically, by your estimate, to $30. You could just sell the stock outright with an at-market order, but you don't want to because you're a bit greedy and don't want to miss out on any gains in case you're wrong. An at-limit order could be the answer. Here, you'd instruct your broker to sell the stock if it fell to, say, $45 a share. If you're right, and the stock falls to $45 a share, your online broker will sell as many shares as possible at that price. You can also set a time limit on at-limit orders and tell your broker to let them expire after a few days or weeks.

  The precision of at-limit orders can be a shortcoming, too. At-limit orders are filled only at the price you set. If the stock falls further than the price you set, the broker may be able to sell only some of the shares, or none, at the price you set. If that happens, you're stuck with the stock. In the preceding example, if XYZ opened for trading and plunged straight to $25, never stopping at $45, you'll still be holding the stock. This possibility is a serious limitation. Also, some brokers charge extra for at-limit orders, so check the commission fees before you start trading. And some brokers don't offer at-limit orders at all.

✔ **Good-for-day orders** consist of an at-limit order that expires at the end of the trading day. If the order isn't filled by the close of trade, then ITS cancels the order, meaning that, if you still want to go ahead, you need to enter it again the following day. Because good-for-day orders refer to the length of time an order is in the system, they don't attract separate charges.

✔ **Default-expiry orders** stay in the system for a maximum of 20 days if not executed. After 20 days the order is cancelled. As with good-for-day orders, default orders also refer to the length of time an order is in the system, so they don't attract separate charges either.

Tailoring your trades even more

In 2004, Australia's two largest brokers, CommSec and E*TRADE, introduced a new feature to online investors. Called *conditional trading* or *conditional orders*, the feature incorporated stop-loss functions that were previously only associated with traditional brokers. A *stop-loss order* allows an investor to create an order that executes automatically when a stock reaches a certain price, which 'stops' whatever losses you may take on a particular investment, hence the name.

Investors employ many different strategies with conditional orders, but you need to be prepared to pay for the privilege. Conditional orders will cost you upwards of $10 on top of the regular broking fees associated with the trade. This feature is often marketed at investors who don't have time to watch the market carefully or are going on holidays and don't want to miss an opportunity.

But conditional trading can be dangerous. Having too many conditional orders active at the same time is never a good idea, because keeping track of them can be difficult.

Some brokers allow you to place conditional orders only when your 'trigger price' is within an arbitrary range they set. Long-term investors rarely use conditional orders because they believe their investments will display good value over the long term and aren't affected by short-term drops in price.

The following variations are all types of conditional-trading instructions (stop-loss orders) you can give your broker.

- **Falling-sell orders** are the most popular. They appeal to investors looking to limit losses in a particular stock. With a falling sell, your holdings will be sold when the stock passes a certain level that you set. Conditional orders require you to input a trigger and a limit. Say you buy XYZ for $8 and want to limit your downside to 10 per cent, if the price begins to fall. Setting a trigger of $7.30 and a limit of $7.20 accomplishes your aim. If XYZ falls to $7.30, then the stop-loss order would begin selling your stock, selling as much as possible above $7.20. If XYZ falls and your stop-loss order sells the stock at $7.26, then you have taken a loss of 9.25 per cent, which you may consider a good result if the stock keeps falling.

- **Rising-sell orders** help when you decide that you want to take profits when your shares hit a predetermined price. For example, if you buy XYZ securities for $8 and want to sell them after a capital gain of 15 per cent, then setting a rising-sell trigger price of $9.45 and a limit price of $9.40 achieves your goal. When XYZ hits $9.45, your broker fills as much of your order as possible with a lower limit of $9.40.

- **Falling-buy orders** are useful when you believe that, at a particular price, XYZ securities represent good value. If you think that, at $8, XYZ is overvalued by 10 per cent, a good strategy is to create a falling-buy order of $7.15 with a limit of $7.20. When XYZ hits $7.15, your broker fills as much of your order as possible, with an upper limit if $7.20.

- **Rising-buy orders** are used by *momentum traders*. These traders believe in the 'weight-of-money' argument, which says that, as funds are invested in a particular stock, the price rises and attracts more money, creating upward momentum in the share price. You may think that XYZ securities are languishing at $4 but, when the price hits $4.25, it should push towards $5. You create a trigger price of $4.25 and a limit of $4.30. As the stock rises past $4.25, your broker fills as much of your order as possible, with an upper limit of $4.30.

Markets can move pretty fast, so conditional orders aren't really suitable for most investors. Think of them as like placing a For Sale sign on your house or car, or any other asset you own. You don't want to forget about them and find out that someone has taken you up on the offer!

Part II
Using Online Investment Resources

Glenn Lumsden

'I've invested 50 per cent in raincoats and 50 per cent in zinc cream ... regardless of climate change, we can't lose.'

In this part ...

Opening an online brokerage account doesn't suddenly make you an online investing master. To get to the next level and boost your sophistication and success investing online, you need to upgrade your knowledge of the tools used by online investors and understand how to use the internet to your advantage.

The chapters in this part help you lift yourself above the click-happy masses of online investors who just buy and sell stocks willy-nilly. You find out what forces drive stock prices and how to track those forces by using online calculators and communities on the internet. We then introduce you to one of the most important, and most ignored, skills that all online investors need — measuring the risk and return of stocks and your portfolio. You find out how to use the internet to design an asset allocation, a (boring-sounding) step that determines your success as an online investor.

Chapter 5

Connecting with Other Investors Online

· ·

In This Chapter

▶ Considering the advantages of networking

▶ Discussing stocks with others on stock message boards

▶ Tapping into internet newsgroups

▶ Discovering investors through Web 2.0 social networking sites

▶ Joining investment clubs

▶ Reaching out to special-interest investing groups

· ·

*T*he ways in which online investors can connect with each other continues to evolve because of the myriad tools now available on the internet. Online investors often rely on *stock message boards*, also called *chat boards*, to trade stock tips, gossip and hunches with each other. In this chapter, we show you how to get online with stock message boards, including how to contribute to them, how to network using them and what to watch out for. We also explore the dangers of penny stocks, which are some of the favourites on stock message boards and other online forums. Later in the chapter, we look into online newsgroups, investment clubs and sites for special-interest groups.

Finding Kindred Investment Spirits Online

Whenever you're about to try something risky, or at least something you've never done before, talking to people with experience brings you a certain sense of comfort, which is also why many investors attempt to connect with each other. You have several ways to develop this connection — online through stock message boards and social-investing sites, as well as through investment clubs.

Here are a few things to consider when thinking about adding a social aspect to your investment strategy:

- **Moral support:** Many beginning online investors are bewildered by the things they need to remember. By connecting with other online investors who've already done what you're thinking about doing, you can gain first-hand knowledge of the risks and rewards.

- **A new perspective:** You may think you know the best way to manage your money. But why not run your strategy by others and make sure you're not overlooking anything?

- **New ideas for investments:** Members of online communities come from different professions and from all over the world. You can use this diversity to your advantage, and you may even find out about investments you've never heard of.

Getting the Message with Stock Message Boards

When you think of connecting with other investors, you probably instantly think of stock message boards — and for good reason. These informal, anonymous forums were an early way for investors to chat with each other online. They give you an instant way to brag about your returns, promote a stock you own, or *flame* (to make critical comments about) a stock you sold for a loss.

Stock message boards aren't for everyone

Australian investors can tap into dozens of message boards, but they're not all created equally. Generally speaking, message boards are controlled by administrators or moderators who may have different ideas about what's acceptable and what isn't. For example, some message boards tolerate members using profanities, whereas others don't. In a case where a member's behaviour isn't consistent with what's expected, the moderator may give that member a warning or impose disciplinary action. On the one hand, message boards that have an anything-goes attitude can be overrun with useless information. On the other, message boards that are heavily moderated can often stifle interesting discussion. The key is to find a balance.

Some investors, especially passive investors, described in Chapter 1, may not care what other investors think about their stocks. They've formed their asset allocation — as described in Chapter 7 — and they're going to stick with that no matter what.

But, if you're an active investor and see online investing as a hobby, you may be very interested in the chatter surrounding stocks you're considering. Stock message boards are suited to you if you

✔ **Are a speculator.** Some investors buy and sell stocks not so much to accumulate a nest egg, but for speculation. Speculators often use discretionary funds, not core savings.

✔ **Don't want to hassle with sign-up procedures.** You can be up and running with most stock message boards in just minutes and usually don't even have to identify yourself with anything other than your chosen username.

✔ **Know the rules.** Investors who understand that many of the things said on stock message boards are exaggerations, manipulations or just plain wrong have a better chance of finding worthwhile nuggets of information.

Blindly following what other investors are doing, generally speaking, isn't a good strategy and can be dangerous. If you're looking for stock message boards for stock recommendations, you're likely going to be disappointed with your results.

Understanding the types of stock message boards

Although stock message boards have been around essentially since the start of online investing, they morphed quite a bit through the past bull and bear markets. The rise of the first generation of text-heavy internet message boards coincided with the dot-com-inspired bull market of 1995–2000, also referred to as the 'tech wreck' when it was eventually undone. Then a prolonged bear market began, which was fanned by the fallout of 11 September 2001 and other geopolitical events. From January 2003 to November 2007, the market entered another extended bull run, during which much of today's feature-rich applications were trialled and tested. Today, they're available on a number of different platforms. The following sections explore the various corners of the internet where investors congregate to swap info.

Using online stock message boards as the key to your investment strategy isn't a good idea. Listening to so many other opinions may cause you to second-guess yourself and prompt you to buy and sell stocks too often. But, more importantly, you don't know who you're chatting with, and such boards are havens for scammers and fraudsters such as insider traders (see the sidebar 'Insider messes with message boards'). Always consider the source when using information from stock message boards.

Insider messes with message boards

In November 2007, Peter Woodland pleaded guilty to one count of insider trading and one count of communicating inside information to other persons. Woodland came into possession of information about Kanowna Consolidated Gold Mines, now known as Andean Resources, through irregular contractual work with the company. After acquiring approximately $27,000 worth of securities, he communicated the information to members of the HotCopper message board. Woodland was given a suspended sentence of 18 months' imprisonment and a two-year good behaviour bond.

Just starting out

The moderation on the following message boards isn't too stringent, and they're easy to use if you're just starting out. Both enjoy good volumes of traffic, which means more opportunities to connect with investors just like you! So, if you want a safe place to get started, check these sites out:

✔ **ShareScene** (www.sharescene.com)**:** ShareScene began life as ASXboard.com in 2003 before evolving to its current format. Today it combines a popular message board with various multimedia applications. You can search for discussions by ASX code, read just the most active topics, view video market reports that are updated several times a day or participate in polls and stock-tipping competitions. ShareScene has around 14,000 users and was the winner in the 2008 Traders' Choice Awards for the best stock forum.

✔ **Aussie Stock Forums** (www.aussiestockforums.com)**:** Aussie Stock Forums is an independent message board that has been around since 2004 and remains one of the most user-friendly examples for Australian investors. It has a dedicated beginners' section (select Forums and go to the Beginners Lounge), as well as sections that feature discussions about commodities and international markets. The membership of Aussie Stock Forums tends to be both knowledgeable and helpful. Aussie Stock Forums was the runner-up in the 2008 Traders' Choice Awards for best stock forum.

Getting more confident

If you're getting more confident about investing online, then the following boards are for you. They make reference to more complicated strategies and rely heavily on jargon and abbreviations. Members swap tips, strategies and even the odd insult! They're likely to be moderated less, which means you really need to have your wits about you, but check them out:

✔ **HotCopper** (www.hotcopper.com.au)**:** HotCopper is one of the most well known and highly trafficked Australian stock message boards. It has a focus on commodity stocks and is largely frequented by daytraders, who profit from short-term movements in stock prices. It's been criticised for not being moderated heavily enough and frequently attracts controversy.

✔ **Yahoo!7 Finance** (http://au.messages.yahoo.com/finance)**:** Yahoo!7 Finance operates a series of message boards that cover topics such as personal finance, taxation and stocks. The site isn't heavily trafficked or moderated like some others, but it does offer detailed charting, news and data services on each page.

Stock message boards and the Enron debacle

Despite the many problems with stock message boards, sometimes they can contain very valuable pieces of information. You ought to carefully monitor the boards for comments that appear to be from informed employees. Stock message boards, in fact, were one of the only places where investors were warned about the coming collapse of Enron in 2001, one of the largest bankruptcies in US history.

Between 1997 and 2001, ahead of Enron's fall, more than 129 detailed posts appeared on Enron's stock message board on Yahoo!, according to James Felton and Jongchai Kim in their article 'Warnings from the Enron Message Board'. These posts, many appearing to be from employees, indicated serious problems at the company, even while most Wall Street analysts rated the stock 'buy' or 'strong buy'.

In April 2001, for example, an anonymous post read, 'It will soon be revealed that Enron is nothing more than a house of cards that will implode before anyone realizes what happened. Enron has been cooking the books with smoke and mirrors. Enron executives have been operating an elaborate scheme that has fooled even the most sophisticated analyst.'

That post appeared online four months before Enron employee Sherron Watkins wrote the famous warning letter to Enron CEO Ken Lay. You can download the article at `http://papers.ssrn.com/sol3/ papers.cfm?abstract_id=918519# PaperDownload`. Click on Choose Download Location and select Korea University.

Knowing the ulterior motives of some online stock message board members

Although many of the people who use online stock message boards may be upstanding individuals just looking to help their fellow investor, you can avoid heartache by being cautious. People can abuse online stock message boards for personal gain in several ways, including the following:

- **Hyping stocks they own:** Some members can exaggerate or even make up good news regarding a stock they own, hoping to fool others into buying the stock. This type of scheme is commonly called a *pump-and-dump scheme*, or *ramping scheme*.

- **Disparaging stocks they're shorting:** Investors can profit from a falling stock by shorting shares, as described in Chapter 15. Some investors spread false rumours about a company with hopes that such rumours are going to cause a panic and get others to sell. Speculation that such activities were driving down the value of stocks in Australia and the US led regulators to ban short-selling outright during periods of 2008.

✔ **Promoting companies that pay them:** Some message boards have been known to accept advertising dollars from investment companies and derivatives trading firms. So, if this is the case, reading anything impartial about those companies or their products on these message boards is unlikely.

Determining what exchange or market a stock trades on

The big successes in the stock market become well known quickly and are referred to often by US and Australian message board users, but they may be of little use to you if you're a beginner. For example, familiar stocks such as Berkshire Hathaway and Google have provided many shareholders with a great deal of success. But these stocks trade on different exchanges in the US, not in Australia. Warren Buffett's company, Berkshire Hathaway, trades on the New York Stock Exchange (NYSE), which is the largest stock exchange in the world, where the combined total of all companies listed on it exceeds $25 trillion. Google trades on the NASDAQ, which is smaller but no less active, featuring 3,200 mostly technology-oriented stocks. This point is important because starting your trading with Australian stocks is easier. (For all about trading on overseas markets, see Chapter 18.)

If you're asking the question, 'What trades on the Australian stock market then?' the answer is easy because, fortunately for all Aussie investors, the Australian Securities Exchange (the ASX) is one of the most active stock markets in the world. A defining feature of the ASX is the number of resource or commodity stocks listed. Because of Australia's unique geology and large land mass, opportunities for mining and exploration companies abound. This scenario gives exposure to one of the first booms of the 21st century — the commodities boom — which is being driven by the need for raw materials (such as iron ore, coal and gas) from countries like China and India.

To find out if a stock trades on the ASX:

1. **Visit the ASX website (**www.asx.com.au**).**

2. **Click on Find a Code.**

   The search page (www.asx.com.au/asx/codeLookup.do?) opens, as in Figure 5-1.

3. **Type the first few letters of the company's name (for example, 'BHP' for BHP Billiton) and click the Go button.**

   The search provides you with the ASX code or codes of stocks that match those letters. (If the code doesn't appear, either you may not have the correct name or the stock trades on another exchange.)

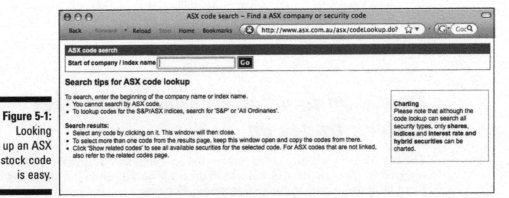

Figure 5-1:
Looking
up an ASX
stock code
is easy.

How the ASX is different from other exchanges

The ASX began life in 1861, when the Melbourne Stock Exchange came into existence (and, coincidentally, the same year as the first Melbourne Cup!). Today, more than 2,200 stocks trade on the ASX with a combined value of $1.5 trillion, making it the eighth-largest market in the world. This pales in comparison with the big markets of the world like the NYSE, which has roughly the same number of companies listed but is worth many times more.

The reason for this seeming dichotomy is that some of the companies listed on the ASX would never be allowed to list on a stock exchange like the NYSE because requirements for turnover and company value are higher on those exchanges. Compare the requirements of the NYSE, the NASDAQ and the ASX:

To list on the NYSE, a company must

✔ Have made US$10 million over the previous three years.

✔ Be valued at US$100 million.

To list on the NASDAQ, a company must

✔ Have made at least US$11 million over the previous three years.

✔ Be valued at US$70 million.

To list on the ASX, a company need only

✔ Have made A$1 million over the previous three years.

✔ Be valued at A$10 million.

So, although just as many stocks trade on the ASX as on other exchanges, not all companies are created equally.

A penny saved: Beware of penny stocks

If you spend much time looking at online stock message boards, you notice that many of the messages are posted about stocks that trade for less than 20 cents — so-called *penny dreadfuls*. They're popular discussion points on message boards partly because penny stocks, due to their tiny share prices, allow investors to buy large numbers of shares. Owning large chunks of stock is appealing to the same speculator types that flock to stock message boards to begin with.

Penny dreadfuls are rarely covered by reputable broking houses for two reasons:

- ✔ The sheer number of them means they can't be researched thoroughly.
- ✔ Smaller companies are extremely volatile. Mining companies can soar on a single discovery and industrials can rocket up after a key contract is signed. This makes things very difficult for analysts, whose hard work is quickly rendered useless or out-of-date.

Penny dreadfuls can be popular on stock message boards also because they're easily manipulated. Unlike giant stocks such as BHP or National Australia Bank (which are so valuable you need hundreds of millions of dollars to budge the stock), penny stocks can be nudged with just a few hundred bucks. And, therefore, just a small amount of hype or negativity can have a large effect on a penny stock's share price. A stock has to move only from one cent to two cents to double a fraudster's money.

You're best to avoid investing in penny stocks but, if you can't resist, be sure to

- ✔ **Locate some broker research.** If a stock is likely to have earning potential, reason says that one of the many broking houses has already begun to provide coverage or research. Tips from message boards or acquaintances can never replace comprehensive coverage from a respected analyst (see Chapter 13).
- ✔ **Do your own research.** You can research the company fully at the following websites:
  - **ASX (**www.asx.com.au**):** On the homepage, click on Prices, Research & Announcements and choose Announcements to search for a company's announcements page, which contains a list of all the material disclosures a company has made for the previous seven years, giving you a good overview of how the company has performed.

- **Australian Securities and Investments Commission** (www.asic. gov.au/asic/asic.nsf): ASIC is the government's consumer protection regulator. Use the search window to research a company you're interested in.

- **Google News** (www.google.com.au): Click on News and choose Business to get an idea of market sentiment surrounding the company and look for comments from the chief executive. Do a search on individual company directors' names to get an understanding of their experience and value to the company.

✔ **Double-check that you can't do better.** With thousands of stocks listed on the ASX, you ought to be able to find a comparable listed stock in the same sector with good disclosure levels that you want to invest in.

Don't be fooled:
Fortescue Metals wasn't a penny stock

Some penny-stock investors claim many big companies, such as Fortescue Metals, started out as penny stocks. They look at long-term charts and say those stocks started trading at less than 5c a share. That claim is simply not a true representation of the historical facts.

Some investors look at the long-term chart and claim that the iron ore player was trading for 5c on 30 June 2004, before breaking out to its current range. And, if you chart the stock yourself, the data appears to support this claim. But this 'result' is an illusion caused by a *stock split*. When a stock splits, the company cuts its share price and increases the number of shares. A stock split has no effect on the value of the stock or company, but changes historical prices because most charting services split-adjust historical stock prices. Fortescue Metals shares underwent a 10-for-1 stock split on 19 December 2007.

To find out what the actual closing price of Fortescue Metals was on 30 June 2004, you must undo the effect of the 10-for-1 split that occurred in 2007. To do that calculation, you simply multiply the split-adjusted stock price for any period prior to 19 December 2007 by the split amount — in this case, the number is 10 — $10 \times 5c = 50c$ — which means Fortescue Metals closing price on 30 June 2004 was 50c, not 5c.

Tapping into Online Newsgroups

Newsgroups are similar to stock message boards in that they're giant online bulletin boards where members can post largely anonymous comments. But, unlike stock message boards, which run on websites, most newsgroups live on a pretty ancient network, called Usenet. *Usenet* is a corridor of the internet roped off for discussion groups.

Usenet hosts newsgroups pertaining to just about any topic you can imagine, and some you can't. You can find forums where members talk about grooming their pets, tuning their cars and, oh yeah, investing online.

How to locate specific online newsgroups

Because thousands of newsgroups are available on Usenet, they're all carefully categorised by topic. Usenet uses a very precise naming convention so you can zero in on a topic quickly and find the appropriate forums. Usenet forums are given a three-part address, much like a street address. First up is the broad category, or *section*, which is equivalent to the state on your home address. Beneath this main section is the secondary section. Using my address metaphor, the secondary section is like your city. Then the groups are broken into very specific topic areas, much like your street address.

A typical newsgroup address looks like this: `section.second_section.topic`. For instance, a newsgroup dedicated to options is `misc.invest.options`, where `misc` is the section, `invest` is the secondary section and `options` is the topic.

 In case you haven't noticed yet, the whole newsgroup address naming convention is bit of a hassle. You're probably better able to access newsgroups using Google Groups, as described in the following section. Google Groups handles the whole Usenet address nightmare for you.

Some sample investing newsgroups you may consider include the ones in Table 5-1. Be aware that only the first newsgroup listed, aus.invest, deals exclusively with Australian stocks. Although the remainder are US-based, they still contain discussion of global themes and strategies that you may find interesting.

Table 5-1	Select Investing Newsgroups
Newsgroup Address	*Topic*
`aus.invest`	Stock analysis and broader market themes
`misc.invest.mutual-funds`	Choosing and investing in managed funds
`misc.invest.stocks`	Analysing and picking stocks
`misc.invest.options`	Understanding complex options-trading strategies

How to participate in online newsgroups

So, you understand how Usenet addresses work and the kinds of topics that are available. But how do you access these newsgroups? Because newsgroups are essentially in the public domain, you can access them in many ways, including the following:

✔ **Google Groups (**`http://groups.google.com`**):** Probably the best way to access Usenet newsgroups, Google Groups (see Figure 5-2) lets you search all available newsgroups by entering the group name or topic in the search field — all without installing any special reader software often required by browsers. Try terms like 'investing', 'investing online', and 'money'. You don't need to remember or look up the complicated Usenet addresses. Google Groups also organises newsgroups by topic area. Just sign up for the service or log in using your Google Gmail account information — although some newsgroups may require additional registration.

If you know the Usenet newsgroup address, such as `misc.invest.stocks`, Google Groups can still help. Just enter the Usenet address in the search field and you can access the newsgroup.

✔ **Yahoo! Groups (**`http://groups.yahoo.com`**):** Yahoo! Groups doesn't actually connect to Usenet; rather, it links you with groups created within Yahoo!. In this particular corner of the Yahoo! portal, you can find newsgroups that discuss everything from technical support to trading advice.

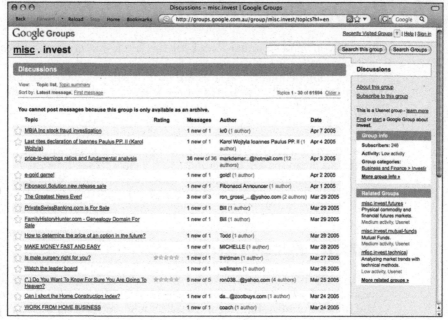

Figure 5-2:
Google
Groups can
track down
Usenet
newsgroups
for you.

Although newsgroups can be okay sources of investment chatter, moderated message boards are typically better bets because they make their users more accountable. Generally, newsgroups are best suited for getting technical help when you're having computer problems — when you have questions about personal finance software, for example. Just post a question to a group listed in Table 5-2, and the experts flock to help you out. You can also use newsgroups to hear what people are saying about a company's products to give you the inside track.

Table 5-2	Select Useful Technology Newsgroups
Newsgroup Address	*Topic*
`alt.comp.software.financial.quicken`	Help with using Intuit's Quicken
`comp.sys.mac.system`	Forum regarding Apple Macintosh computers
`microsoft.public.windows.server.sbs`	Discussion about Microsoft's Windows operating system

The Brave New World of Web 2.0

Unless you've been under a rock for the last few years, you've heard about websites like MySpace and Facebook. A big hit with students and other young people, these sites are part of what's called Web 2.0, the second generation of websites where *you* create the content, whether it's photographs from a birthday party that you want to share with friends or an online diary that you want to share with the world.

The different ways this technology is being used is growing just as quickly as the applications are being built, so it's easy to see how they could be used for more than just keeping in touch with friends. With more than 200 million users worldwide, it was probably inevitable.

Social networking

In the beginning, social networking was used to keep in touch with those who moved away or to reconnect with old school friends. But, since then, the big end of town has begun to take social networking seriously. Many politicians have a Facebook page and several leading financial institutions have embraced staff use of such sites. You'll also find heaps of Facebook groups dedicated to investing, trading and other topics related to finance. MySpace, so far, is still more of a youth-and-music site.

Although social networking offers a slightly higher degree of transparency than other methods of online communication, you should always be cautious about the personal details you give out and the information you choose to take away from it. You can take a number of precautions to make sure your social-networking experience is both fun and safe:

- ✔ Make your profile private.
- ✔ Do not become friends with people you don't know.
- ✔ Do not enter your full birthday.
- ✔ Do not enter your full address.

Social networking can be great, but if you place too much information 'out there' it's possible that you could become a victim of identity fraud. If you follow these four simple rules, your details will be secure and your risk greatly reduced. In general, the same guidelines that apply to message boards also apply here (refer to the section 'Getting the Message with Stock Message Boards' earlier in this chapter).

Social investing

One of the more exciting developments in the world of online investing since the ability to trade online is called *social investing*, which aims to combine the transparency of social networking with the information flow you get from message boards.

Unlike stock message boards, where you have no way of knowing someone's motives or of qualifying their claims, social investing provides the platform on which investors can track their performance against each other and against the index. Anyone can boast about having traded their way from the poorhouse to a townhouse but social investing sites let your trades do the talking. That's not to say you can't still boast about it, with many incorporating *blogs* (web logs), which are their personal narratives on how to invest. Refer to Chapter 2 for more on blogs.

One of the best elements of social investing is the ability it gives you to track other successful investors in real-time across a number of categories, using several variables — based on particular markets, return or sector focus. Searching for buy-and-hold investors who have an expertise in commodity stocks, for example, reveals that all investors could probably learn something from a 40-year-old from Zagreb, Croatia, who has produced an annualised return of 205 per cent.

Social-investing sites can be found much like any other web-based application. You may come across them using Google, advertised on another website or recommended by a friend. They come in two flavours:

- ✔ **Standalone sites:** If you want to test the social-investing waters or are concerned about security, investigate a standalone site. This type of site gives you the opportunity to evaluate it safely by keeping your social-investing account quite separate from your online-broking account.

- ✔ **Broker-sponsored sites:** If you can't be bothered with signing up to another service and are comfortable with the security of your online broker, you may be happy to sign up with a broker-sponsored site.

Up until recently, Australian investors weren't very well catered for in the world of social investing. But one of the biggest (and in James' opinion, the best) sites has recently opened its doors to Aussies — Covestor.com (www.covestor.com).

Follow the simple steps below to get started on Covestor.com or any other social-investing site:

1. **Register.**

   Most social-investing sites require you to give more details about yourself than some stock message boards do. That might be a slight burden at first, but it's also one of the ways these sites eliminate users who insist on being cloaked in privacy.

2. **Create a profile.**

   Here you describe yourself, giving only details you're comfortable sharing with the rest of the social-investing site. Typically, you might say how long you've been investing, what kind of investor you are and what types of stocks you prefer.

3. **Enter your transactions.**

   The biggest thing that separates social-investing sites from stock message boards is that other users can see your real trades if you give permission. For Covestor.com that means you have to enter your trades manually and then attach copies of the buy or sell confirmation from your broker. This sounds like a bigger hassle than it actually is — the confirmation is normally a small PDF document sent to you from your broker at the time you made the trade.

4. **Set your permissions.**

   The most important aspect of social investing is to give careful thought to the level of 'permissions' that you apply to your account. Your permissions provide others who use the site with certain pieces of information about you — your name, email address, portfolio and location. Giving away all of these details on the internet to a group of people you've never met isn't a very smart idea. You may like to give yourself a nickname or 'handle', restrict your location to a particular state and provide percentage figures rather than dollar sums of your portfolio breakdown.

5. **Look around.**

   After you're set up with a profile, you can peruse the community to find people you may want to be 'friends' with. These are investors you think are worthwhile listening to. You can also read other investors' blogs and search users based on what stocks they hold, what sectors they invest in or their returns.

Starting an Investment Club

If online stock message boards seem too wild and scary but you still want to connect with other investors, consider starting an *investment club*. Investment clubs are typically gatherings of investors in a certain geographic area who meet at a local restaurant or a member's house to 'shoot the breeze'. Members pitch stocks they think the group should buy or sell. Investment clubs also have a bit of a party feeling to them, because they're usually designed to be fun, educational and, oh yeah, profitable.

In Australia — unlike the United States — you don't find publicly available, centralised databases of investment clubs, and they don't operate online as such. Although the success of investment clubs is well publicised, unless you know someone in an investment club, you can't approach a club cold. This etiquette isn't without reason either. After all, would you be prepared to give your money to a group of people you don't know, and trust them to make decisions about where it should be invested?

For this reason, starting up an investment club yourself is often easier. Initially, you may feel you don't know anyone who's going to be interested. However, your friends, family, colleagues and club acquaintances are a good starting point. This central network can often turn up a number of leads that can get you on your way to starting your own investment club.

Using investment club resources

As the demand for investment clubs began to rise, the ASX responded by creating a comprehensive online resource. It offers information about:

- The benefits of joining an investment club
- A step-by-step guide on how to set one up
- The legal responsibilities of its members
- Downloadable forms that you need to get your club off the ground

But, first, you need to register for a free ASX membership. Here's how:

1. **Visit the ASX website (**www.asx.com.au**).**

   While you're there, bookmark the site by clicking on Bookmarks (or Favorites) in your browser's menu bar. The site contains a wealth of information for new investors, including tutorials and factsheets. Even experienced investors can learn a lot from this excellent resource.

2. **To enter the site, click on the Sign Up link in the Log In To ... panel, which is found on the right-hand side of the page (see Figure 5-3).**

3. **Fill in some personal details.**

4. **View the investment club resources available on the site by choosing Investment Clubs from the Sign Up for MyASX panel on the right.**

Figure 5-3:
How to bookmark and sign in to ASX's online investment club resource.

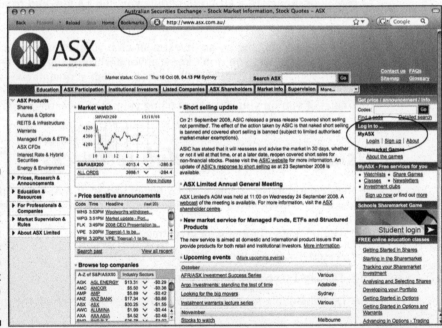

Understanding the drawbacks of investment clubs

Before you rush out and join an investment club, be aware of the potential drawbacks:

- ✔ **Bad decisions by others cost you.** If the loudmouthed guy in the club talks the group into buying a stinker, you're going to take a bath, too.

- ✔ **The very nature of an investment club promotes regular buying and selling.** Club members may consider themselves individually to be long-term investors but, as a group, clubs rarely hang on to a stock for much longer than 12 months. After all, an investment club isn't much fun if the members never buy or sell anything. As a long-term investor, buying and selling so frequently can feel like a betrayal of your investment ideals, but it's a conflict that many club members face at one time or another.

- ✔ **Compromise can hurt.** Most group decisions involve some form of compromise, whether it's asset allocation, stock selection or the duration of the actual investment. Having several people steering a portfolio sometimes means a single and coherent strategy becomes elusive.

- ✔ **Members' investing skill levels can vary.** Some investment club members are only there for the fun, food and friends. That level of non-involvement can leave much of the grunt work for the few members with the skill or desire to make money for the club.

Finding Information for Investors Like You

Online investors are typically in one of two categories, active or passive. But investors can classify themselves in many other ways, be it by age, experience level or gender. Plenty of websites are dedicated to serving specific demographics.

Sites for kids

Encouraging young people to start investing is exciting and prudent. Several sites are dedicated to the young investor:

- ✔ **mtrek** (www.mtrek.com.au): This website from ING DIRECT provides kids with an entertaining way of learning about money. It includes information about saving, credit and investing. With colourful characters and easy-to-understand language, this site is recommended for younger children.

- ✔ **Know your money** (www.knowyourmoney.com.au): This website from the Commonwealth Bank provides teenagers with information about creating a budget, taking out a personal loan, tax, superannuation and investing. The site uses realistic scenarios and testimonials from real young people.

- ✔ **FIDO** (www.fido.gov.au): This website from ASIC contains information about investing for young people who already know the basics of money management. Click on About You and select Young Adults from the dropdown menu.

Some parents get their kids interested in investing by splitting their allowance into two parts. One part is paid in cash and the other is automatically deposited into a savings account that the child chooses. This method is a good way to show children how money saved diligently can snowball into growth.

Sites for women

To be honest, how a man or woman invests isn't really much different. But some sites are tailored to females and provide various money-management suggestions:

- ✔ **FIDO's Women and Money** (www.fido.gov.au): This website is a great starting point for those beginning to get a feel for finance, and tackles some important topics. Load up the homepage, run your cursor over About You and select Women and Money.

- ✔ **Femail** (www.femail.com.au/moneyfinancearchives.htm): This website from Femail contains a collection of articles about saving, superannuation and investing.

✔ **Wire** (www.wire.org.au): Click on Women's Information and select Finance from the dropdown menu. This website provides an introduction to financial issues for women who are working, at home with children or going through a separation.

Sites for seniors

The financial goals and objectives of senior citizens are completely different from those of a 20-something just entering the workforce. These sites address the unique situation of older investors:

✔ **Seniors.gov.au** (www.seniors.gov.au): This website is produced by the Department of Health and Ageing and provides the community with access to Australian government information and services relevant to older Australians. Click on Your Finances and select Financial Planning. This portion of the site contains specific information about investing, and features a list of programs, resources and associations available to seniors.

✔ **FIDO** (www.fido.gov.au): Click on About You and select Retirees from the dropdown menu. This comprehensive website from ASIC contains information about how to spot a dangerous investment, planning for retirement and *reverse mortgages* (an agreement that releases equity from your home). It also contains a list of approved government agencies that can help you plan your finances for free, as well as information about insurance and superannuation.

Seniors are constant targets for opportunists, so they need to be extra vigilant regarding possible scams (see the sidebar 'Vigilance is a virtual virtue'). Operators such as David Tweed are known to mass mail shareholders of particular companies with offers below the current market value. Never, ever agree to sell your shares to someone who approaches you without checking the stock's true market value.

Vigilance is a virtual virtue

Australia has one of the largest proportions of shareholders in the world, largely as a result of *privatisation*, when government assets go private via the stock market, and also because of *demutualisation*, when insurance companies list on the market and give shares to former policy holders.

Because of this scenario, many shareholders aren't especially active or sophisticated investors. Even if you receive an official-looking letter in the mail from an official-sounding company with a form containing your details already filled out, don't sign on the line without first checking the true value of your shares.

Although, in many cases, the legality about making such offers to shareholders isn't in question, this type of approach is generally viewed as unscrupulous and unethical. If you receive any correspondence that you think is suspicious, don't hesitate to contact ASIC on 1300 300 630.

Chapter 6

Measuring Your Performance

- -

In This Chapter

▶ Seeing the importance of tracking your performance

▶ Figuring out the best way to calculate investment performance

▶ Using online tools that can measure your risk and returns

▶ Choosing the right benchmark

- -

Y ou'd be surprised how many investors keep buying and selling
stocks online even when they have no idea whether they're beating
the market. They brag at dinner parties about the winning stocks they've
bought. But, if you ask them what their rate of return is, they look at you
blankly. Most online brokers don't necessarily help either, because many
don't have tools that accurately measure your returns.

Investing online without knowing how you're doing is like driving with your
eyes closed. As an online investor, it's pretty much up to you to calculate
your own returns. To help you get back in control, this chapter first shows
you how to manually calculate your returns and how much risk you've
taken to get those returns. If you want more support, we also discuss online
sites and software that do all the calculations for you. Either way you
choose, you'll be miles ahead of other investors who keep investing without
knowing whether they're successful.

The Importance of Tracking Your Performance

You figure out from an early age to monitor your progress with most things.
As babies, your height and weight were plotted on charts to illustrate how
quickly you were growing and how your size ranked with other infants. In
school, your progress was constantly monitored using grades and tests.
And, at work, annual reviews and pay increases often reflect the job you're
doing and show what's working and what's not.

That's why it's so strange that many people don't monitor their investment performance. Investors often look through their portfolios, see a few stocks that are up since they bought them and assume they're beating the stock market.

Psychology plays a big part in investing. Many online investors tend to get overly confident if they've recently picked a few lucky stocks. That prompts them to take more uncalculated risks in the future, which may cost them dearly. Investors also tend to wipe out painful losses from their memories. They remember only the winners. And other investors beat themselves up for losing money on a stock, blaming something that had nothing to do with the loss. By measuring your performance, you can try to remove some of the emotion from investing. The US website for Morningstar, the independent investment research outfit, has a great little lesson on how human nature can affect your success investing online. Follow these steps:

1. **Go to** www.morningstar.com.

2. **Click the Personal Finance tab at the top.**

3. **Scroll down to Investing Classroom and choose Course Catalog.**

4. **Select Course Level 400 followed by 407: Psychology and Investing.**

Some investors don't bother monitoring their investment performance because it requires some maths and a few scary-looking formulas that a lot of people don't understand. This chapter, though, demystifies how to track your portfolio's risk and return. We start by showing you how to do the calculations yourself.

Understanding how all the calculations are done is important, so you don't blindly rely on websites to do it for you, but we also know that not everyone has the time or the willingness to crunch down performance stats themselves. And that's why we include online tools that do the maths for you. If you get confused at any point in this section about calculating performance manually, don't dismay. Just skip ahead to the section 'Using Online Tools to Calculate Your Performance'.

Why measuring your returns is worth the trouble

Studies have shown that people who regularly weigh themselves tend to have more success reaching their fitness goals. Investing online is similar. If you take the time to measure your results, you'll likely be a better investor. After all, even if your investments aren't doing well, if you track your performance, you may be able to adjust your strategy. Some investors, for example, may find that constantly buying and selling stocks isn't working for them. These investors can adjust accordingly and may find more success being passive investors. (You can review the difference between active and passive investors in Chapter 1.)

If you take the time to measure your performance, you'll be able to figure out whether you're going to

- **Reach your financial goals.** When you invest, you typically estimate the rate of return you need to reach your goal, such as funding retirement or paying for uni. By tracking your returns, you can see whether you're on the right path or not. And, if you're not, you can consider ways to improve your results, including changing your *asset allocation*, the split of different types of assets in your portfolio. We discuss how to design the right asset allocation for you in Chapter 7.

  One of the first things you should do before you start investing is decide how much risk you can tolerate and what rate of return you need to meet your goal. You can find out how to do this in Chapter 1.

- **Hurt yourself more than help.** If you're an active investor who's constantly buying and selling stocks, you may be wasting your time and hurting your portfolio. If you find that your returns are lower than what you could get by just buying an index managed fund, you may be better served following a more passive approach.

- **Find your mistakes.** You might have a good investment plan that's working, except for a few investments or stocks that are killing your performance. By tracking your results, you can find what's hurting you and make adjustments if needed.

  Curious what the top mistakes investors make might be? Check out the US CFA Institute's not-to-do list, compiled by prominent professional money managers, at www.cfainstitute.org. Click the About Us tab at the top, select Investor Tools from the list at the left and click on the link for Crucial Information to find the factsheet. You'll also find our own take on the top ten mistakes made by investors in Chapter 19.

Why you want to measure your risk, too

Investors get so obsessed with the potential return for winning stocks that they forget the other side of the picture, the risk. After all, you can get a great return by putting all your chips on black at the roulette table. But are you willing to risk it all? By measuring how much risk you're taking on with your investment, you'll know whether you are

- **Getting adequate returns.** When you invest in a savings account, you're not taking any risk, so you shouldn't expect a giant return. But, if you invest in a risky stock, you should demand to be compensated with a bigger return. If you're not, you're being short-changed.

- **Invested properly.** Some investors aren't matched up with their investments very well. If you're risk-averse and can't stomach it when your portfolio falls just 5 per cent in value in a year, you shouldn't be invested in risky stocks that go up and down wildly. You might consider changing what types of investment you own so you can smooth the bumps. This is done by creating your asset allocation. (You find out how to use online tools to create a portfolio that fits your personality in Chapter 7.)

- **Prepared for volatility.** If you know how risky your investments are ahead of time, you won't be surprised when the value of your account swings up and down. That foresight helps stop you from doing something in haste that you may regret, such as selling all your stocks in panic.

To get higher returns, you must accept more risk. Return and risk are tied at the hip. However, investing in a risky asset doesn't always mean you get a higher return. As you find out if you read Chapter 7, many risky assets have generated poor returns over the years. Avoid these investments because they're bum deals.

Why stocks move in the short term

On average, shares of large Australian companies gain about 12 per cent a year, as we explain in Chapter 1, but don't expect your stocks to gain 1 per cent each month — stocks aren't cuckoo clocks! The ups and downs over the course of a year can be extreme, as investors react to news, corporate events and economic data.

Stock prices can be volatile in the short term because investors are reacting to hundreds of different things. Stock prices reflect what investors know and expect from the company, but they can change the second an unexpected piece of news emerges, altering the company's prospects in an instant. Here's a selection of factors that can influence short-term direction:

- **Movement by the rest of the stock market:** If the rest of the market goes up or down, most stocks move in the same direction. Likewise, movement in the big US indices like the Dow Jones Industrial Average and the S&P 500 can influence the market.

- **Earnings:** These reports are released by companies twice a year to give investors a status report on the business. They're usually released during February–March and July–August. Investors react quickly to the results.

- **Industry developments:** What's happening to the industry as a whole can affect every company in the field. If one company, for example, creates a new product that makes rivals' offerings obsolete, the reaction can be swift.

- **Management changes:** Who gets hired and fired at the top can be critical because such moves may signal poor performance or a change in direction.

- **Raw materials:** Changes in the price of raw materials can significantly affect companies that must buy basic ingredients to make their products.

- **Trading momentum:** When a certain stock gets going, it may seem unstoppable. Often companies become darlings with investors and enjoy big rallies as everyone piles on.

- **Merger chatter:** When the buzz tells you that a corporate wedding is in the offing, that can be market-moving information because companies are usually bought out for a premium to the existing share price.

- **Bond yields:** The yield on bonds determines how much stocks are worth to investors, so a move in yields has a swift effect on stocks.

- **Economic reports:** Official pronouncements about the state of the economy, including changes in the official cash rate from the Reserve Bank or economic data from the Australian Bureau of Statistics.

- **Buying or selling:** When corporate executives are doing a lot of buying or selling of their company's stock, that's worth watching closely. When the company's chief executive officer (CEO) is buying, for example, investors assume he knows what he's doing and may want to go along for the ride. Similarly, institutions buying large stakes in a company can also be a vote of confidence. Of course, this cuts both ways, so the selling of stock by either group can be a negative.

Calculating Your Performance Yourself

If websites and software programs can calculate your portfolio's risk and return for you, why bother learning to do it yourself? We've found that many of the automated ways of calculating performance use slightly different methods, so you're not always clear what's going on. And, with something as important as your investments, you don't want to rely solely on a website that may or may not be accurate. If you know how performance is measured and can approximate your performance yourself, you'll know if you're getting the right information from the automated tools.

If you don't care to know how portfolio returns are measured and just want to do it online, try MoneyChimp's Portfolio Performance Calculator (go to the homepage at www.moneychimp.com, click on Calculator in the top menu bar and choose Portfolio Performance from the list at the right). It automatically calculates your portfolio's return if you enter your portfolio's beginning and ending balance and indicate whether you deposited or withdrew money.

The easiest way to calculate returns

If you haven't deposited money into or taken any money out of your brokerage account, measuring your rate of return for the year is relatively easy. Just follow these steps:

1. **Get your account balance at the end of the financial year and write it down.**

   You can get your year-end balance from your online broker's website or from a printed statement.

2. **Get your account balance at the end of the previous financial year and write it down.**

   Again, this information is available from your broker's website or from a printed statement.

3. **Subtract the answer to Step 2 from the answer to Step 1, divide that difference by the answer to Step 2 and then multiply by 100.**

   Say your portfolio was worth $10,000 on 30 June 2007, and it was worth $12,000 on 30 June 2008. You subtract $10,000 from $12,000 to get $2,000. Divide $2,000 by $10,000, multiply by 100 and the answer is 20 per cent. You earned a 20 per cent rate of return in that year.

Don't worry about dividends and splits when using this approach. And don't concern yourself if you've bought or sold stocks. As long as your dividends and sale proceeds go into the brokerage account, this way of calculating your return reflects all these things.

An easy way to calculate returns if you deposit or take out money

You're probably already asking the logical question: What if you deposit money into or withdraw money from your brokerage account? It complicates things a bit, but it's still not hard. There's an easy way to calculate your return when there are deposits to or withdrawals from your account.

Say your portfolio was worth $10,000 on 30 June 2007, and it was worth $12,000 on 30 June 2008. But you made the withdrawals and deposits to your account shown in Table 6-1.

Table 6-1	Changes in a Sample Portfolio	
Date	*Action*	*Amount*
30 June 2007	Account balance	$10,000
20 Sept 2007	Deposit	$1,000
25 Dec 2007	Withdrawal	$500
1 April 2008	Deposit	$1,000
30 June 2008	Account balance	$12,000

Okay, time to start crunching some numbers:

1. **Get your account balance at the end of the previous financial year.**

   Using the example, you'd write down $10,000, which was your balance on 30 June 2007.

2. **Get your account balance at the end of the current financial year.**

   You'd write down $12,000, which was your balance at 30 June 2008.

3. **Add all the money you've added to your account during the year.**

   In the example, you'd write down $2,000 ($1,000 from 20 September plus $1,000 from 1 April). Only include fresh money you've deposited into your account. Don't include dividends that were paid.

4. **Add up all the money you've withdrawn from your account during the year.**

   In the example, you'd write down $500. That's the only withdrawal you made. Include just withdrawals from the account or cheques you've written against the account. Don't include stocks you've sold if you left the proceeds in your account.

5. **Subtract the answer to Step 4 from the answer to Step 3. Divide the result by 2 and write down the answer.**

   In the example, you'd write down $750. You'd get that by subtracting the $500 in withdrawals from the $2,000 in deposits and dividing the answer, $1,500, by 2.

6. **Add the answer to Step 5 to the number from Step 1.**

   You'd write down $10,750, by adding $750 to the $10,000 from Step 1.

7. **Subtract the answer to Step 5 from the number from Step 2.**

   You'd write down $11,250. That's $12,000 minus $750.

8. **Subtract the answer to Step 6 from the answer to Step 7.**

   You'd write down $500. That's $11,250 minus $10,750.

9. **Divide the answer to Step 8 by the answer to Step 7 and multiply by 100.**

   You'd get your 4.7 per cent rate of return by dividing $500 by $10,750 and multiplying by 100.

You may want to calculate how your portfolio is doing before the end of the year. For example, in December, you may want to get your mid-year performance. That's no problem. Just use the value of your portfolio at any date in the year in Step 2. All the formulas remain the same.

Calculating How Risky Your Portfolio Is

The returns you get from investing online are only half of what you need to know. Just as important, if not more so, is how much risk you took on to get those returns. Measuring risk is a little more controversial. There are many ways to do it, and investors generally disagree on the best way.

Most investment professionals, though, acknowledge the value of measuring risk by studying its *standard deviation*. Yikes, that's a scary term and one that may conjure up memories of statistics class. But, by using readily available online tools, you can use standard deviation as a way to get a handle on how much risk you're accepting in investing. Standard deviation is a mathematical way to determine how much your portfolio swings in value from its average return.

Just know this: When your portfolio's standard deviation is a large number, there's a good chance you can see some big ups and downs in your portfolio's value. And, when the standard deviation is low, you have a good idea your portfolio will pretty much give you your average return every year.

Statistics state that, 68 per cent of the time, your portfolio shouldn't rise by more than its average return (plus the standard deviation) or fall more than its average return (minus the standard deviation). And, 95 per cent of the time, your portfolio shouldn't rise by more than its average return plus two times its standard deviation or fall by more than its average return minus two times its standard deviation.

For example, if you put your money in a five-year term deposit that pays 5 per cent interest, the standard deviation of your return would be 0. In other words, you'll get 5 per cent a year no matter what. But, if you invest in a stock that returns 15 per cent a year on average, your standard deviation might be closer to 40. That means 68 per cent of the time you can expect your portfolio to be up 55 per cent (the 15 per cent average return plus the standard deviation) or down 25 per cent (the 15 per cent average return minus the standard deviation).

A simple way of calculating your average return

Before you can measure how risky your portfolio is, you must first calculate its average yearly return. Earlier in the chapter, you find out how to calculate your portfolio's annual returns. Next, you need to use those annual returns to measure your portfolio's average annual return. You can do this easily by taking all your annual returns, calculated using the directions in the earlier sections, and analysing them.

After you calculate your portfolio's annual returns for each year, write them down or put them in a spreadsheet. The returns listed in Table 6-2 are an example.

Table 6-2	Returns in a Sample Portfolio
Year	*Return*
2003–04	16.8%
2004–05	19.7%
2005–06	20.0%
2006–07	23.8%
2007–08	−16.9%

Source: Compiled from Bourse Data.

If the returns above look familiar, they should. Those are the annual returns of the S&P/ASX 200 index, which tracks the 200 biggest Australian stocks, over the past five years.

How do you measure your average return over five years? You can't just take a simple average by adding up all the returns and dividing by five. Doing that gives you the wrong answer. Instead, you must calculate the geometric mean. The *geometric mean* is the way to correctly measure stock return, trust us. We could explain the technical difference between simple averages and geometric means, but we'll all get headaches for no good reason. If you're truly curious, Deborah Rumsey does a nice job explaining it in her book, *Statistics For Dummies* (Wiley Publishing, Inc.).

If you don't want to go to the trouble of measuring geometric mean, as we describe shortly, the Average Return Calculator at Hugh's Mortgage and Financial Calculators can do it for you. Go to the homepage (www.hughchou.org), click on Mortgage and Other Financial Calculators, and scroll down to Saving and Investing to find the Average Return Calculator. Just enter your returns for each year, and the site calculates the geometric mean, or what it calls the 'true average return'. Easy Calculation (www.easycalculation.com) can also calculate the geometric mean. Choose from the list of Online Statistics Calculators.

You can calculate geometric means using a financial calculator or a spreadsheet. But this is *Online Share Investing For Dummies*, right? So, we show you how to do it online by using Horton's Geometric Mean Calculator, which you see in Figure 6-1 (available at www.graftacs.com/geomean,php3).

Before you rush and type the returns from Table 6-2 into Horton's Geometric Mean Calculator, you need to follow an additional step. Horton's Geometric Mean Calculator can't handle negative numbers. We know you don't think you'll ever have a negative return, but most investors have a bad year sooner or later. Just add 100 to each of the returns, giving you what you see in Table 6-3.

Table 6-3	Returns Converted to Get Geometric Mean
Year	**Plus 100 (Adjusted Return)**
2003–04	116.8
2004–05	119.7
2005–06	120.0
2006–07	123.8
2007–08	83.1

Enter those returns in the blanks in Horton's Geometric Mean Calculator labelled Point 1, Point 2 and so on, as you see in Figure 6-1. After you've entered the returns, scroll to the bottom of the page and click the Submit button. At the top of the page, you see the geometric mean, from which you subtract 100. In this example, the geometric mean is 111.53. You just subtract 100 from 111.53, and you find out your portfolio has a geometric mean return of 11.5 per cent.

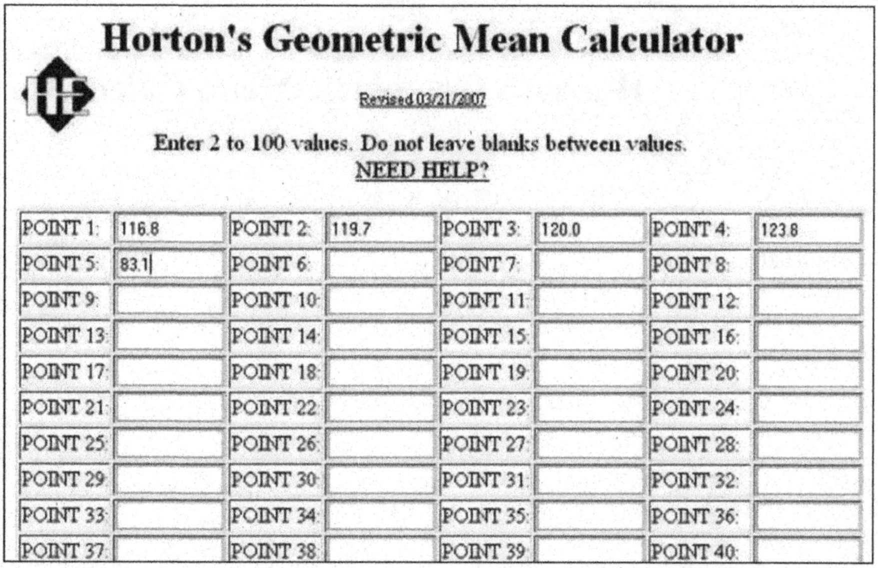

Horton's Geometric Mean Calculator

Revised 03/21/2007

Enter 2 to 100 values. Do not leave blanks between values.
NEED HELP?

POINT 1:	116.8	POINT 2:	119.7	POINT 3:	120.0	POINT 4:	123.8
POINT 5:	83.1	POINT 6:		POINT 7:		POINT 8:	
POINT 9:		POINT 10:		POINT 11:		POINT 12:	
POINT 13:		POINT 14:		POINT 15:		POINT 16:	
POINT 17:		POINT 18:		POINT 19:		POINT 20:	
POINT 21:		POINT 22:		POINT 23:		POINT 24:	
POINT 25:		POINT 26:		POINT 27:		POINT 28:	
POINT 29:		POINT 30:		POINT 31:		POINT 32:	
POINT 33:		POINT 34:		POINT 35:		POINT 36:	
POINT 37:		POINT 38:		POINT 39:		POINT 40:	

Figure 6-1: Horton's Geometric Mean Calculator can do much of the work for you.

If you'd rather measure your portfolio's geometric return in a spreadsheet, Microsoft Excel has a GEOMEAN function that will do it for you. Choose Function from the Insert dropdown menu and select GEOMEAN from the Statistical functions. And, if you don't have Microsoft Excel, you can download a fairly capable spreadsheet program for free. It's called OpenOffice (go to www.openoffice.org and click on Download). And, although it's not as slick as Excel, it's hard to argue with the price. (OpenOffice's Calc spreadsheet program calls it the GEOMEAN function as well.)

Calculating your risk

If you used Horton's Geometric Mean Calculator to measure your portfolio's average return, you've also measured your risk. At the top of the page, right below the geometric mean, is the risk, or standard deviation. In this example, the standard deviation of the portfolio is a modest 16.72 per cent, as shown in Figure 6-2.

Microsoft Excel has a function that measures risk. The STDEV function can measure the standard deviation of returns that you enter.

Figure 6-2:
Horton's
Geometric
Mean
Calculator
crunches
down your
portfolio's
risk (standard
deviation)
as well as
the return
(geometric
mean).

Geometric Mean Calculator Results				
Number of points	5	Arithmetic mean	112.68	
Geometric mean	111.53	Maximum value	123.80	Graphs are currently not available.
Standard deviation	16.72	Sum of points	563.40	
Minimum value	83.10	Equation is	y=-6.33 x + 131.67	

Horton's Geometric Mean Calculator

Revised 03/21/2007

Enter 2 to 100 values. Do not leave blanks between values.
<u>NEED HELP?</u>

POINT 1:		POINT 2:		POINT 3:		POINT 4:	
POINT 5:		POINT 6:		POINT 7:		POINT 8:	
POINT 9:		POINT 10:		POINT 11:		POINT 12:	

Standard deviation works best as a measure of risk if you have many years of data to study. If you've been investing for only a few months or years, you can convert your quarterly results into a yearly or *annualised* number. David Harper's Investopedia article shows you how to do this. Go to the homepage (www.investopedia.com), type in **The Uses and Limits of Volatility** and scroll down to the link in Articles. If all this seems like too much effort, just use the online risk-measurement tools described in the section 'Using Online Tools to Calculate Your Performance' a little later in this chapter.

What does it all mean? Sizing up your portfolio

You did it. You measured your portfolio's average return and risk. But don't start bragging to all your friends just yet. You also need to compare your portfolio's risk and return with another investment so you can put it into perspective. You can see how your performance stacks up by comparing it with a benchmark called an index. An *index* is a basket of stocks used to measure your success. If your portfolio's risk is higher than the index's risk, you want to make sure you're also getting a higher return.

Chapter 2 describes most of the popular market indices. The S&P/ASX 200, due to its general acceptance and the fact that it closely tracks the stock market, is the most common index used to size up investors' returns. If you want to compare your portfolio's risk and return with the S&P/ASX 200 for the same period, you can download the S&P's annual returns from Standard & Poor's by first going to the homepage (www2.standardandpoors.com) and then clicking on Australia & New Zealand. Select Indices from the list at the left, click on the link for the S&P/ASX 200 and choose Data. This displays a table of the sectors that make up the S&P/ASX 200 with the index itself in the top row. By using the dropdown date windows, you can select the various points you need to compare with your own returns. The column on the far right headed YTD (year to date) provides you with the returns, which you can then enter into Horton's Geometric Mean Calculator. The result you get is the S&P/ASX 200's risk and return for the same years.

If you want an easier way to compare returns, you can see how your portfolio fared relative to the returns of major types of investments since 1950, such as the ones in Table 6-4.

Table 6-4	Long-Term Risk and Returns of Different Investments	
Investment	*Return*	*Risk (Standard Deviation)*
S&P/ASX 200	13.5%	20.6%
S&P 500	13.0%	22.2%
Cash	5.5%	5.0%

Source: Compiled from Andex Charts.

Are your returns lower than the long-term returns on the S&P/ASX 200? If so, you want to make sure your risk is lower too. You can see that the Australian sharemarket also offers relatively better performance for less risk than the US sharemarket. The lower long-term returns of cash are balanced out by its low volatility.

Finding other things to compare your returns with

You don't have to compare your stock portfolio with the S&P/ASX 200. Investors commonly choose different indices to compare their performance. It's important to rank yourself against the right index in order to get a good understanding of how you're truly performing. For example, if you want to know how fast your sports car is, you compare it with another sports car, not a four-wheel drive. You can benchmark your returns against

✔ **More specific indices.** If you're investing mainly in small company stocks, you'll want to compare your results against an index that tracks small company stocks. The US iShares website includes an Index Returns Chart, which is a colourful and easy-to-use way to find out how specific areas of the market have performed. Go to the homepage (http://us.ishares.com), click on Tools & Charts at the top and select Index Returns Chart. You can track stocks of different sizes, sectors, industries, regions, countries and commodities. You can also measure different timeframes, such as five days or five years.

Russell's Index Returns Calculator can also help you do this. Go to www.russell.com, choose Indexes from the top menu bar, and click on the Index Returns Calculator. You can download a series of annual returns from many types of stocks, including large company stocks (measured by the Russell 1000) and small company stocks (measured by the Russell 2000) going back 13 years. You can then enter those returns into Horton's Geometric Mean Calculator to see how your portfolio stacks up.

Some investors choose to slice the market even more finely when selecting a benchmark. For example, if you invest mainly in large undervalued stocks, you want to compare your performance to a large *value* index that owns similar stocks.

✔ **Broader indices.** The Capital Markets Index (www.cpmkts.com) gives you an idea of how a diversified basket of stocks, bonds and money-market investors have performed. You can use this index to measure your portfolio's returns.

Using Online Tools to Calculate Your Performance

If you understand the inherent value of tracking your portfolio's performance but maybe the maths involved is just too onerous, you've come to the right section of this chapter. Here we show you automated tools that will crunch your performance numbers for you. Letting your computer do the heavy lifting in measuring performance has three main advantages:

✔ **Ease:** All you have to do is enter your trades, and the computer does the rest. There's no need to look up formulas. You also don't risk making a mistake in the calculations.

✔ **Speed:** The calculations are already programmed in so, after the data is entered, the system can spit out your performance. There's no need to fire up a calculator.

✔ **Customisation:** You can tinker and have the system calculate what your performance would have been, for example, if you didn't have that one stinker in your portfolio.

Completely relying on online tools to tell you something as important as your portfolio's risk and return isn't ideal. Different sites may use different methodologies and it can be difficult to find out what precisely is being measured. With that said, relying on online tools is better than not measuring your portfolio's risk and return at all.

Looking at online tools to measure your performance

Because many new investors are just now getting interested in tracking their performance, a flurry of new tools promising to do the job have popped up on the web. They generally fall into these four categories:

- **Financial software:** This is software you install on your computer that crunches the numbers. It includes personal finance software (refer to Chapter 1) that contains performance-tracking abilities. Specialised software designed just to track returns is also available.

- **Online stock simulations and social-investing sites:** Most of the stock-simulation sites (refer to Chapter 2) and social-investing sites (refer to Chapter 5) have adequate performance-measurement capabilities. We single out a few later in this chapter.

- **Portfolio-tracking sites:** These services allow you to enter your stock holdings and help measure your returns. Portfolio-tracking sites are kind of like Swiss Army knives: They include a variety of portfolio-tracking tools in addition to measuring your portfolio's returns. Many portfolio-tracking sites, for example, alert you if a stock is about to pay a dividend or provide links to online news stories about stocks you own.

- **Performance-tracking websites:** These websites are designed with the express purpose of tracking portfolio performance. Because performance-tracking sites focus on performance tracking, they tend to give a great deal of information on your portfolio's risk and return and are very precise and exacting.

Using personal finance software and performance-tracking software

If you choose to go the software route, it stands to reason that you're going to be buying and/or downloading software and installing it on your PC. This software runs on your computer and crunches down your returns and sometimes your risk, too. Examples include the following:

- **Intuit's Quicken (**www.quicken.com**):** A major player in the financial software field, Quicken Personal Plus monitors all your returns. What makes Quicken unique is that it measures the expected risk, or standard deviation (refer to the section 'Calculating How Risky Your Portfolio Is' earlier in this chapter), of your portfolio in addition to returns. Quicken compares your portfolio's risk with the risk of different benchmarks, including small and large stocks. You can access this feature within Quicken by choosing the Portfolio Analyser feature on the Investing tab. Refer to Chapter 1 for more information on Quicken.

✔ **Analyze Now! (**www.analyzenow.com**):** Technically, Analyze Now! doesn't offer a software program; rather, it provides you with a collection of free spreadsheets. Use the free Return Calculator to calculate your portfolio's returns even if you moved money in and out of your account. Select Free Programs on the left-hand side of the website to find the spreadsheets.

✔ **Spreadsheet data:** If you're already a spreadsheet jockey and want to track your performance that way, you need a place to download current stock quotes into your spreadsheet. Yahoo!7 Finance offers a good, free service at http://au.finance.yahoo.com. Just enter the ASX code for each stock, then click on the Historical Prices link in the left-hand column. When you've entered the range of dates you're interested in, click on Get Prices, scroll to the bottom of the page and click on Download to Spreadsheet.

✔ If bringing up individual stock prices is a chore, you can download the prices of each stock in the S&P/ASX 200 with one click. The catch is that the web page is complicated to get to, so make sure you bookmark it for later use. First go to the homepage (www2.standardandpoors.com) and then click on Australia & New Zealand. Select Indices from the list at the left, then Equity Indices and click on Australia. Choose S&P/ASX 200, click the Overview tab and then Constituent List. Select the date you require, click the green Update button and then click on Download Table just below that. Easy peasy.

Using stock-simulation and social-investing sites

Most stock-simulation and social-investing sites offer performance-tracking tools. We describe stock simulations in Chapter 2 as a way to get your feet wet by choosing stocks and investing online. And we cover social-investing sites in Chapter 5 as a way to connect with other investors.

Covestor (www.covestor.com), in particular, is emerging not only as a leading social-investing site that accommodates Australian users but also a very good performance-tracking tool. It provides data on risk and return using standards recognised by fund managers around the world, giving you highly accurate results.

Online brokers are so competitive they often look at what others are doing and match it. Be sure to check with all the online brokers to see whether they have added any portfolio performance-tracking tools.

Using portfolio-tracking websites

Just about all the sites that track market information, described in Chapter 2, contain portfolio trackers. These sites allow you to enter your holdings or transactions and then sit back, waiting for them to tell you how much your stocks are up or down for the day and year, and several, including Yahoo!7 Finance, let you download your portfolio into a spreadsheet. Portfolio-tracking sites do many things in addition to measuring performance. Still, some of these portfolio-tracking sites can also have advanced capabilities, including the following:

- ✔ **Trading Room (**www.tradingroom.com.au**):** This website not only lets you track your stock and managed-fund portfolios but also contains an excellent portfolio tracker that you can customise to your needs. Register by clicking on the Login link at the top of the page and then click on Become a Member. After you've registered and entered your portfolio data, click the New button next to the heading Column Layouts. In addition to measuring how much your stocks go up or down, you can also view highs and lows for the week, month and year, as well as rolling averages and a host of other items.

- ✔ **ninemsn Money (**http://investorv2.ninemsn.com.au**):** This site also has a portfolio manager that displays individual stock and overall portfolio returns, as well as fundamentals like annualised dividend figures, yield and price-to-earnings (PE) ratios, which we discuss in Chapter 10. It's also handy because you can export your portfolio as an Excel spreadsheet.

- ✔ **Google Finance (**http://finance.google.com**):** Like all Google applications, this site is sparse but nothing is wasted. You can view your portfolio's performance by looking at gains over the day and year to date. You can make notes against individual transactions, view fundamentals, highs and lows, and breaking news tailored to your portfolio.

By keeping tabs on your portfolio's risk and return, you're already way ahead of many other online investors. You have the know-how to tweak and refine your investments to make sure you get the optimal return for the risk you're taking.

Chapter 7

Choosing an Asset Allocation

*Y*ou wouldn't sail a ship without a map or bake a cake without a recipe, but so many online investors do the equivalent when they buy and sell stocks and other assets without understanding how they fit into a broader plan. That plan, in investment language, is called an *asset allocation*. Your asset allocation determines how much of your portfolio is placed into different types of *asset classes*, or types of investments — typically stocks, bonds and cash. By following this plan, you can make sure you get the maximum return for the amount of risk you're taking. One controversial study even claims more than 90 per cent of a portfolio's swings, on average, are due to the asset allocation.

In this chapter, we show you how an asset-allocation plan can improve your success investing online. You also find out how to build your ideal asset allocation using online tools to help you find an allocation that's right for you.

The Recipe for Your Online Investing: Asset Allocation

Many investors make the mistake of chasing random stocks they hear about, buying them and throwing them into their portfolios. They pick up stock tips from TV and neighbours, and blindly invest. Some of these investors wind up owning so many stocks they have an unmanageable portfolio, which generates disappointing returns. Others try to be more selective and invest in just a few stocks they think are promising, but they later find out their portfolios are too risky for their taste.

The answer is simple: Approach investing like a chef with a recipe in hand. Rather than tossing all sorts of ingredients into your portfolio pot and guessing what it will taste like, know what needs to go into the pot to produce a lip-smacking result. In investing, these ingredients make up your asset allocation.

An asset allocation may be general and tell you what percentage of holdings to put in stocks, how much in property and how much in fixed-interest securities. But the recipe may become more detailed and exotic, calling for a dash of large Australian company stocks, a pinch of international stocks and just a touch of fixed interest.

Asset allocations are designed to let all the investments in your portfolio blend together into a dish that will be most likely to generate the highest possible return for the lowest amount of risk.

The advantages of creating and sticking with an asset allocation include:

- ✔ **Diversification:** Hands down, diversification is the biggest advantage of having an asset allocation. An asset allocation calls for certain percentages of your portfolio to be in certain investments. For example, you might put 70 per cent in stocks and 30 per cent in fixed interest and bonds (a *bond* is when you agree to lend money to the government or a corporation in exchange for a regular payment). You want your investments to be spread into different investments that tend to move up and down at different times. That mix will hold the value of your total portfolio steady — and reduce risk — over time.

- ✔ **Rebalancing:** A great way to boost your returns without taking on additional risk, rebalancing pretty much does what the term implies. Periodically, one group of investments in your asset allocation will fall in value. Stocks may fall and bonds rally, for example. When that happens, the percentage of your portfolio in stocks will fall below your plan and the percentage in bonds will rise. To stick to your allocation and maintain the percentages, you need to buy more of the investments that have fallen in value and sell those that have gained. And, when you do that, you're buying investments when they're cheaper and selling them when they get pricier, which isn't a bad strategy.

- ✔ **Discipline:** Staying in control is priceless with online investing. Because trading online is so inexpensive and easy, chasing after popular stocks that are in the news or new investments other investors are talking about is tempting. Many of those investments end up disappointing investors, though, because they're overvalued. We explain how to measure a stock's value in Chapter 11 but, if you stick with your asset allocation, you can avoid this pain.

What's so great about diversification?

If you were to design the perfect portfolio, you'd certainly want the maximum returns for the least amount of risk. The way you do this is by *diversifying*, or spreading your risk over a wide swath of investments, which certainly can reduce risk.

The first aspect of diversification is the idea of safety in numbers. As you add more stocks to your portfolio, you reduce the odds that a vicious decline in any one stock will depth-charge your portfolio.

Before you rush out and buy thousands of stocks, though, you need to be aware of two things. First, your portfolio's risk falls by smaller amounts as you add stocks. For example, the reduction of risk when you go from 30 stocks to 40 is less impressive than when you go from 1 stock to 2. Also, before you start buying every stock you can get your hands on, remember that there are better ways to buy hundreds of stocks at a time: You can buy *managed funds* and *listed managed investments*. These single investments are like baskets that own hundreds of stocks. So, with just one trade, you get the same benefit as an investor who spends hundreds of dollars in commissions building a massive portfolio of stocks. For many investors, buying an index fund or a listed managed investment is the optimum strategy, for just this reason. (We talk about index managed funds in Chapter 8 and listed managed investments in Chapter 9.)

Zigzag: The second element of diversification

Diversification isn't just the result of owning many stocks. You can reduce your risk further by combining different types of assets that zig when the others zag. Stocks that move differently from each other are said to have little *correlation* with each other. Investors build asset allocations by piecing together investments from popular asset classes, such as the following:

- **Cash** is typically parked in funds that buy short-term IOUs, such as term deposits.
- **Bonds** are generally longer term IOUs issued by governments and companies.
- **Australian stocks** are the shares of the thousands of companies that trade on the Australian Securities Exchange (ASX).

✔ **Foreign stocks** are shares in companies that trade on exchanges in other countries. Foreign investing is covered at more length in Chapter 18.

✔ **Emerging-market stocks** own pieces of companies in up-and-coming economies. The risk is very high, but the returns can be high too.

✔ **A-REITs, or Australian real estate investment trusts,** own commercial property such as shopping centres, apartment buildings and offices. They tend to have low correlation with other asset classes, making them attractive in many asset allocations. PIR (www.pir.com.au), a group that specialises in providing research about A-REITs, offers a page that explains the benefits of property investment trusts. Go to the homepage, click on Products & Services in the menu bar and then select Guide to Investing in A-REITs from the menu at the left.

Smart asset allocations put the asset classes together in optimal ways. For example, Australian and US stocks don't move in lockstep with each other, so they work together well in a portfolio. Cash and stocks also move differently. Blending the right doses of these different investments together helps give you the perfect portfolio and is the very purpose of diversification.

The degree to which investments move together is called the *correlation* (or *R-squared*). This complicated mathematical formula is discussed in more length at www.investopedia.com; click on Dictionary and type **correlation** in the search window.

Just know this: When an investment moves identically to the market, it has a correlation of 1 with the market. When an investment moves exactly opposite to the market, it has a low correlation, or –1. If you can find investments with a low correlation and add them to your portfolio, you may be able to reduce your portfolio's risk.

The secret to creating a portfolio is a balancing act between three factors — expected returns, risk and correlation. Sure, you want to pick asset classes with high returns and low risk, but you also want those asset classes that tend to move differently from each other. That way you get the best return and lowest risk possible. Designing a perfect asset allocation can require more maths skills than a university physics final exam. To make things easy, in the section 'Using guidelines' later in this chapter, we show you websites that can do the number crunching for you.

But, for now, just know that most asset allocations recommend you own a certain percentage of stocks, fixed interest, property and cash. Some asset allocations, though, dissect some asset classes, especially Australian stocks, with even more precision (see the section 'Picking investments with the right styles' later in this chapter).

Bigger isn't always better: Understanding size

You'll often see references to *large-cap*, *mid-cap*, *small-cap* and *micro-cap* companies when you're researching asset allocations. Those terms are critical to asset allocations and are the basis on how online asset-allocation sites work.

When you hear reference to large-cap companies, for example, it's a way to describe the company's total market value, or *market capitalisation*. The market cap is the total price tag the stock market places on a company, and is calculated by multiplying the stock price by the number of shares the company has outstanding (in the hands of stockholders). Market cap is a valuable way for investors to look at stocks, because studies show that companies with similar market values have similar returns, risk and correlations. For example, small companies tend to have higher returns than large companies, but they're also riskier.

That raises the question: What's a small company and what's a large company? The answer changes over time as the stock market rises and falls, which can be as much as 30 per cent at times. But Table 7-1 gives you a general idea of where the lines are drawn.

Table 7-1	What's Big and What's Small?
Asset Class	*Market Value Is . . .*
Large cap	Greater than $5 billion
Medium cap	Greater than $1 billion but less than $5 billion
Small cap	Greater than $250 million but less than $1 billion
Micro cap	Less than $250 million

Generally speaking, those companies in the S&P/ASX 50 are the large caps. Those companies that are in the S&P/ASX 100 but not found in the S&P/ASX 50 are the mid caps. They can also be found in their own special index called the S&P/ASX Midcap 50. The next 200 companies are referred to as small caps. These are companies that are in the S&P/ASX 300 but not in any of the other indices. They also have their own index called the S&P/ASX Small Ordinaries.

Want to know whether a stock you own is a large or small company? Nearly all the quote services described in Chapter 2 can give you the market value. You can even type a stock's code (we show you how to find a code in Chapter 5) into the search window in Google Finance (http://finance. google.com/finance), add **ASX:** before the code to denote the ASX, click the Google Search button and the market value will appear below the stock price. Use that figure to see where it ranks in Table 7-1.

Picking investments with the right styles

Companies' market values aren't the only thing that matter when it comes to asset allocations. Some investors also pay attention to stocks' *styles*, such as *value* and *growth*. The definition of what makes a value or growth stock isn't as cut and dried as market cap.

Chapter 13 discusses ways to decide if a stock is considered to be a value stock or growth stock but, for now, just know that *value stocks* are those that are generally bargain-priced. Value stocks tend to be cheaper relative to the earnings and dividends they're generating. Value stocks, though, are cheaper for a reason: They're perceived as being risky because they're in trouble or in a mature industry. *Growth stocks*, on the other hand, generally command lofty prices relative to their assets and earnings because investors expect them to grow rapidly in the future. *Core stocks* fall somewhere in between the two.

You can see how stocks can fall into a number of different categories in Table 7-2. Each box in the table contains a *size*, such as large or small, and a *style*, such as value or growth.

Table 7-2	Popular Ways to Categorise Stocks		
	Style		
	Value	*Core (between value and growth)*	*Growth*
	Large value	Large core	Large growth
Size	Mid-sized value	Mid-sized core	Mid-sized growth
	Small value	Small core	Small growth

When you put market value, style and correlation together, you have everything you need to construct a perfect portfolio. These components are the building blocks that help you get the highest return for the amount of risk you're taking on. Table 7-3 shows the long-term returns, correlation and risk of some of the types of investments suggested by asset-allocation sites.

Table 7-3	Stocks that Zig When the Market Zags		
Asset Class	Long-Term Return	Correlation with Large Stocks (S&P 500)	Risk (Standard Deviation)
Large company stocks	10.3%	1.0	19.2
Large value-priced stocks	11.5%	0.81	25.7
Micro-cap stocks	12.8%	0.62	33.0
Small value-priced stocks	29.6%	0.68	29.6
International value-priced stocks	11.4%	0.61	25.9
Emerging-markets stocks	15.2%	0.56	28.7

Source: IFA.com.

You can read more about how asset allocations balance the three factors at the following sites:

- **Vanguard's guide to asset allocation (**www.vanguard.com.au**):** Visit the Vanguard site and click the Tools and Education tab, then select Plain Talk Library from the left-hand navigation bar and scroll down to Building Your Investment Portfolio. This downloadable document gives you a comprehensive guide to asset allocation from index fund pioneers Vanguard. As an added bonus, you can print out this report as a reference.

- **ASX and Russell Investments long-term investing report:** In conjunction with the ASX, Russell puts out a report each year on the role asset allocation plays in long-term investing. It contains an excellent overview of the performance of different asset classes over the previous 20 years. To access the report, visit the ASX website (www.asx.com.au) and select Shares from the left-hand menu, followed by What Are Shares. Under the heading Benefits of Investing in Shares is a link to the latest Russell report.

✔ **Investopedia (**www.investopedia.com**):** This site provides a comprehensive explanation of how an asset-allocation plan is created. Load up the homepage, click on Articles on the left-hand side and then choose Personal Finance. Scroll to the bottom of the page and count back up 25 articles for the one titled 'Achieving Optimal Asset Allocation'. Note that this is a US site and US conventions apply, such as the US definition of large caps, which start at US$10 billion, as opposed to Australia's A$5 billion.

✔ **IndexInvestor.com (**www.assetallocation.org**):** Here you find in-depth explanations of why asset allocation is so important, as well as guidelines for creating your own asset-allocation plan. Another US site, so the same caveats apply as for Investopedia.

✔ **Path to Investing (**www.pathtoinvesting.com**):** The people at Path to Investing summarise the asset-allocation process and describe how it's done. Choose Portfolio Management from the menu bar and click on Asset Allocation & Diversification (see Figure 7-1.)

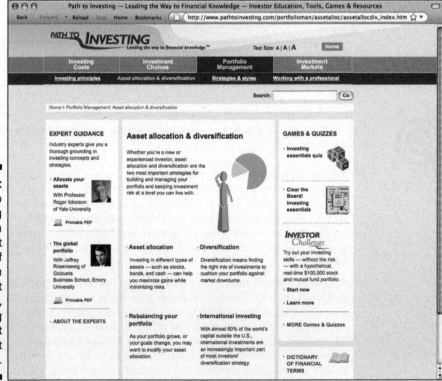

Figure 7-1:
Path to Investing is a convenient source of information on asset allocation, including how to do it and why it works.

Investors commonly make the mistake of thinking their portfolios are diversified if they own shares of companies in many different industries, such as energy, finance and technology. But, if you own only the shares of a large energy company, large finance company and large technology company, you may not be truly diversified.

How rebalancing steadies your portfolio

When you have an asset allocation, you're given a recipe that you stick with. And doing this forces you to be a smart investor by buying more of certain asset classes when they're down. Buying investments when they're down may seem counter-intuitive. And, to be clear, buying individual stocks when they're plunging can be hazardous. But, if you invest in index managed funds or exchange-traded funds that own large baskets of hundreds of stocks, buying when shares go on sale can be smart because you lower your cost. This approach, called the *rebalancing bonus* by respected financial historian William Bernstein, is described fully in his article 'Portfolio Rebalancing: Theory and Practice' (www.efficientfrontier.com — select September 1996 from the Back Issues list to locate the article).

Rebalancing is only advised when you're buying diversified baskets of assets, such as managed funds or exchange-traded funds, which track sections of the market. Buying individual stocks is completely different. Buying when a stock is nose-diving is called 'catching a falling knife' and can be hazardous to your financial health.

How discipline saves your portfolio from getting spanked

An asset plan gives you something to stick to if the markets get choppy. Sometimes that saves you from yourself and helps you resist the temptation to chase after the hot stock or an index your neighbours are talking about. And that's a good thing, because investing in last year's winner is a good way to find this year's loser.

For example, if you look at the performance of stocks by capitalisation over the last five years, you can quickly see how last year's out-performing asset class was the following year's dog (see Table 7-4). Using Standard & Poor's indices, you can see that small caps out-performed large caps by more than

10 per cent in 2003–04 and 2006–07. In 2004–05 and 2005–06, mid-cap stocks were the place to be. But, by the time the market went into a significant correction in 2007–08, large caps recorded less than half the losses recorded by the small- and mid-cap sectors.

Table 7-4	Best Performance by Capitalisation, 2003–08		
	S&P/ASX 20	**S&P/ASX Mid Cap 50**	**S&P/ASX Small Ordinaries**
2003–04	13.27%	20.08%	21.55%
2004–05	16.21%	28.88%	22.53%
2005–06	20.60%	22.48%	20.62%
2006–07	19.71%	28.51%	39.13%
2007–08	−11.83%	−21.39%	−23.32%

Using and Finding Your Perfect Asset Allocation

You can use one of three main ways to design your asset allocation:

- **Following guidelines:** These simple rules, available on websites we point out in 'Using guidelines' later in this section, are great if you just want to keep things simple.

- **Taking a risk-based approach:** Calculate how much risk you can tolerate and select a blend of investments to give you the highest return for that risk.

- **Taking a return-based approach:** You can work backwards and measure how much return you need to meet your goal and design a portfolio that will get you there.

In this section, we help you choose an asset allocation that gives you a roadmap of the types of investments you should buy to get the returns you're looking for. But an asset allocation doesn't do you any good if you don't act on it. In Chapter 8, we show you how to buy the investments your asset allocation calls for by picking the right managed funds. Chapter 9 gives you the lowdown on listed managed investments, and, in Chapter 11, we show you how to find individual stocks that match your asset allocation.

Determining your current asset allocation

If you own any investments now, you already have an asset allocation. It just might not be what you think it is, and it might not be designed to give you the returns and risk you want. It's important to understand what types of investments you own currently and what your current asset allocation is. You can do this by using the following:

- **Personal finance software:** The big players here are Microsoft's Money and Intuit's Quicken. Both can classify all the stocks, bonds and managed funds in your portfolio and tell you what percentage of your holdings are in each. You can read more about both in Chapter 1.

- **Morningstar's Portfolio X-Ray®:** Morningstar offers a handy tool called the Portfolio X-Ray® for premium subscribers, but you can access it when you take out a free trial. After you've registered, from the homepage (www.morningstar.com.au), click on the Portfolio tab and follow the steps to create your portfolio.

  Click on the X-Ray tab, and your holdings are broken down into the major categories, such as cash, stocks, bonds and other. You also see how much of your stocks are in value-priced or growth stocks, as well as whether they're large, mid-sized or small companies. A breakdown of what industries your holdings fall into is also given. (You can see a sample in Figure 7-2.) You can also enter your fund codes into the X-Ray tool. Being able to see both your stocks and your funds is really the power of the tool. It shows you how much of an individual stock you're exposed to.

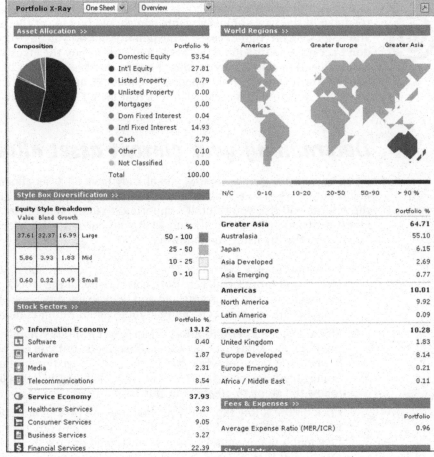

Figure 7-2: Morningstar's Portfolio X-Ray dissects your portfolio by looking for patterns in the types of stocks, industries and regions you're invested in.

Using guidelines

If you're the kind of investor who wants to have an asset allocation but doesn't want to delve into all the complications, this method is for you. The resources covered here make asset allocation easy, by either suggesting a general-purpose asset allocation that will work for most people or letting you choose from simple but effective allocations.

Intuit's Quicken financial software

Quicken has a helpful Asset Allocation Guide that lets you choose from several off-the-shelf asset allocations. You can look them over and decide which one gives you the level of return you're interested in at the amount of risk you can tolerate, such as conservative, moderate or aggressive.

Efficient Frontier

Efficient Frontier (`www.efficientfrontier.com/ef/996/cowards.htm`) is a site managed by well-known and well-respected market scholar and adviser William Bernstein. He suggests a Coward's Portfolio, which he says is designed to be an easy way for investors to build a solid portfolio with international exposure. He also suggests which managed funds to buy to match the portfolio.

MoneyChimp

Okay, MoneyChimp isn't a big player, but the folks there know investing. Visit `www.moneychimp.com/articles`, click on Modern Portfolio Theory and then Build a Portfolio. The Asset Allocation page gives you a simple calculator to provide a general breakdown of what types of assets you should own at your level of risk tolerance.

Gummy Stuff

Coming straight from Canada, the Gummy Stuff site is chock-full of tutorials, spreadsheets and financial tools, including an asset allocator (`www.gummy-stuff.org/allocations.htm`). It lets you play with different asset allocations to see how you would have done.

Picking an asset allocation based on your risk tolerance

Some investors may decide they want to tailor their asset allocation with a bit more precision for their individual taste. And, if you're like most investors, the disappointment you feel when your portfolio falls more than you'd like is definitely greater than any happiness you might feel at eking out a slightly better-than-expected return. That's why online tools that assess your appetite for risk, and then design a portfolio, make sense for many investors. Here are a few to try.

- ✔ **ASIC's Risk and Return Calculator** (www.fido.gov.au): Select from the dropdown menu for Calculators. This handy Excel spreadsheet is a very basic but helpful method to gauge levels of risk in your investment plan. It lets you select an asset allocation, the type of return you're expecting and the investment timeframe, before placing them in the general context of risk. A helpful starting point for beginners.

- ✔ **Colonial First State's Risk Profiler** (www.colonialfirststate.com.au): Click on Calculators and choose What Investments Suit Your Risk Profile? It examines your risk profile in relation to your investment horizon, goals and how much volatility you're prepared to tolerate. At the end of the questionnaire you're given a summary of your risk profile and the recommended asset allocation for your needs.

- ✔ **AXA Investor Profile Calculator** (www.axa.com.au): Choose from the Calculator options. This application from AXA provides you with information that can inform your ideas about your asset allocation for superannuation. It takes into account your timeframe for investment, your investment experience and your attitude to risk, as well as your own view of how long you expect to rely on your superannuation. A worthy exercise for anyone interested in superannuation — and that should be everyone!

- ✔ **BT Risk Profiler** (www.bt.com.au): Click on Tools & Resources, select Calculators and choose Risk Profiler. This tool from BT Financial Group (owned by Westpac) goes a bit deeper to establish your level of investment experience and overall tolerance for risk. At the end of a series of questions, you're shown your ideal asset allocation in the form of a pie chart. But, be warned, the site works only in Internet Explorer, which is frustrating if you're using Firefox or Safari.

- ✔ **Index Funds Advisors** (www.ifa.com): Click on Risk Capacity Survey from the homepage. IFA's survey — mentioned in Chapter 1 — is another way to determine what kind of investor you are. The survey asks you a battery of questions to assess how much risk you can take, which is the way it recommends a portfolio to you. The Quick Risk Capacity Survey has just 5 questions, and a longer survey has 25 questions. After you answer the questions and submit them along with your contact details, the website provides an automated analysis of your responses and suggests one of several predetermined portfolios. The most risk-tolerant investors are pointed to Portfolio 100 and risk-averse investors to Portfolio 5.

  IFA's asset allocations are much more detailed than some of the sites that provide guidelines. For example, rather than suggesting owning large-cap stocks, IFA distinguishes between large-cap stocks and large-cap value-priced stocks. The portfolios also recommend specific index funds sold by asset-management firm Dimensional Fund Advisors, which you can buy through a financial adviser licensed to sell them.

✔ **Vanguard's Investor Questionnaire (**https://personal.vanguard.com.us/home**):** Choose Planning & Education from the menu bar, click on Create Your Investment Plan, choose Complete the Investor Questionnaire and follow the instructions. This section of the Vanguard site, shown in Figure 7-3, asks you ten questions in an attempt to try to figure out how much risk you can stomach. At the end, the site recommends that you own certain mixes of short-term reserves, stocks and cash. You can view all the recommended portfolios by going back to Create Your Investment Plan, selecting Choose Your Asset Allocation and scrolling down to the link Find the Right Mix.

✔ **Analysis of Asset Allocation (**www.asset-analysis.com**):** With a name like Analysis of Asset Allocation, you can't go wrong, right? Under Tools on the right-hand side of the page, click on the Asset Allocation option. This section of the site steps you through five questions that measure your appetite for risk. When you're done, the site determines how much risk you can take and tells you how much of your portfolio should be invested in cash, bonds, emerging markets, domestic stocks, real estate and international stocks.

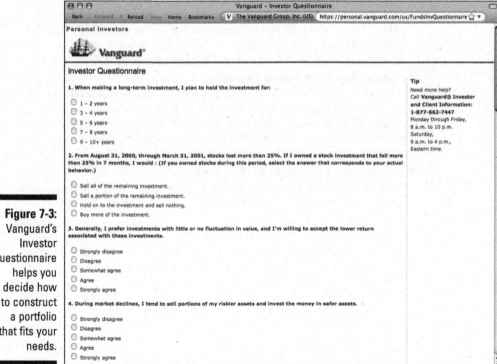

Figure 7-3:
Vanguard's Investor Questionnaire helps you decide how to construct a portfolio that fits your needs.

Picking an asset allocation based on your goals

The other way to figure out how to allocate your portfolio is to first determine what rate of return you need to reach your goal and then pick an asset allocation that will get you there. Several of the asset allocation sites take this approach:

- ✔ **FIDO's Compound Interest Calculator** (www.fido.gov.au): Want to calculate the rate of return you need to reach a goal? Try FIDO's Compound Interest Calculator (select from the Calculators dropdown menu). Just enter how much money you have now, how much you need to have and when you need to have it, and the calculator tells you the rate of return you need.

- ✔ **ING DIRECT's Savings Goal Calculator** (www.ingdirect.com.au): Select Savings from the list of calculators and click on Savings Goal Calculator. This tool, shown in Figure 7-4, does much the same thing as FIDO's calculator, but on a web-based application.

- ✔ **TIAA CREF's Asset Allocation Evaluator** (www.tiaa-cref.org): This tool designs your allocation based on your investment philosophy by asking you a series of questions before advising you. Visit the TIAA CREF homepage and then click on Education & Support, followed by Tools, and then click Asset Allocation Evaluator to get started.

- ✔ **Forbes' Asset Allocation Calculator** (www.forbes.com/tools/calculator/asset_alloc.jhtml): Forbes' calculator asks you to enter the current mix of investments in your portfolio. The site then estimates how much you'll earn based on 50-year historical returns of cash, stocks and bonds. You can then tweak the allocation to see whether you can get the rate of return that you need.

- ✔ **Fidelity.com's Portfolio Review** (http://personal.fidelity.com): Select Investment Products from the menu bar, choose Mutual Funds, click on Design Your Portfolio and then Build Your Own Portfolio.

The Portfolio Review helps you plan for a wide array of goals, ranging from retirement and education to more specific things like a holiday, wedding or wealth accumulation. The Portfolio Review also studies how much risk you can stomach. The site can analyse your current portfolio, make suggestions on ways to improve, and suggest an asset allocation. You don't have to be a Fidelity account holder to use the system; you can sign up for a free membership instead.

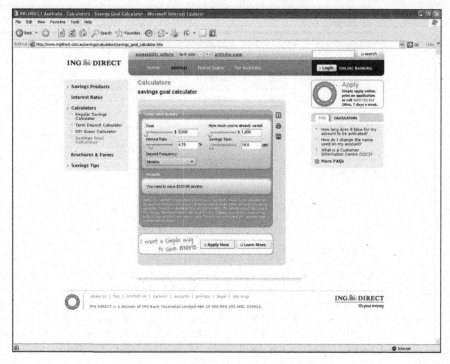

Dollar-Cost Averaging: Reducing Your Risk

After you've decided on the optimum recipe for your investments, rushing out to the sharemarket to buy everything on your shopping list isn't always a good idea. When buying stocks, you should be just as careful about protecting your *downside* (losses) as you are about achieving the *upside* (gains). Let's say you had $20,000 on 28 September 2007 and you were interested in buying shares in BHP. At the time, BHP shares were trading for $44.55. When you flip forward to the end of the financial year, nine months later, BHP is trading for $43.70 — your portfolio has lost 1.9 per cent, or $380 for the period.

But, if you were to split your funds into equal amounts and buy the stock at regularly spaced intervals over those nine months, that's *dollar-cost averaging*. In this case, let's say you were to buy $5,000 worth of BHP every three months from 28 September 2007, as Table 7-5 shows.

Table 7-5	Dollar-Cost Averaging			
Date	Buy Price	30 June 2008	Gain/Loss	Profit/Loss
28 September 2007	$44.55	$43.70	−1.9%	−$95.00
31 December 2007	$40.14	$43.70	8.9%	$443.00
31 March 2008	$35.81	$43.70	22.0%	$1,101.50
30 June 2008	$43.70	$43.70	0.0%	$0.00

Source: Compiled from Bourse Data.

By 30 June 2008, you've made a net profit of $1,449.50 — that's a gain of 7.2 per cent compared with a net loss! Dollar-cost averaging is an effective way of de-risking your portfolio while building it, but many investors find it very difficult to do for two reasons. First, it's not something that can be done immediately. It takes a long time — in fact a whole year or more! Many investors don't have the discipline to hold on to capital in this manner for an extended period. Second, when you dollar-cost average, your investment plan will often require you to buy into a stock when it's falling, which can be counter-intuitive. But, if you stick to your original investment plan, it can be both a prudent and profitable method of buying shares.

Part III
Finding the Right Investments

Glenn Lumsden

*'My online stock screen tells me to invest in
Village Roadshow, but only if you
stop stealing movies.'*

In this part ...

If you're the kind of person who can't stop after just mastering the basics, you'll find yourself at home in this part. Here we dig in deeper and take on more-advanced topics that savvy investors rely on when choosing investments and constructing their portfolio. You get tips on how to research and buy managed funds and listed managed investments, including exchange-traded funds, online.

We also show you how to use online tools to closely examine companies' earnings, cash flow and financial statements to get a clearer picture about whether a stock is for you. You get exposure to advanced online techniques used by the pros to measure stocks' prospects, including assessing their risk, potential cash flow and valuation. You find tutorials on how to make your computer do much of the hard work for you by building online screens that unearth stocks and investments from thousands of candidates. We show you how to find out whether certain experts and analysts are worth listening to by using online tools that evaluate their performance. And, for investors looking for more stability, this part tackles the topic of bonds and other fixed-interest investments.

Chapter 8

Finding and Buying Managed Funds

*O*nline investing isn't just for individual stock pickers. The internet can also be used to pick, track and monitor investments in *managed funds* — funds that pool money from many investors so that it can then be invested in stocks, bonds or other assets. By pooling money, managed funds give small investors some of the benefits enjoyed by larger investors, especially the ability to spread money over many investments, or *diversify*.

Most Australians have invested money in managed funds without even knowing — through superannuation. According to the Australian Bureau of Statistics, in March 2008, more than $1.2 trillion was pooled together by Australians into managed funds. When you consider that a trillion equals one thousand billions, that's quite a lot of money in anyone's language!

In this chapter, we explain how online tools can maximise your success investing in managed funds. We also show you how to use online tools to pick the right investments for you and walk you through the process of setting up an account to buy or sell the funds.

Understanding Managed Funds

If all the work it takes to pick individual stocks, described in Chapters 10 and 11, sounds exhausting, managed funds may be for you. By their design, managed funds give investors what they're looking for with minimal work. Most managed funds own large baskets of stocks, giving investors the benefit of diversification (refer to Chapter 7) right off the bat. And managed funds come in many flavours, allowing investors to buy exactly what they want, such as specific types of stocks or industries. Want to own small value-priced stocks? No problem, there's a managed fund you can buy that takes care of it. Passive investors can also buy *index funds*, which match market indices and charge low fees. Active investors can choose from *actively managed funds* that rely on human stock pickers who try to beat the market (although very few do and they charge like wounded bulls).

There's just one problem. The sheer number of managed funds is so enormous that it's hard to know where to start. More than 6,000 managed funds are available for retail investors. That's five times the number of stocks trading on the Australian Securities Exchange (ASX)! Meanwhile, the amount of money invested in funds, called *net assets*, also continues to swell.

Considering the pros of managed funds

Just because managed funds are popular, though, doesn't mean they're right for you. You may decide that buying individual stocks is more your style. Even so, first considering what you gain and lose by investing in managed funds is worthwhile. First, what you gain:

- **Instant diversification:** If you buy just one managed fund, you own a piece of dozens, if not hundreds, of stocks. Buying a share of a fund is more cost-effective than buying and managing hundreds of stocks yourself.

- **Easy asset allocation:** As we explain in Chapter 7, it's important to have an asset allocation that helps guide you in what kinds of stocks you should buy to get more return for the amount of risk you're taking on. Some of these asset allocations get pretty specific, calling for a certain percentage of your portfolio to be in small value-priced stocks or large stocks. You can easily pick up the right exposure by buying managed funds dedicated to these *sizes* and *styles*. Buying just five or more managed funds can give you an easy-to-manage and completely diversified portfolio.

✔ **Low fees:** By pooling your money with many other investors, you gain significant cost savings. Large managed-fund companies can save money on commissions, research and other fees, which means they pay less than what you'd have to pay if you were doing all this on your own. Managed funds must also disclose their fees, so you can quickly find those that are the most efficient. ASIC's FIDO website (www.fido.gov.au) contains an excellent calculator that shows you how high fees can eat into your returns. Select Managed Funds Calculator from the dropdown menu.

If you're interested in keeping your costs down, index managed funds have extremely low fees, sometimes less than 0.5 per cent a year. If you have $1,000 invested and a fund charges 0.5 per cent, that means you pay just a $5 fee that year.

Drawbacks of managed funds worth considering

Despite managed funds' advantages, they have some significant drawbacks:

✔ **Lack of control:** When you buy a managed fund, you're putting your investment in the hands of an investment company. If you invest with an actively managed fund, which hires a professional portfolio manager to select stocks for the fund to buy, you don't have much say in investment decisions. If the manager sells a stock — one you think is a good long-term hold, for example — you can't do anything about it. This is the case with index managed funds too. If a stock is added to the S&P/ASX 200, for example, your S&P/ASX 200 index fund will buy the stock too.

✔ **Tax inefficiencies:** When managed funds buy and sell stocks during the year, their actions often result in tax bills you aren't expecting. The most unfortunate type occurs when a fund sells a stock for a gain.

Yes, you have to pay tax when you sell an individual stock for a gain also. But *you* decide when to sell that stock. Managed funds may sell stocks for gains anytime, including a time that's not good for you. That gain is then distributed to you, the managed-fund owner, and you must pay tax on it. *Capital gains distributions* often come with no warning and can spoil a well-thought-out tax plan. This tends to be much less of an issue with index managed funds because the *turnover*, or number of stocks bought and sold, tends to be lower than with actively managed funds.

Realised capital gains nightmare

Realised capital gains distributions are one of the biggest drawbacks of actively managed funds. These distributions can be very large and unexpected, two things you don't want when it comes to managing your taxes.

Consider the whopper of a capital gains distribution paid by AXA's Australian Equity Fund in 2008. After the fund manager cleaned house and sold off giant chunks of stock, the fund delivered distributions of 12.6 per cent in a year when average returns should have been closer to 4 per cent.

Making things worse, if a portfolio manager sells stocks owned for a year or less for a gain, shareholders who own the funds in a taxable account can get hit with high short-term capital gains tax. Capital gains tax is explained in detail in Chapter 1.

Types of investment companies

Investment-fund companies are usually structured in one of three ways. The structure dictates how the value of the fund is determined and how you buy and sell your shares. The main types of structures are:

- **Listed or unlisted:** If the fund trades on the ASX, it's described as *listed*, and *unlisted* if it's bought and sold through the fund manager (companies like AXA, Colonial First State, Macquarie and Vanguard). The value of a listed fund, like a company's share price, is determined by market forces. What investors are prepared to pay for it. In an unlisted fund, the *unit price* is determined when the fund manager divides the total value of the fund by the number of units.

- **Open or closed:** *Open-ended* funds continually take on more funds for investors over the life of the fund. *Closed-end* funds only take on investors during a set period of time. Once they close, that's it.

- **Indexed or actively managed:** One of the big questions to face investors throughout the ages is whether to choose an index fund or an actively managed fund. An *actively managed* fund contains shares specifically selected by the fund manager. Funds like these are more expensive because you're paying for the fund manager's expertise. On the other hand, *index funds* replicate the performance of an index like the S&P/ASX 200 or the US S&P 500. What these funds do is pool investor money together and replicate the entire index in a portfolio by buying a certain amount of every stock in a particular index weighted according to the size of the company. Essentially, the fund managers of an index fund are continually balancing and rebalancing the fund to ensure that it closely mirrors the index.

Index shadowing is a sinister activity in which managed funds pretend to be adding value by picking winning stocks but are actually just tracking or shadowing the market. This practice isn't good for investors because they're paying for the expertise of a fund manager but not getting anything in return. These investors could get the same results, and save money on fees, by investing in low-cost index funds.

If you want to find a managed fund's unit price, check out the websites that provide stock quotes, described in Chapter 2. Nearly all those sites provide the managed fund's unit price if you enter the fund's code. Some sites provide additional information about the fund. For example, visit the free service provided by Morningstar (www.morningstar.com.au) and use the Fund Screener at the bottom of the homepage to find your fund. The site tells you the following information about the fund:

- **Performance:** The site will track performance going back six months, one year, three years, five years and seven years.

- **Net assets:** This is a tally of how much investor money is invested in the fund.

- **Category:** The site displays the type of fund, such as equities, property or bonds.

- **Fees and expenses:** This covers entry fees, exit fees and the management-expense ratio (MER), which is discussed more fully in the section 'Deciphering the morass of managed-fund fees' later in this chapter.

- **Distributions:** The site lets you know how often you receive dividends.

- **Initial investment:** This is the minimum amount you can choose to invest in the fund.

Categorising Managed Funds

Because managed funds outnumber stocks, the fact that many types of managed funds are on offer is probably not too surprising. Managed funds at their most basic level come in four basic flavours — those that invest in stock funds, bond funds, money market funds or hybrid funds. But, if you drill down, you find even more categories. The following sections give you a sense of how categories and subcategories branch off from each other.

Stock funds

Stock funds invest in shares of publicly traded companies. These funds typically go for large gains by pursuing one of a number of strategies:

- ✔ **Growth funds** are filled with shares of companies that investors generally expect to expand their earnings the fastest. Portfolio managers of actively managed growth funds are typically willing to pay higher valuations for *growth* stocks because they think the companies are worth it. Growth index funds buy shares of companies that have the highest valuations, often measured by the price-to-book ratio, a concept we explain in more detail in Chapter 11.

  If you're young and retirement is still years off, many experts advise to invest in growth funds. The trouble, though, is that academic studies have shown growth funds, including growth index funds, tend to own the most overvalued stocks. That means they tend to have lower future returns and higher risk than value funds that own less glamorous stocks.

- ✔ **Value funds** own companies that are usually out of fashion or considered by the market to be ho-hum and mature. Fund managers of this type are trained to identify *undervalued* stocks, stocks that are sold for less than their intrinsic value, or *net tangible assets (NTA)*, which means they're sold for less than they're actually worth. Value index funds usually own stocks that have the lowest valuations.

- ✔ **Income stock funds** seek to invest in companies that pay fat dividends, such as utilities and real estate investment trusts (REITs). Income stock funds aren't looking for stock price appreciation.

- ✔ **Region funds** look to take advantage of economic conditions in a certain geographical area. Some may look for a recovery in the US economy and invest in US stocks that could benefit most from a turnaround in that economic environment. Separately, many funds are available to investors that are solely focused on the emerging economic strength of nations like Brazil, Russia, India and China (the so-called BRIC nations). Some funds are focused on all of the BRIC nations at once, diversifying by selecting a basket of stocks from each country.

- ✔ **Sector funds** concentrate on a particular industry or theme that the fund manager believes in or has particular expertise in. Sectors can include such themes as uranium, biotechnology or energy.

- ✔ **Diversified funds** take a more balanced approach, spreading risk across a number of asset classes, regions and sectors. Examples include bonds, real estate, currency and stocks selected from different corners of the world.

- ✔ **Fund of funds** invest across a range of different funds, once again spreading your risk. This approach can give you access to funds that aren't normally available to you at a retail level. It's also viewed as the easiest way to access a group of assets classes at once.

Bond funds

The US has a long tradition of investors buying bonds directly from the issuer, including from the government, private companies or utilities. Bond funds own diverse baskets of bonds, which usually have similar characteristics. Bond funds are generally seen as a way to reduce risk because they collect income from a variety of borrowers. If one borrower defaults on the loan, you own many other bonds and aren't wiped out. Bond funds are often where an institution will put your money when you take out a term deposit or any other type of fixed-interest instrument. Many types of bond funds exist, which we discuss in more detail in Chapter 14, but the main types are characterised as follows:

- ✔ **Government bond funds** tend to invest in debt issued by the US government. These funds usually invest in treasuries that mature in the short term, intermediate term or long term, or a blend of each.

- ✔ **High-yield bond funds**, nicknamed *junk bond funds*, generate higher returns by investing in debt issued by companies with shakier finances. The overall risk is reduced by spreading the investment over many companies' debt.

- ✔ **Corporate bond funds** own bonds issued by large companies. Their yields are usually higher than those paid by government bonds but less than high-yield bonds.

More kinds of funds

In Australia, around five times as many funds exist as do stocks. That's because financial institutions are continually coming up with new ideas to attract investor funds and, hence, make more money. Here are just a few more funds that have emerged over the last few years that might interest you:

✔ **Capital-guaranteed funds** are for the most risk-averse of all investors. Capital-guaranteed funds are closed-end funds that promise that you won't lose any of your money! Sound great? Well, there's a catch. Your downside is limited, so your upside is too — you may be eligible for a 12 per cent return at best. Say a fund is capital guaranteed, with a headline rate of 12 per cent fixed over five years. You invest $10,000 and, if everything goes to plan, the best possible outcome you can hope for is a return of $17,623.

But say the investment turns sour in the second year. Which is a pity, because your money is tied up for another three years. But that doesn't matter, because your capital is guaranteed, right? Wrong. Unfortunately what's known as the *time value of money* comes into play, which, in this case, means accounting for inflation. When you get back your initial investment of $10,000 it's only worth $8,587, because inflation is running at 3 per cent per annum. If you put your $10,000 in the bank at 9 per cent interest, you walk away with $15,386 after five years, with arguably less risk and much more flexibility.

✔ **Alternative funds** invest in opportunities found outside the stock market. Typically this means private-equity funds or hedge funds.

- **Private-equity funds** often look for under-performing listed companies, buy them and 'take them private'. This means taking them off the stock market. The funds believe that listed companies are so focused on short-term gains that they ignore the bigger picture. Often, after taking them private, the funds perform radical restructuring and cost-cutting measures before returning them to the stock market years later. Private-equity funds typically have timeframes of five years or longer.

- **Hedge funds** are often called absolute-return funds, which means they aim to turn a profit in good times and in bad. They're often involved in currency, commodity or derivatives trading. For many years these funds were only available to the very rich but, in recent years, some hedge funds have opened their books to the average investor. Because of their specialised nature, hedge funds charge the highest fees of all funds, what's known in the industry as *2 and 20*. This means an ongoing fee of 2 per cent of your initial stake and 20 per cent of everything over the *benchmark*, which is often an index like the S&P/ASX 200.

So, if you invest $10,000 in a hedge fund, your annual maintenance fee is $200, leaving you with $9,800. If the benchmark returns 12 per cent and the fund returns 18 per cent, then the fund will charge an additional fee of $117.60 ($1,764 – $1,176 = $588 × 0.2). Your net gain becomes $1,646.40, which equates to a return of 16.8 per cent.

✔ **Ethical funds** are a relatively new invention. In an age when people are genuinely interested in doing their bit to reduce their impact on the environment, ethical funds seek to invest only in companies that are doing the same.

However, it turns out that many shades of green colour the ethical-funds industry. Some Australian funds that claim to be ethical have big investments in companies like BHP and Woolworths. We're not suggesting these companies are in any way unethical, but investors who seek out ethical funds may not expect uranium mining and gaming operations to be included.

As two of the biggest listed and best performing companies on the ASX, BHP and Woolworths have many interests. BHP has an interest in the world's largest uranium deposit at Olympic Dam and recently has ramped up its oil production and exploration activities. And Woolworths, which is normally associated with well-run supermarkets, generates a significant slice of revenue from the sale of alcohol and tobacco. Recently it has also become involved in the operation of poker machines, activities that may not sit well with some investors. At the same time, ethical funds that have stringent requirements for their investment strategy typically under-perform other investments, so you want to make sure that you're on the same wavelength at the very least.

✔ **Cash-management trusts** are yet another type of fund, although many people view them like savings accounts. These are high-yielding accounts where money is 'parked' while you work out where you want to invest it, or if you want to invest it at all! In the past, Macquarie Bank dominated this space with its product, called, appropriately, Macquarie Bank Cash Management Trust. However, following the deregulation of the banking sector and the rise of the internet, many other options are now available giving you at-call access to your money and the protection of the government guarantee, such as ING DIRECT's Savings Maximiser and Bank West's Telenet Saver. Both of these accounts offer high headline interest rates but are online only. If you require extra features like credit cards, then a cash-management trust may be more appropriate, but you will pay for the extra features.

What to Look For in a Managed Fund

When you're shopping for a fund, you want to have a checklist of all the things that are important. Pay attention to the following characteristics:

- ✔ **The fund's style:** If your asset allocation calls for investing in international equities, you want to go with a fund that does exactly that. Sounds easy, right? Watch out, though, because the name of a managed fund may make it sound like one thing, when in reality it's something else.

  How could this 'what's in a name' business affect you? Say you're debating between two managed funds that claim to invest in international equities. Both have the word 'international' in their names, but the funds may have completely different strategies.

  Finding out which one is truly international is easy. Log on to the site of managed-fund tracker Morningstar (www.morningstar.com.au), as shown in Figure 8-1. Enter the first managed fund's name or APIR code (kind of like a company code for managed funds) and click the arrow. Underneath Asset Allocation will be a breakdown of how the fund invests its money. It's not unusual for some funds to have significant portions of capital in cash, but if it's international equities you're after, make sure you get what you're paying for!

- ✔ **Long-term performance:** Chasing after managed funds that did the best last year or over the last decade is tempting. But studies have shown explosive managed funds are rarely able to maintain their streaks. Concentrate on a fund's five- or ten-year track record, at the least. If you can get performance data going back further, even better. And always compare a managed fund's performance with the comparable index. If you're looking to buy a managed fund that invests in large value-priced stocks, you should compare its performance with a large-value index like the S&P/ASX 20.

- ✔ **Turnover:** The amount of buying and selling a fund does is called its *turnover*. It's important to keep turnover low because, when your fund sells stocks, you can face serious tax consequences if it causes capital gains distributions.

- ✔ **Ratings:** Morningstar (www.morningstar.com.au) ranks managed funds based on many dimensions of their performance. Although you can't rely solely on these rankings, they're worth paying attention to. Plus they're easy to understand.

✔ **Size:** When shopping for *actively managed* funds, you'll often come across a dilemma. When they get too large and have huge chunks of money to invest, performance usually suffers as they struggle to find enough investments to plough the money into.

A general guideline on this is, if you own a fund that invests in large companies, it may be getting too big when it has $5 billion in assets. You can find out how much money is invested in a fund by logging on to www.morningstar.com.au, entering the fund's name or code, and clicking the arrow to bring up the Morningstar Fund Report, which includes net assets.

Popular funds attempt to stop themselves from getting too bloated by *closing* to new investors. When this happens, if you're already an investor in the fund, you can add money, but you can't buy into the fund if you're not already an investor.

Being too small can be a problem, too. If a fund doesn't attract enough assets, it may be shut down.

✔ **Fees:** The fees charged by your fund to invest your money are typically taken annually, no matter what. That means, even if the fund falls in value, you pay fees. That's why fees are one of the most important things to pay attention to. They're so important that the next section is dedicated to understanding them.

Actively managed funds tempt investors with the promise that their portfolio managers are so smart they can beat the market. The reality, though, is that very few beat the market consistently, and they wind up charging investors fees for a promise that's never realised. A look at history shows how the odds are stacked against active managed-fund managers. Of the funds that existed in 1970, only 37 per cent were still around by 2005, according to John Bogle, founder of Vanguard, which pioneered the low-cost index managed fund. The other 63 per cent of managed funds were shut down due to poor performance. Even if you picked one of the survivors, you didn't necessarily score. Of the funds that lasted, 45 per cent lagged behind the stock market, and 36 per cent turned in performances that nearly matched the market. That means just 7 per cent of the funds that existed in 1970 beat the stock market by more than one percentage point a year. That's why investing in a low-cost index fund, for many investors, is often the best option. Check out the full article at the Vanguard website (www.vanguard.com/bogle_site/sp20060515.htm).

Figure 8-1:
Morningstar
lets you
dig deeper
and find
out precise
details
about
managed
funds.

Deciphering the morass of managed-fund fees

Managed-fund performance swings up and down, along with the stocks and bonds the fund is invested in. But one thing is for sure — the managed-fund company will certainly collect its cut.

If you're not careful, managed funds can sting you with all sorts of fees. The good thing, though, is that all fees must be disclosed ahead of time so you can avoid expensive funds if you know what to look for. The shortlist of things to be on the lookout for includes the following:

- **Entry fees** are charged to investors immediately when they buy units in a fund. These fees, also called *front-end loads*, are the most sinister because a bite is taken out of your portfolio even before you get started. Investor outcry helped to drive these fees down to 2 per cent in 2008. Entry fees may also include a fee for reinvesting your returns in a fund.

- ✔ **Exit fees** are essentially commissions charged when you redeem units. They're also called *back-end loads* and will sometimes be waived if you own the managed-fund units long enough. For example, you'll be socked with a 3 per cent fee if you redeem units in a year or less and 2 per cent if you redeem in two years, falling to 1 per cent after three years.

- ✔ **Redemption fees** are charged when shareholders *redeem*, or sell, their units. Redemption fees are technically different from exit fees because the fees go to paying the costs that arise from your redemption. But they sting just the same.

- ✔ **Management fees** are the ongoing fees the managed fund charges you to run your money each year. These fees can also include trustee fees.

- ✔ **Trailing commissions** are fees of around 0.5 per cent per annum for the life of the investment and are often hidden in the management fee. These are paid to the person who sold the fund to you.

- ✔ **Other fees** include exchange (or switching) fees if you shift money into a different fund owned by the same managed-fund company, or an account fee if you, for example, don't meet a minimum account balance.

Although it may seem like the number of charges levied by managed funds is limitless, managed-fund fees have fallen. In the US, the average fees and expenses collected by stock managed funds were 1.5 per cent in 2008, down from 2.3 per cent in 1980. And the fees of bond funds fell to 0.8 per cent from 2.1 per cent during the same period.

No-load managed funds don't charge entry or exit fees. But that doesn't mean they're free. Even no-load funds can charge redemption, exchange and management fees, which are often higher than those of other funds.

You can easily find out online how much a fund charges in fees. Go to www.morningstar.com.au and enter the APIR code or part of the fund's name and click through to the Morningstar Fund Report. At the bottom of the page is a summary of the fund's fees and expenses (see Figure 8-2). When a fund indicates an ICR (indirect cost ratio), this usually replaces the management fee and, in most cases, is similar to the *management-expense ratio*. MER is a figure that represents the level of fees you need to pay as a percentage of the funds you invest. MERs for most funds are typically around 2 per cent.

Morningstar Fund Report

AXA Generations - Bernstein Aust Equity Value

Equity Region Australia Large Value | Retail

Fund Report | Report generated 12 Jan 2009 | 🖨   ⊞ Read the Analyst Research Report

Risk Relative to Category	as at 31 Dec 2008
1 Year	Above Average
3 Year	Average
5 Year	Average

Morningstar Ratings	
Overall	★★★★
3 Year	★★★
5 Year	★★★★

Fund Details	
Fund Inception	28 Jul 2003
Manager	AXA-Nat Mutual Funds Mgmt
Base Currency	$A
Net Assets $Mil (as at 30 Nov 2008)	27.88
Minimum Investment $	2,000
Regular Savings Plan (Yes/No)	Yes
Cash Distributions	6 Monthly

Fees & Expenses	
Entry Fee %	4.4000
Exit Fee %	5.2800
Switching Fee %	--
Reinvestment Fee %	--
Management Fee $	--
Trustee Fee %	--
ICR % pa	1.9000

Figure 8-2: Morningstar's Fund Report shows you what fees funds are charging.

Before paying a fee, be absolutely certain there isn't a less expensive managed fund or index managed fund that will accomplish the same thing for you.

Finding managed funds that work for you

With so many managed funds to choose from, you need your computer's help to find the ones best suited to you. You can use computerised *screening tools*, which scour a database of all managed funds looking for criteria you select. A number of websites provide such screening tools, including the following:

✔ **Morningstar (**www.morningstar.com.au**):** That Morningstar is on the list shouldn't come as a surprise. To pinpoint the types of funds you're looking for, just click on the Fund Screener link at the bottom of the Morningstar homepage. You can screen managed funds based on everything from the type of fund, such as large-value, to funds with expense ratios below certain levels and even seven-year returns. You can exclude funds that charge loads or only view funds that receive Morningstar's highest ratings. When you're done entering all your criteria, click the Show Result button and you get a list of all the funds that meet your standards.

Sticking with managed funds that charge total fees of well below 2 per cent is generally a good idea.

✔ **Aegis (**www.shareanalysis.com**):** Aegis usually provides professional-level research, but this site is focused strictly on retail investors. A full membership is expensive at $699 a year, but they do have a free-trial service, which may be all you need to make your first foray into the world of managed funds.

✔ **Lonsec (**www.lonsec.com.au**):** Lonsec is another research house with a particular focus on managed funds, which also offers a two-week trial subscription. It offers research on around 7,700 funds.

Many of the discount online brokers provide free access to managed-fund screening tools, most of which are based on Morningstar data.

How investors used to buy managed funds

The key difference between buying managed funds and buying stocks is that in order to buy managed funds you need to open an account with the fund manager before you make a purchase — with the exception of listed funds that trade openly on the stock market like a regular stock. But more of that in Chapter 9.

In the past, investors looking to buy a managed fund visited a traditional broker or financial planner and asked for a prospectus. The prospectus contained an application form that the investor filled out with bank account details and handed across the table. The financial planner stamped it and sent it off.

The broker, for his services, then charged you a *trailing commission* of around 0.5 per cent for the life of the fund. Many investors were happy to write these fees off as the cost of doing business but, over time, they can seriously erode your returns.

If you had $200,000 invested in a managed fund being charged 0.5 per cent per annum as a trail, that's $1,000 a year evaporating from your nest egg. And for not much work on the behalf of the sponsoring broker, we might add. But, today, there's a way around it, as we explain next.

How investors can buy managed funds today

For those investors used to buying stocks online, the old system of buying units in a fund probably seems a bit old fashioned. Unfortunately, things haven't changed all that much, but you can avoid many of the fees (including the trailing commission) by going directly to the fund manager.

Most fund managers now have a significant online presence; in order to open an account with a fund manager just visit its website. Most fund managers will allow you to open an account with them via one of three ways.

- **By phone:** It might seem antiquated but it's still often the best way to get something done fast.
- **By mail:** Snail mail can also be useful for sending documents, like a photocopy of your driver's licence, if required.
- **By registering online:** This is certainly the easiest way, but on occasion will require a follow-up phone call.

For any of these methods, you'll need the same kinds of identification that you would use to open an online trading account (refer to Chapter 3), including driver's licence, tax file number, bank account details and the BSB number of the account you want to transfer the money from.

Other ways to buy managed funds

In 2003, a business called InvestSMART began selling funds with the intention of returning entry fees to investors in the form of more units in the fund. It waived these fees in order to gain access to the trailing commission of the fund, which was capped for InvestSMART clients at $395 a year. Of anything paid in fees over this figure, 50 per cent was rebated in cash.

For a company like InvestSMART, the angle was pretty simple. Many investors are aware that they pay far too much in fees and, if a company promises to rebate a portion of the fees normally reserved for financial advisers, it could do pretty well.

The rebate sounds like a good deal, and in some cases it is. Investors who get rebates or cash payments reserved for *originators* (brokers and financial planners) are pretty pleased with themselves. InvestSMART has gained access to the capped trailing commission and everyone's happy. But does the maths really stack up? Let's take a closer look.

If you invest $10,000 in the A1 Managed Fund, which has an entry fee of 4 per cent, by the time your money is invested it's already been whittled down to $9,600. But with InvestSMART that fee is rebated in the form of units so your initial investment is still worth $10,000. The trail on this fund at 0.5 per cent is $50 per annum. So, in order to gain the advantage of InvestSMART's trailing-commission cap, you need a stake of $100,000 to deliver an annual saving of $100 per annum. Hmmmmm. This particular innovation doesn't save you much, but it's certainly better than nothing.

The discount brokers who were, up until this point, simply selling stocks realised the potential of a volume business like InvestSMART and began to offer variations of the program themselves. However, the number of funds offered, the specific fees rebated and the proportion of fees rebated all differed (see Table 8-1).

Of course, any of the funds that offer rebates through these providers are just as likely to offer rebates to you if you contact them directly. In many cases, the trailing commission is waived in these circumstances. In other less frequent cases, the fund manager would keep the trail for themselves, at their discretion. Most online brokers allow you to track the performance of any managed-fund units that you bought elsewhere through their portfolio software. So, unless you have a really good reason for using any of these services, approaching the fund directly is usually the best option.

Table 8-1		How to Buy Funds		
Purchase Method	**Rebates**	**Who Gets the Trail?**	**Number of Funds**	**Sell Fees**
E*TRADE	Entry fees	E*TRADE takes 0.66% per annum	550+	No
CommSec	Entry and contribution fees	CommSec takes the trail	550+	Yes
InvestSMART	Entry fees	InvestSMART takes 0.2%–0.6%	4,000+	Yes
Direct	At the fund's discretion	Waived in most cases	Unlimited	Yes

Some managed funds can't be bought directly by individual investors. A few managed-fund companies sell their funds only through certified financial planners.

Comparing Managed Funds

When you're choosing a managed fund, a good idea is to always compare several similar funds to make sure you're getting the best one for your needs. You want to consider both the characteristics and risk of the funds.

Putting funds' characteristics side by side

InvestSMART (www.investsmart.com.au) provides a very good device that allows you to compare aspects of the various funds it offers (see Figure 8-3). Select Find a Managed Fund from the dropdown menu for Managed Funds. If your browser uses tabs, open a tab with the same web address (or open a second window), then enter the fund names or APIR codes in each window to bring up the funds you want to compare (you can also select the fund manager using the Manager dropdown menu). When you see the fund, click on Fund Name. This provides you with easy-to-digest information on fund size, fund performance and asset allocation (refer to Chapter 7) at a glance.

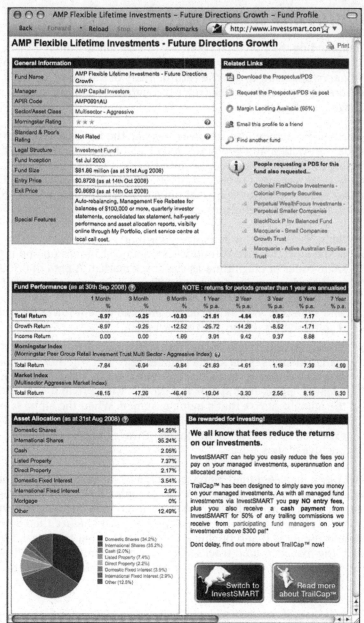

Figure 8-3:
Invest-
SMART
provides
information
in a manner
easy to
take in at a
glance.

Analysing a managed fund's risk

Understanding the potential returns you may enjoy from a fund is just half of the equation. Equally, if not more, important is knowing how much risk you're taking on to get the return. Many of the same methods used to measure your portfolio's risk (refer to Chapter 7), can be used to gauge your managed fund's risk too.

In particular, you need to use measures like the fund's average return, standard deviation and geometric mean, all of which you can gather by entering the year-on-year returns into Horton's Geometric Mean Calculator (available at www.graftacs.com/geomean.php3 — refer to Chapter 6). But funds also have their own special units of measurement, which are often used in broker research. Here are some of the more important ones:

✔ **Beta:** Measures how sensitive your fund is to movements by the rest of the stock market. A fund with a beta of 1 moves up and down by the same order of magnitude as the stock market. A beta of 0.75 shows the fund tends to under-perform by 25 per cent when the market gains but also declines 25 per cent less when the market falls. If you want fewer wild swings in your financial life and can accept lower returns as a result, look for a fund with a low beta.

✔ **Alpha:** Definitely one of the best statistics out there for measuring managed funds. This single number tells you whether the portfolio manager is adding value or destroying value. When a fund has a negative alpha, that means it performs worse than it should, based on the amount of risk that's being assumed. When the alpha is positive, the manager is adding value by getting a better return than would be expected for the risk being taken. Always look for managed funds with positive alphas.

Don't pay a managed-fund manager high fees for just shadowing an index. You could pay much less and just buy an index fund. To know whether your manager is shadowing the market, look at its *correlation*, or *R-squared*. If an actively managed fund you own has an R-squared higher than 80 per cent, consider dumping it and buying an index fund. What this measures is the extent the managed fund tracks the index. R-squared is commonly found in broker research. See Chapter 11 for more on correlation and how it affects your portfolio.

Getting More Information about Funds

Managed-fund companies are required by regulators to clearly explain to investors, in writing, everything an investor would need to know. This information is contained in a *prospectus*. This document is very detailed and worth reading before you invest in a fund.

Nearly all the most vital data contained in managed-fund prospectuses are captured by the managed-fund websites we describe in the preceding sections. You don't have to dig through a prospectus to get things like fees or investment objectives. But a section of the prospectus that's often left out of the websites is the risks section, which outlines all the things that could go wrong. That's worth checking out.

The funny thing about managed funds is that they can be extremely hands-off — or an addiction. On the one hand, you can buy into an index fund, set up a regular contribution via direct debit and never think about your managed fund again. But you can also read about the ins and outs of managed funds and keep up on all the new developments. If you're interested in studying funds, some of the sites to check out include the following:

- **Egoli** (www.egoli.com.au) is a general online finance and business news website. Choose Managed Funds from the Investing dropdown menu to view a special section to keep you up-to-date on all the latest moves and product news in the world of managed funds.

- **Business Spectator** (www.businessspectator.com.au) monitors news 24 hours a day across 25 categories. By drilling down to Financial Services from the list under Industry & Category on the left-hand side, you can keep in touch with what's happening in managed funds globally.

- **The Australian Financial Review** (www.afr.com) kindly collates all its coverage on managed funds in the one place for you. Select Financial Services from the menu bar, scroll down to the Weekly Sections and choose Managed Funds. The only catch is that you need to be a subscriber to access the articles. Or you could take out a two-week free trial while you do your research.

- **Investor Daily** (www.investordaily.com) is a free online news service aimed at the financial services industry. It's also a good place to pick up on emerging trends and themes in the sector.

✔ **Money Management** (www.moneymanagement.com) is another free news service aimed specifically at financial advisers. But, if you're planning on going it alone, you should at least be aware of what the advisers are reading.

✔ **ASIC's FIDO** (www.fido.gov.au) is an excellent resource when you're ready to take the plunge. Click on Calculators on the left-hand side and select Managed Funds Calculator to calculate fees charged by a managed fund.

✔ **MAXfunds.com** (www.maxfunds.com) features a blog that constantly presents new developments regarding the managed-fund world.

✔ **Vanguard** (www.vanguard.com) features a collection of Vanguard founder John Bogle's speeches. Select Other Sites from the list at the bottom right of the homepage. This page is an invaluable source for investing insights, not just for managed-fund investors, but for everyone.

✔ **TheStreet.com** (www.thestreet.com) features a section on managed funds, called *mutual funds* in the US. Click on Life & Money in the menu bar and choose Mutual Fund Center from the More Investing Education list. This section provides a good selection of stories written about managed funds.

Chapter 9

Finding and Buying Listed Managed Investments

*I*f you're looking to diversify your holdings but aren't interested in buying managed funds, you can buy instruments called listed managed investments, or LMIs. Like managed funds, LMIs invest in baskets of stocks. But LMIs differ from managed funds in that they trade during the day just like an individual stock. This important difference gives LMIs an edge over managed funds for some investors.

More than $140 billion of investors' cash is invested in LMIs on the Australian Securities Exchange (ASX), almost 10 per cent of its total market value! In this chapter, we explain why they're so popular and how online tools can maximise your success investing with them. We help you use online tools to pick the right investments for you and show you how to set up an account to buy or sell them.

Locating Listed Managed Investments You Can Trade

Listed managed investments are baskets of stocks, much like managed funds, that trade like stocks. You can buy and sell them using your online broker just like you would with other stocks. All LMIs have company codes and qualify for the low commission rates you can get from online brokers. You can even get price quotes by using your favourite stock-tracking websites, including those listed in Chapter 2.

You can buy and sell LMIs by using the online broker you're already signed up with. Just enter the LMI's company code, and you can buy and sell just like you would shares of a company's stock.

Investors like LMIs because they're easy to buy without the hassle of signing up for accounts with managed-fund companies or checking to see whether they're loaded up with fees. Unlike managed funds, which update their price once a day after the market closes, LMI prices are constantly updated during the trading day. That means investors can just buy LMIs and sell them whenever they want during the day.

LMIs have the same advantages of managed funds, as described in Chapter 8. That includes diversification and access to specific corners of the stock market, such as certain sizes of stocks or industries. LMIs, though, offer several advantages over managed funds, including the following:

- ✔ **Intraday trading:** Managed funds price once a day, meaning you don't know how your portfolio has done until the markets close and the fund companies get around to publishing the net asset value (NAV) for the day. The prices of LMIs constantly update during the day just like stocks.

- ✔ **Access to tougher areas of the market:** Investors interested in buying commodities, bonds and currencies can buy them easily, just like buying a stock, thanks to LMIs. And, because LMIs are priced during the day, speculators can get in and out of risky positions anytime they want. LMIs are a great way to add foreign exposure to your portfolio.

- ✔ **Low fees:** If you think the fees on index managed funds are low, in some cases the fees associated with LMIs are even lower. It's not unusual for some LMIs to charge lower maintenance fees than managed funds that mirror the same stock index by owning all the stocks in the index.

- ✔ **Tax advantages:** Due to their structure, LMIs rarely stick investors with capital gains distributions. That helps investors plan tax strategies. Keep in mind, though, that many LMIs still pay dividends, which are usually taxable.

- ✔ **Advanced trading options:** A lot of LMIs offer *options*, specific trading vehicles we discuss in Chapter 15. That's attractive to investors who want to do more than just buy or sell the investments. LMIs can also be *shorted*, a technique used to bet an investment will decline in value, which we also explain in Chapter 15.

What's the big idea? Investing in a theme

Although diversification is a powerful incentive to invest in LMIs, the potential to invest in a theme is another great drawcard. As specialised vehicles emerge with specific strengths, investors find they're also a great way to invest in a theme.

As stockbroker and commentator Marcus Padley once said, 'You make more money thinking about the big themes in business than you ever do trying to keep on top of every single detail.' Themes are all around you and can be discovered simply by talking to people. A conversation with a young parent may reveal the growing expense and reliance on childcare. That's a theme that may bear up under further examination.

The biggest theme in Australia over the last six years has been the performance of the resources sector, because of the demand for building materials, like steel, coming from China. Although plenty of people have opinions about the length of the boom, as long as the industrialisation of China progresses, it will continue to demand raw materials from Australia.

Listed managed investments can help you access themes while diversifying your risk and lowering your costs. There are LMIs to assist your entry into sectors like mining, regions like China or even classes of property like commercial real estate. If you have a big idea or a theme you want to invest in, you can be sure that an LMI exists that suits your needs.

Core and satellite: Supercharging your returns

How much of your portfolio you can afford to invest in a theme depends on your investment horizon and tolerance to risk. A theme shouldn't totally inform your investment selections, but most asset allocations allow for some form of alternative investment, as we cover in Chapter 7. In the cases where an investor is comfortable with some risk, a 'core and satellite' approach can be used.

Essentially, this approach means investing a small portion of your investment capital into higher risk asset classes. This may include absolute-return funds (hedge funds), foreign currencies, emerging markets and micro-cap companies — anything associated with a higher than normal risk.

The idea is that, although the majority of your portfolio consists of low-risk (core) investments like an index fund, property and fixed-income securities, a small portion is invested in higher risk (satellite) asset classes. The higher risk component can add significant out-performance to your portfolio over the long term without overpaying for management or compromising your long-term investment strategy.

For example, if you have a $100,000 portfolio and $90,000 is invested in low-risk asset classes, $10,000 of that may be invested in an absolute-return fund. While the core component of your portfolio returns a steady 12 per cent, your emerging-market absolute-return fund might return 30 per cent. Your core holdings go from $90,000 to $100,800, while your satellite holdings go from $10,000 to $13,000. A total profit of $13,800.

In using this approach, you increase your return from 12 per cent to 13.8 per cent, or an additional 1.8 per cent. The power of compound interest in a long-term investment plan can be a powerful thing.

Using the Right Tool for the Job

As with managed funds, one of the toughest things about LMIs is just finding the one that's right for you among the 200 or so available on the ASX. Fortunately, the ASX publishes quarterly updates on their performance. Go to the homepage (www.asx.com.au), click on ASX Products on the left and choose Managed Funds & ETFs. Scroll down to Research and Tools on the right, click on Current & Historical Data and select the most recent Performance Returns document, shown in Figure 9-1.

The update provides an excellent overview of LMIs as a sector, because it not only lists all of them according to type, with a record of returns over one, three and five years, but it lists their size, year high and low, and the dividend yield.

When you're looking for a fund, ask yourself what *you* are investing for. Are you investing for your retirement and looking for an LMI that generates regular income? Are you investing to pay for the education of your children, seeking maximum capital growth over the longer term? Or do you want a combination of both?

For some investors, LMIs represent too much of a temptation to trade. Although, in most cases, *liquidity* — the ability to be traded quickly — is a good thing, some investors hop from investment to investment, looking out for the next best thing. These investors may be better suited to the low-cost managed funds we cover in Chapter 8.

Listed Managed Investments (LMI)
Quarterly Update - June 30, 2008 ASX

			Prices		Dividend Yield %		Returns (pa%)		
		Size ($mil)	Last	Year High	Year Low	Cash	Grossed	1 Year	3 Year	5 Year
Listed Investment Companies (LICs)										
Australian Shares										
ALR	Aberdeen Leaders	96	1.67	2.25	1.65	5.99	8.55	-9.66	17.90	20.27
ALF	Australian Leaders Fund Limited	65	0.82	1.24	0.78	9.82	14.02	-22.44	7.47	n/a
AMH	Amcil	116	0.67	0.88	0.60	8.96	12.79	-3.96	18.01	26.67
ARG	Argo Investments	4,041	7.09	8.49	6.50	4.09	5.84	-8.89	12.95	13.24
AUF	Asian Masters Fund	45	0.90	1.20	0.90	n/a	n/a	n/a	n/a	n/a
AFI	Australian Foundation	4,867	5.02	6.58	4.50	4.18	5.98	-7.69	14.40	12.22
AUI	Australian United Investment	732	7.70	9.60	7.17	3.12	4.45	-10.12	14.50	15.74
BKI	Brickworks Investment Company	355	1.22	1.55	1.04	4.67	6.67	-16.34	8.13	n/a
CIN	Carlton Investments	443	16.71	28.21	16.20	3.77	5.39	-20.33	6.50	10.78
CYA	Century Australia	197	1.06	1.44	1.01	10.38	14.82	-16.36	9.20	n/a
CHO	Choiseul Investments	421	5.16	7.05	5.10	4.55	6.51	-13.60	6.38	11.06
CAM	Clime Capital	34	0.90	1.63	0.76	3.06	4.37	-34.55	4.59	n/a
CTN	Contango MicroCap	140	1.18	2.33	1.15	6.78	9.69	-36.39	18.01	n/a
DUI	Diversified United Investment	468	3.34	4.40	3.26	3.74	5.35	-13.96	15.01	17.78
DJW	Djerriwarrh Investments	871	4.27	5.40	3.97	6.09	8.70	-9.63	9.46	9.82
ELI	Emerging Leaders Investments	37	0.97	1.16	0.93	6.70	9.57	-8.57	n/a	n/a
FAT	Fat Prophets Australia Fund	32	0.98	1.08	0.90	4.62	6.59	-2.78	n/a	n/a
HIC	Huntley Investment Company	128	0.75	0.97	0.70	6.67	9.52	-16.34	6.96	10.23
HIP	Hyperion Flagship Investments	40	1.40	2.12	1.25	6.07	8.67	-26.81	8.78	12.70
IBC	Ironbark Capital Limited	74	0.47	0.71	0.46	10.00	14.29	-19.54	2.10	5.47
MLT	Milton Corporation	1,639	19.38	25.00	17.00	4.44	6.34	-10.34	10.07	12.79
MIR	Mirrabooka Investments	229	1.85	2.69	1.75	5.41	7.72	-20.73	9.94	15.05
MMA	MMC Contrarian	146	0.58	0.98	0.57	13.79	19.70	-30.48	-4.46	n/a
OEQ	Orion Equities Limited	16	0.90	1.50	0.90	3.89	5.56	-31.73	23.30	n/a
OZG	Ozgrowth Limited	80	0.20	0.30	0.18	n/a	n/a	n/a	n/a	n/a
PRV	Premium Investors	178	0.80	1.26	0.78	10.63	15.18	-29.08	2.77	n/a
SCB	Scarborough Equities Limited	12	0.61	1.10	0.61	4.30	6.14	-41.49	11.55	-3.34
SYL	Sylvastate	67	3.80	5.56	3.70	5.26	7.52	-25.90	3.87	3.57
VTP	Van Eyk Three Pillars	127	0.95	1.43	0.91	10.53	15.04	-20.88	9.71	n/a
WAA	WAM Active Limited	14	0.89	1.01	0.86	n/a	n/a	n/a	n/a	n/a
WAM	WAM Capital	117	1.11	1.96	1.10	14.48	20.69	-33.08	5.96	8.14
WHF	Whitefield	219	3.14	4.87	3.06	5.13	7.32	-31.99	1.06	3.43
WIL	Wilson Investment Fund	87	0.71	1.19	0.71	8.10	11.57	-36.37	-2.91	n/a

Figure 9-1:
You can find all sorts of details about LMIs at the ASX website, including past returns over one, three and five years.

You can find out about upcoming LMIs on the ASX site. Go to the homepage again (www.asx.com.au), click on ASX Products on the left and choose Managed Funds & ETFs. Scroll down to New Listings and click on the link for upcoming and recent listings.

Understanding the Different Types of LMIs

Six different varieties of LMI are available, each with its own unique set of risks and rewards. Whether a specific variety of LMI is suitable for your portfolio depends on your investment horizon, risk tolerance and asset allocation (we explain these in detail in Chapter 7). Your tax considerations are also important because some LMIs offer specific tax advantages that can make them more or less attractive, depending on your personal circumstances.

Income from listed property trusts, now known as REITs (real estate investment trusts), for example, offers the advantages of *tax deferral*. This means that part of these dividends reduce your cost base, ensuring that you don't pay tax on this portion of the dividend until you sell the trust, when you pay *capital gains tax (CGT)* on half your profits at your marginal tax rate (we explain how CGT works in Chapter 1).

For example, let's say you put $10,000 in a REIT that pays a 6 per cent distribution of $600, which is 40 per cent tax-deferred. Tax is payable on the remaining 60 per cent, or $360, but 40 per cent, or $240, is not taxable in the year it's earned; rather it goes towards reducing your cost base.

After five years, say the value of the securities has risen to $12,000. Assuming there are no changes in the amount of distribution or the tax-deferred portion, then the cost base is reduced by $1,200 ($240 × 5). The sale of the securities ($12,000) minus the new cost base ($10,000 – $1,200 = $8,800) gives you a capital gain of $3,200. This leaves you with a 50 per cent discounted capital gain of $1,600 to be taxed at your marginal tax rate.

Now, if this investment didn't offer a tax-deferred component, the capital gain would be the sale price minus the original cost ($12,000 – $10,000), producing a gain of just $2,000, leaving you with a discounted gain of $1,000 subject to your marginal tax rate. In addition, without the advantage of tax deferral, $240 per year ($1,200 over five years) would have incurred normal income tax at your marginal rate without the 50 per cent CGT discount.

Listed investment companies: Purest of the pure

Listed investment companies (LICs) are the purest form of LMI and the closest in concept to the managed fund. LICs are a portfolio of assets that are generally available at lower cost to their managed-fund cousins. Listed investment companies invest in Australian shares, international shares, fixed-interest securities, private companies and even property.

LICs generally take one of two approaches — a passive buy-and-hold strategy with a view to the long term or a more aggressive active-management style focused on delivering consistent returns. Like managed funds, LICs are often viewed as a one-stop-shop for investors seeking instant diversification but, of late, more-specialised LICs have emerged that concentrate on particular areas, like the energy sector or international markets. Investors are drawn to them because the LIC may have particular expertise in that field.

Investors are paid regular dividends twice or four times a year. These payments can be used as income or reinvested in the fund, a flexibility that offers LICs an advantage. Investors also like LICs because transaction costs are often lower than those that can be achieved through building your own portfolio or going through a managed fund.

One of the biggest bug-bears for LICs in recent times has been gearing levels. As credit markets seized up following the sub-prime implosion, companies like Allco Finance found itself unable to meet its obligations and subsequently went into receivership amd voluntary administration.

Australian real estate investment trusts: A-REITs by any other name

A-REITs have been around for a long, long time. You may not recognise them because, up until very recently, they were called *listed property trusts*, in line with US terminology. In the past, these vehicles were considered quite boring by the investment community because the business model simply consisted of owning assets like CBD office blocks and shopping centres, and collecting the rent, which was distributed to investors. In the 1980s, financial advisers would recommend them for 'widows and orphans'.

But *A-REITs* are considered to be among the most innovative investments in the world and account for some 12 per cent of the world's total listed real estate. These days, they're involved in development, fund management, building maintenance and administration. Investors are often attracted by the income generated by this asset class but, between the years 2001 and 2006, A-REITs had an outstanding period of capital growth and were, in fact, the best performing asset class, year after year.

Most LMIs offer investors the benefit of diversification, but A-REITs offer an entry directly into an asset class that is both prohibitively expensive and incredibly illiquid. Almost all asset allocations recommend some exposure to property; A-REITs can offer you that exposure with low transaction costs and *T+3 liquidity*, which means you can turn your investment into cash in around three days (refer to Chapter 4).

In late 2007, the sub-prime crisis hit A-REITs hard. While some of them, like Stockland, enjoyed modest gearing levels, others, like Centro, struggled in the credit environment and the share prices were savaged. One of the problems was the diversification by A-REITs into new areas like development and funds management. Investors found the entire sector to be wanting in terms of disclosure and opacity and the markdowns were quite widespread.

A-REITs that use lower ratios of gearing, employ dependable management teams and avoid the more speculative ventures will be the first to emerge from this cyclical downturn. However, in doing that they will no longer offer the returns that made these vehicles so attractive to investors in the first place.

Infrastructure funds: Building for the future

Infrastructure funds are a relatively new phenomenon, at least in comparison with A-REITs. *Infrastructure funds* invest in public assets such as toll roads, utilities and airports. Often they take advantage of government privatisations but they're just as likely to purchase assets from the private sector. The projects themselves are often expensive, which creates a high barrier to entry for competitors.

Infrastructure funds are attractive to investors because they generate steady streams of revenue. The assets are usually *counter-cyclical*, or recession-proof, which means that profits are generally not under threat in the case of an economic downturn. In times such as these, people still need to drive their cars, use electricity and fly. Infrastructure funds can concentrate on one asset, one type of asset or a whole smorgasbord of assets.

Like A-REITs, investors often turn to infrastructure funds when they're looking for a regular income stream; however, the underlying assets do also have the potential for capital appreciation.

The structure of these vehicles is often criticised for the way-hefty fees paid to the manager. Macquarie Bank, arguably one of the pioneers of the sector, is one of the groups that has been singled out the most for the quite generous streams of fees that wind back to the manager. A float of road and transport assets known as BrisConnections in July 2008 was a notable flop — which may have had something to do with the fact that for every $50,000 invested around $8,700 was going in fees.

Pooled development funds: Small ponds

In 1993, the Australian federal government created a scheme designed to promote long-term investment in small to medium-sized companies in Australia. The investors it attracted banded together as *pooled development funds*. Essentially a reworking of an earlier concept (the Management and Investment Companies Program), the scheme offers the lower corporate tax rate of 15 per cent and restricts investments to be made in companies with a market capitalisation of less than $50 million.

Investor profits are tax-free provided they're held longer than one year; however, capital losses can't be claimed as a tax loss. Despite the attractive concessions on offer, the scheme hasn't been a success, with less than ten pooled development funds listed to date. The funds tend to concentrate on single sectors, like biotechnology, mining or wine.

In some cases, the companies that the pooled development funds invest in are so successful that their market cap exceeds $50 million. If the pooled development fund fails to bail out of the investment at the cut-off point, it's excluded from the program and forced to become just another garden variety LIC in the process.

Absolute-return funds: Hedging it

Absolute-return funds, or *hedge funds*, promise investors the holy grail of investing: They promise to generate positive returns in both rising and falling markets. They achieve this by investing in asset classes that retail investors may not be able to access because of their large minimum investment requirements, such as commodities like oil and coal. They also tend to invest heavily in *derivatives*, which are financial instruments, such as options, that derive their value from an underlying instrument, such as shares, but are not shares as such. We talk more about options and derivatives in Chapter 15.

These funds are usually structured along two lines, a so-called *single-strategy fund*, where the fund manager invests capital directly, or a *fund of funds*, where the fund manager invests in a number of different absolute-return funds. Absolute-return funds are among the most expensive, and generally operate on a *2-and-20* approach to fees — 2 per cent entry fee and a performance fee of 20 per cent of anything above the benchmark, often an index like the S&P/ASX 200 (refer to Chapter 8 for more on this calculation).

Despite their name, funds such as these should attract only investors with a high tolerance for risk. The funds are expected to have little if any correlation with the market, thanks to their use of strategies such as *shorting* (profiting from an investment that loses value, as we explain in Chapter 15) and investment in complex securities. James knows of some funds that buy only assets that could be considered the opposite of ethical. These vice funds concentrate their investments in alcohol, tobacco and firearms. Others specialise in so-called *disaster bonds*, where insurance companies lay off risk by issuing a high-yielding security. If a hurricane or earthquake strikes, then the bond is cancelled and the insurance company uses the capital to pay out insurance holders. Disaster bonds have been referred to as 'Nature's casino'.

The real incentives for the fund manager come from the fund's performance — that is, anything above the benchmark. In April 2007, MFS Group (now known as Octaviar) launched an absolute-return fund called the MFS Water Fund. Not only did this fund have a 3 per cent up-front fee, it also had an annual management fee of 1.25 per cent. Financial planners who recommended the fund were eligible for a 0.44 per cent annual *trailing commission*, a kind of perpetual kickback paid to those who sell financial products. For performance, the fund manager took 10 per cent. In industry-speak, the fund was *benchmark unaware*. This meant that the fund did not compare itself with the S&P/ASX 200 or the S&P 500. The fund manager simply took 10 per cent of any return that was above zero.

Looking very carefully at the track record of the fund manager and the fees they charge is important. Ask yourself if they're really worth it. If the manager isn't consistently out-performing the market by more than they're charging you, then this is not a good sign.

Counting the Costs

As with all investments, it pays to look very carefully at what you're buying. Although LMIs are billed as low-cost investments, that doesn't mean that someone won't try to charge you more than they should. For the more exotic investments in emerging markets, for example, it pays to shop around.

In addition, these investments aren't necessarily the holy grail of investing. They may offer you instant diversification and low-cost entry into hard-to-reach markets but they have their own specific sets of risks attached.

Watch out for the crunch

The amount of debt your company has presents its own particular set of challenges. Although the amount of debt in a vehicle increases investor returns, or ROI (see Chapter 11), when interest rates rise or credit becomes more expensive, it can have a devastating effect on the price of the security.

This has been particularly evident in the cases of Allco Finance Group, Centro and Babcock & Brown. As sources of capital dried up in the credit crunch of 2007, it became almost impossible for these groups to find new financing and carry on normal operating activities.

LMIs have fees too

The fees involved in listed managed investments aren't immediately identifiable because they're built into the structure of the investment. By the time you receive a dividend, or distribution, the fees have already been taken out. Although they're typically less than 1 per cent per annum (with the exception of hedge funds of course), digging around a little to find out exactly what they are is a good idea.

All LMIs provide you with information about fees in their prospectus or product disclosure statement (PDS). You can find this information from the company website or by typing its company code into the Get Price/ Announcement/Info box on the ASX website (www.asx.com.au). When the page opens, click on the code, then scroll halfway down the page to Search for Past Company Announcements. Click on that link to find the LMI's prospectus and PDS.

Because you buy LMIs on the exchange, commissions become important again. If you're looking to invest $1,000 in an LMI from a broker charging a commission of $30, that's an up-front fee of 3 per cent, not much better than an expensive managed fund! To get around this, you need to either shop around for a broker who offers you the best deal, as we explain in Chapter 3, or buy in larger quantities to offset the costs.

Risk wears many hats

All investments carry with them certain risks, and particular LMIs carry their own specific risks within the areas they operate. Several risk areas exist, and some apply more to one style of LMI than another:

- **Market risk** refers to the overall health of the market and investor sentiment. There are *always* going to be periods when markets drift, or move backwards. This can be offset by both diversification and time in the market. In fact, some LMIs, like A-REITs, are a natural hedge against market risk.

- **Currency risk** is an important one to remember, especially if your LMI has considerable assets overseas. A-REITs, in particular, despite the 'Australian' in their name, are largely invested offshore. Over the last few years as the US economy has weakened, the US dollar has also been devalued, meaning that each dollar earned in the US is worth less than it was in previous years. At the same time, the assets owned have also depreciated, hitting investors twice.

✔ **Structural risk** may also present complications for some investors. Features that were once advantages can just as quickly become significant disadvantages to your investment's performance, as with the changed tax treatment of agricultural managed-investment schemes. Investors had enjoyed the 100 per cent tax-deductible status of these investments, which saw them soar in popularity every June. However, with this status now under review, a canny investment could quickly become an albatross around your neck.

✔ **Liquidity risk** works in two ways. First, it refers to your fund manager's ability to buy and sell *positions* in the market; that is, the individual investments or stocks that make up the LMI you purchased. If your LMI is an absolute-return fund or pooled development fund, *exiting* positions, or selling individual investments quickly, may be very difficult. Second, it refers to your ability to buy or sell the managed investment, which can become notoriously difficult when conditions take a turn for the worse.

Getting to Know the Newcomers: Exchange-Traded Funds

Available in particular markets since the mid to late 1990s, exchange-traded funds, or ETFs, are one of the biggest developments in the world of retail finance. In a June 2008 survey of financial advisers, 67 per cent of respondents identified ETFs as the most innovative investment vehicle of the last two decades.

Like the rest of the listed managed investment fraternity, ETFs trade on the stock market like any other share, which means you can track their performance over the course of the day using the tools we show you in Chapter 2. At the end of 2008, 20 ETFs were trading on the ASX. To view the list of ETFs, go to the ASX homepage (www.asx.com.au), select ASX Products from the left and click on Managed Funds & ETFs. Then scroll down to Research and Tools, click on Research Tools and scroll down to the list of ETFs.

Despite their small number, ETFs offer unique access to corners of the market that regular LMIs won't or can't access. The variety of ETFs available means that you aren't just restricted to investing in the S&P/ASX 200 or the S&P 500 anymore. ETFs give your portfolio global reach and that is why, in 2008, around US$750 billion was invested in ETFs worldwide.

So far, most ETFs track a stock market index much like an index fund, but others focus on particular commodity plays. Most of the oldest and largest ETFs, not surprisingly, track the most popular stock market indices, as well as commodities such as gold. The market is dominated by two companies, Barclays, with their iShares product, and index fund specialists State Street, with their StreetTracks offering, as shown in Table 9-1.

Table 9-1			Popular ETFs
ETF Name	*Size*	*Symbol*	*Detail*
iShares MSCI Emerging Markets	$20 billion	IEM	An index developed by Morgan Stanley that represents countries such as Brazil, China, India, Russia and others
iShares S&P 500	$15.5 billion	IVV	An index of the top 500 large-cap companies in the US as maintained by S&P
iShares FTSE/ Xinhua China 25	$5.8 billion	IZZ	An index of the largest 25 companies in the Chinese equity market available to investors
iShares Russell 2000 Index	$10.7 billion	IRU	An index of 2,000 small-cap stocks in the US
StreetTracks 200	$730 million	STW	Modelled on the S&P/ASX 200
StreetTracks 50	$60 million	SFY	Modelled on the large-cap S&P/ASX 50 index
StreetTracks 200 Property	$730 million	SLF	Modelled on the S&P/ASX 200 listed property trust
Gold Bullion Securities	$336 million	GOLD	Each share represents one-tenth of a troy ounce of gold

Don't assume the most popular ETFs are the best

When you buy an ETF, you're most frequently buying a basket of stocks mirroring a stock index. And, when shopping for index funds, you typically want to find the ones that either best track the type of stocks you're interested in or have the lowest fees.

Ask yourself the same questions you consider when buying an index fund:

✔ **How large is the ETF?** In the case of an ETF, the more assets under management, the better. You don't want to invest in a small ETF that doesn't attract enough investors and ends up being shut down. This is becoming more of an issue as more ETFs are rushed to the market.

✔ **What index does the ETF track?** Some small-cap indices, for example, track the Russell 2000, and others track the Standard & Poor's 600. Both track small stocks, but differences exist between the indices themselves. Make sure that you're tracking the index you prefer.

Imagine that you want to buy an ETF that invests in small companies. Checking out the website of the ETF company is a good idea so you can check the average market value of the stocks held by the ETF and compare it with the competition.

✔ **What are the expenses?** If everything else is equal, nothing's wrong with looking at the price tag and going with the ETF that's cheapest. The rampant competition in the ETF business has dramatically driven down fees. That's why it's worthwhile to use one of the screening tools we mention in the section 'ETF fees can vary' to see what fee the fund charges and compare it with other options.

ETF fees can vary

Using screening sites, you can easily find and compare the fees charged by ETFs. Here's how you do it using ETFConnect:

1. **Go to** www.etfconnect.com.

2. **Enter the company code or name of the ETF you're interested in checking fees for in the Search field in the upper-right corner of the page and then click the Go button.**

3. **Look over the screen.**

   The screen shows all the vitals about the ETF, including its price, the fund company that sponsors it, when it was created, what it invests in and what its top holdings are. You also see the breakdown of industries it owns and what countries the stocks are based in.

4. Scroll down until you see the ETF Facts box.

You need to scroll down quite a way — the box is on the right side. The ETF Facts box shows you several things, including the ETF's expense ratio.

The *management-expense ratio (MER)* is a very important number that tells you the annual fee the ETF provider will charge you for owning the ETF. If you invest $1,000 in an ETF with an expense ratio of 0.5 per cent, that means you'll pay an annual fee of $5. You want to compare this ratio with other ETFs you're considering. You can see a sample in Figure 9-2.

Finding out how pricey an ETF is

Stock investors commonly look at the *price-to-earnings ratio*, or *PE*, of an individual stock to find out how expensive it is. The higher the PE, the more richly valued the stock is, as we explain in detail in Chapter 11. But ETF investors can also use PE ratios to find how cheap or expensive the stocks held by the ETF are. The two big providers of ETFs in Australia offer regularly updated price-to-earnings information.

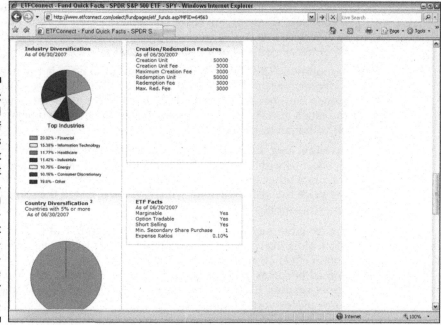

Figure 9-2: You can find all sorts of particulars about ETFs at ETFConnect, including the all-important management-expense ratio, or MER.

To find out the price-to-earnings ratio of an iShares ETF, visit the homepage at www.ishares.com.au. To enter the site proper, select Individual Investor in the Investor Type window, click the Terms and Conditions button and then click Continue. From the left-hand menu, select the name of the fund from either Developed Markets or Emerging Markets. Underneath the heading Fundamentals you'll find the ETF's price-to-earnings ratio.

To find out the price-to-earnings ratio of a StreetTracks ETF, visit the homepage at www.spdrs.com.au and then select the name of the fund from the Fund Information table. Click the Index Detail tab and scroll down to Information, where price-to-earnings data is listed.

ETFs have issues too

ETFs are great for many investors looking for ways to keep their costs down and simplify their lives. After all, you can buy all your stock and ETF investments from the same brokerage account. But ETFs have drawbacks, too, as the following list makes clear:

- **Commissions:** Unlike managed funds, which can often be bought with no commissions through online brokers or directly from fund companies, ETFs are treated like stocks. That means your online broker's standard stock commission applies. That can be a deal-killer if you make frequent and small investments. Unless you use an online broker with free trades, such as those discussed in Chapter 3, you may be better off with an index managed fund.

- **Temptation:** The ability to trade in and out of ETFs is too irresistible for some investors — the kind who can't keep their fingers off their mouse buttons. If the constant pricing of ETFs encourages you to trade too much and veer off your asset-allocation course, you may be better off with managed funds.

- **Invisible cost, the spread:** ETFs come with an invisible but costly fee. Just as with stocks, ETFs have a bid and an ask price. The *bid* is the price other investors are willing to pay for the ETF, and the *ask* is the price the seller will take. The difference, called the *spread*, costs investors money.

    For example, say you bought 100 shares of an ETF at the ask price of $100. Most likely, you'd only be able to sell it for $99.90 or less, costing you in effect 10 cents a share. The less popular an ETF is, the wider the spread becomes, and the greater this cost becomes. Are you curious about what an ETF's bid and ask prices are? They're available from the same places you get stock quotes.

✔ **Premiums and discounts:** An ETF's price is based on what buyers and sellers are willing to pay for the basket of stocks it owns. That means it's possible the price of an ETF might be greater or less than the value of the stocks it owns. When the ETF price is greater than the value of the stocks it owns, that ETF is said to be trading at a *premium* and, when the opposite is true and the ETF is worth less than the value of its stocks, the ETF is said to be trading at a *discount.*

Don't get overly concerned with the premium or discount. Most ETFs' premium or discount is rather small. And, for popular ETFs, it's practically non-existent.

Reading the fine print: The prospectus

One of the reasons ETFs have been so popular is that they make it easy to invest in assets that were difficult to invest in before. By buying a single ETF just as you'd buy a stock, you can instantly invest in a basket of companies working on alternative energy or in financial commodities like gold. Because ETFs have made it much easier to invest in a wide array of investments, knowing how to find out exactly what you're buying when you purchase an ETF is more important than ever — by reading the prospectus.

Like managed funds, ETFs must be fully described to investors in a *prospectus.* These documents describe ETFs' structures, investing objective, fees and all other details to investors — and can be a dry read filled with legalese. But they're worth taking a look at if you're going to invest in an ETF.

You can get the prospectus online through several ways, including from the following sources:

✔ **The ETF provider's website:** If you log on to the website of the company that provides the investment, you can almost always find a link to the prospectus. This is typically the easiest way to find a prospectus.

Figure 9-3 shows the iShares homepage (www.ishares.com.au). From there, just click the Document Library tab and then select Regulatory Documents.

✔ **The ASX:** ETF prospectuses are a legal requirement, so you can retrieve them from many of the same places you'd use to get company announcements, as we describe in Chapter 2. Go to the ASX homepage (www.asx.com.au), select Prices, Research & Announcements from the list at the left, click on Announcements and type in the ETF's code in the text box. For Time Frame, select 2008 and click the Search button. This brings up a list of all the company announcements made by that ETF, and the prospectus is among the first.

Figure 9-3:
The iShares
website
contains
company
announce-
ments
and pros-
pectuses.

Chapter 10

Putting Companies Under the Microscope

*I*f you're the kind of online investor looking to buy the next Google, this chapter offers tips that may help you. We show you how to use online tools to unearth details about companies that aren't picked up by general investing websites, explained in Chapters 2 and 5. We explain how you can glean insights about companies by picking apart financial statements, and we show you how to compare companies with their peers.

Just be careful. Consistently picking winning stocks and buying and selling them at the right times is infamously difficult and time-consuming. If you don't know what you're doing, you may make less money picking individual stocks over the long term than you would if you just bought a managed fund or exchange-traded fund that keeps up with the market. Refer to Chapter 8 for more on managed funds and Chapter 9 for exchange-traded funds.

Understanding Financial Statements

Most investors focus on company earnings results, which are released twice per year. It's understandable. Stocks rapidly respond to whether a company topped, matched or missed earnings expectations. Online tools also make it easy to instantly see how a company did during the period and decide whether that changes your opinion on a stock.

Short-term performance can cause stocks to swing momentarily, but long-term investors know a company's true value is based on how it performs over the years, not just the most recent half year. Examining a company's long-term performance requires a bit more effort and calls for digging into a company's financial statements. Investors who study a company's financial statements are said to analyse the *fundamentals.*

Financial statements are detailed documents that show you all the important numbers from a company, ranging from how profitable it is to how financially secure it is. You can find out when a company is due to report earnings at www.boardroomradio.com.au. Type the company's ASX code (we show you how to find this in Chapter 5) in the search field at the top of the screen and click the arrow. Scroll down the page to Events to find when the company releases annual and interim (half-year) results.

Most of the detailed financial statements are available online at the company's website and at www.asx.com.au on the day they're released. To find a financial statement on the ASX website, select Prices, Research & Announcements from the left-hand navigation bar and then click on Announcements, enter the code of the relevant company and click the Go button (see Figure 10-1).

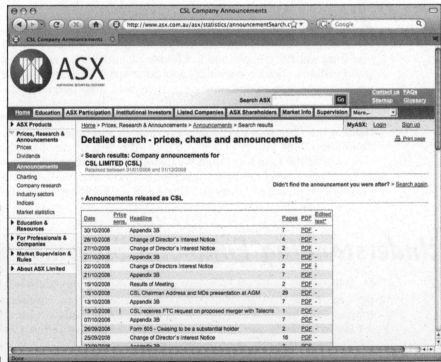

Figure 10-1: The ASX website makes it easy to track down company financial statements.

If you want to go back and look at previous statements, you need to click on Search for Past Company Announcements, enter the company code into the search field (again!) and select the year you're interested in. This process brings up a list of every announcement the company made within a particular year. By scanning the announcements made in February and August carefully, you should find what you're looking for.

The financial statements that must be contained in results include:

- ✔ **The income statement:** This measures the company's bottom line and is also referred to as a profit and loss statement. It tells you how much the company earned during the period or year based on generally accepted accounting principles, or GAAP.

- ✔ **The balance sheet:** This is a snapshot of the company's assets and liabilities at a point in time. The statement shows you what a company owns and owes at the end of the period. Do you want to know how much cash the company has in the bank or how much debt it has? Both numbers are in the balance sheet.

- ✔ **The cash-flow statement:** This tells you how much cash came into and went out of the company during the period. It measures the amount of free cash left over to fund growth and other activities after meeting all its commitments and paying shareholders a dividend. This report is considered one of the most important documents provided by companies. A company's cash flow is more difficult to manipulate using accounting tricks because it's based on the amount of cold hard cash that comes into the company.

You can spend a great deal of time mastering the complexities of reading companies' regulatory filings and financial statements. If that interests you, the ASX provides a number of good resources that can get you started. Typing **Fundamental analysis involves looking** in the search field on any page will return a broad primer on the importance of number crunching written by John Colnan from Shaw Stockbroking. Doing a search on **The balance sheet** returns another good paper on the ins and outs of the balance sheet by John Russell from Aspect Huntley. If you're still hungry for more, try the ASX online class 'Analysing and Selecting Shares'. You need to register first (we show you how in Chapter 2) and then select Education & Resources from the left-hand menu. Choose Education and then Browse the Full List of Online Classes.

Downloading financial statements

Thanks to the internet, investors can get their hands on financial statements at the same instant that brokers and analysts get them, as described in the previous section. Financial statements are usually contained within the larger annual or interim reports, which are really just glossy brochures. They often feature additional, mostly promotional information about the company, such as photos of new products or happy customers, and they can be fun to look at, if you're into that sort of thing.

If you just want the facts, then don't bother printing the whole thing out; annual reports routinely run to more than 100 pages. The financial statements you're looking for will be contained within the report and should be easy to find in the index. That way you can print out just the bits you want, while saving trees in the process.

How to read the income statement

How much money did the company make? That common question is answered, in detail, by the income statement. The income statement matches the company's earnings with its expenses so you can see if it made a profit. The statement itself contains several key components:

- ✔ **Revenue**, or *turnover*, is listed at the very top of the income statement and measures the amount of money generated by the sale of products and services. That's it. You'll hear this referred to by analysts and others as the company's *topline*.

- ✔ **Other** refers to other profits and losses that aren't part of the normal cycle of business, so-called non-recurring items. This could include one-off costs like buying equipment, or a windfall like the sale of property. These irregular occurrences can have a big impact on a company and are therefore given their own lines on the income statement so you can see how the company performed *before* non-recurring items.

- ✔ **Operating profit**, on the other hand, is found down near the bottom of the page and is the sum of revenue minus *operating costs*. These costs can include wages, overheads, raw materials, taxes and so on. If the company lost money, it's said to have a net loss. Whether it's a profit or a loss it's referred to as the *bottom line*, because it's what counts. Hence the phrase 'and that's the bottom line'.

✔ **Diluted earnings per share (EPS)** is what most investors should pay attention to. Diluted EPS converts a company's operating profit into a number that's more relevant to them: The investor's share of the profit. *Diluted EPS* is the earnings number most professional investors watch and is measured by dividing adjusted net income by the number of shares currently in shareholders' hands, as well as those that could be in shareholders' hands if stock options were exercised.

✔ **Basic earnings per share** is arrived at by simply dividing a company's net income by *shares outstanding*, or the number of shares in shareholders' hands. It doesn't factor in the cost of dilution.

Basics about the balance sheet

The balance sheet is the snapshot of the company's assets and liabilities at a particular time, normally at the end of the financial year, or the calendar year. The balance sheet tells you what a company owns and what it owes. The company separates what it owns, called its *assets*, from what it owes, its *liabilities*. The difference between assets and liabilities is that portion of the company shareholders' own, called *shareholders' equity*. The following list breaks it all down for you piece by piece:

✔ **Assets** are objects of value the company owns, including property, equipment and machinery. Assets you can't see or touch, like patents and trademarks, called *intangible assets*, are also included. Assets are further classified as

- **Current assets:** Stuff that's turned into cold hard cash within a year, like inventory, cash and invoices yet to be collected.

- **Non-current assets:** Things like machinery and property that aren't expected to be turned into cash within a year. Often listed as 'Property, plant and equipment'.

- **Intangible assets:** Includes staff, trademarks, brand names, ideas and marketing plans. You may not be able to readily find a buyer for a lot of these things, but they add to the value of the company.

- **Depreciation:** This is the value of an asset after accounting for wear and tear. If you have a car, you may be familiar with this concept. On the other hand, some assets, like property, increase in value. These items are *fair valued* each year to account for any fluctuation.

- **Amortisation:** This is depreciation for intangible assets, similar to how some people buy an item of clothing and then divide the cost by the number of times they wear it to come up with a more palatable figure. Amortisation allows companies to spend up big on assets that will be used for many years.

✔ **Liabilities** are the company's obligations. Liabilities include such things as bank loans, money owed to suppliers, taxes owed to the government or promises to deliver products to customers in the future. These are divided in a similar way to assets, showing

- **Current liabilities:** Bills and other obligations due within a year. The current portion of long-term debt, for example, is the chunk the company must pay off within a year.

- **Non-current liabilities:** Long-term obligations the company doesn't have to pay back within a year.

✔ **Shareholders' equity** measures the value of the investors' ownership of the company. It's kind of the corporate version of your net worth. Your *net worth* is the value of your assets minus your debt. Shareholders' equity is the same: It's equal to a company's assets minus its liabilities.

One of the best things to pay attention to in the balance sheet is the company's number of *shares outstanding*, which is the number of shares that are in the hands of investors. A company's number of shares outstanding is very important because it measures how many pieces the company's profits is sliced into and how big a piece each shareholder gets.

What you need to know about the cash-flow statement

Don't make the mistake of ignoring the cash-flow statement in favour of the other financials. *Free cash flow (FCF)* is the cash left over after meeting all capital expenditure (*capex*) requirements and paying shareholders the dividend.

Despite what you may think, running a business at a profit but running out of cash is possible. Cash is important for funding growth — without it, a company may need to borrow money, which in turn incurs more costs.

The stock buyback blues

You'll want to monitor a company's number of shares outstanding after it says it's buying back stock. Sometimes companies use excess cash to buy their own shares. Investors often applaud stock buybacks because they can, in theory, reduce the number of shares outstanding. And that means each shareholder's slice of the pie gets bigger.

Sounds like a great idea, right? But stock buybacks aren't always what they're cracked up to be. Keep the following in mind when you hear that a company has announced a stock buyback:

✔ **Stock buybacks can distort earnings per share.** If you see a company's earnings per share rise, don't assume that's because the company is more profitable. If a company buys back stock, earnings per share can rise even if net income is flat.

✔ **No rule says the company must follow through.** Just because a company announces it's buying back stock, that doesn't mean it will. In fact, some academic research has found many companies that announced stock buybacks actually increased their shares outstanding as they issued additional shares to give to employees and executives. You can find out more about buybacks at The Buyback Letter (www.buybackletter.com).

Importantly, assets aren't cash. Assets can't be counted as cash until they're sold, including any securities a company may hold. The cash-flow statement is divided into three main parts:

- ✔ **Operating cash flow** tells you how much cash the company used or generated from its normal course of business. This differs from revenue because it represents the actual amount paid by customers, not unpaid invoices. You then subtract the cost of sales, staff and rent, as well as the cost of research and development. Then you subtract the cost of interest on loans and taxes. This figure is called *net operating cash flow*. If it's positive, then the company is generating cash. If it's negative, it's burning cash.

- ✔ **Investing cash flow** is any funds generated by buying or selling shares or businesses, and is only counted when funds are received and banked. This also includes interest and dividend payments received.

- ✔ **Financing cash flow** is a measure of how much cash enters or leaves a company as a result of things like increased borrowings, payment of dividends and repayment of loans.

How free cash flow saved investors from Enron

Investors who compared Enron's free cash flow with net income were glad they did. Enron's quarterly statement from the first quarter of 2001 before its collapse (`http://sec.gov/Archives/edgar/data/1024401/000102440101500014/ene10-q.txt`) is very telling, if you can manage to key in the address correctly! During the quarter, Enron wowed investors with net income of US$425 million. But investors who took the time to study the quarterly report saw the company burned US$464 million in cash from operations and another US$382 million in capital expenditures. That means Enron effectively burned up US$846 million in cash, even while telling investors how profitable the company was.

When you add these three figures together you get *net cash flow* for the period of the financial statement. If you go back to the previous corresponding statement and subtract the old figure from the new figure, you can measure the growth or the contraction of cash flow. Net cash flow can decrease; however, companies should have a good reason for that occurring.

Putting it all together

Some of the real power of financial statements occurs when you take elements of one statement and compare them with numbers on other statements.

The first thing many investment professionals do when they get an annual report, for example, is compare the cash-flow statement with the income statement. If a company is reporting profits on the income statement but not bringing in as much cash, that's a potential red flag. Low cash flow can be a sign that the company has low quality of earnings. A company has *low quality of earnings* when it shows large profits on its financial statements due to accounting gimmicks, not because it's selling a lot of goods and services to actual customers.

Here's an easy way for you to analyse a company's cash flow: Just compare a company's free cash flow (FCF) with its net income.

You can get the data by analysing the financial statements. A company's FCF measures how much cash it brings in the door after paying expenses to keep itself going. FCF is a cousin to cash from operating activities. FCF, however, is stricter than cash from operating activities in that it accounts for the fact companies use cash to buy new equipment and facilities.

To calculate FCF, follow these steps:

1. **Enter the stock's ASX code into the left-hand search box at Yahoo!7 Finance (**`http://au.finance.yahoo.com`**) and click Go.**

   That will take you to the summary page.

2. **Under the heading Financials at the bottom of the page, click on the Cash Flow link.**

   That will bring up a page similar to what you see in Figure 10-2.

3. **Subtract the figure labelled Net Investing Cash Flow from Net Operating Cash Flow.**

4. **Write down the number from Step 3 and then, in the left-hand navigation bar, click on Earnings Summary, which is directly under Financials, and get the figure marked NPAT (net profit after tax).**

   Then compare the number you wrote down with the NPAT. You now have a company's free cash flow (FCF) and net income (NPAT).

Now what? Table 10-1 tells you how to interpret what you've found. It's the same thing many professional investors do.

Figure 10-2:
You can look up a company's cash flow, expenditures and net income at Yahoo!7 Finance.

Table 10-1	Measuring a Company's Quality of Earnings
If Free Cash Flow Is …	*It means the Company …*
Greater than NPAT	Brings in more cash than it reports as profit. That's a good sign and can be an indication of high-quality earnings.
Less than NPAT	Brings in less cash than it reports as profit. This means you want to analyse the company more closely.

A company's FCF not matching its net profit isn't necessarily a deal breaker, particularly when FCF is approaching something resembling NPAT. What's a concern is when a company reports a sizeable profit but has no free cash flow to speak of — this can be an indication of bigger problems lurking within the company.

You can read more about FCF at Investopedia (www.investopedia.com) by doing a search on **Free Cash Flow**. Morningstar's US website also offers a helpful course on the subject. It's hard to get to though, so you'll need to enter the following web address. It's a long one, so prepare to bookmark it or print off the entire lesson if you want to come back to it later. Fingers ready? It's http://news.morningstar.com/classroom2/course.asp?docId=2937&page=1&CN=COM, so good luck!

Spotting trends in financial statements

When you're studying financial statements, you should either look for patterns or look for things that don't fit the company's usual trend. Following are a couple of the things you'll want to pay attention to.

Measuring growth

When you get a raise, what's the first thing you want to know? How much of a percentage increase it is from your previous year's salary. The same goes for the important aspects of a company's income statement and balance sheet. You could go through every item on the financial statements and calculate the change from last year by hand, but it's already been done for you at Yahoo!7 Finance, shown in Figure 10-3. Here's how:

1. **Point your browser to** `http://au.finance.yahoo.com`.

   The Yahoo!7 Finance homepage appears.

2. **Enter the stock's ASX code (the company code plus .AX) into the search box on the left.**

3. **Select the Key Statistics link in the left-hand navigation bar under the heading Company.**

4. **On the Key Statistics page, scroll down to the Growth Rates table.**

   Here you find the growth rates of sales, cash flow, dividends and earnings over one, five and ten years. It also contains two-year forecasts.

Common sizing

Many professional investors compare each item on the income statement with revenue and each item on the balance sheet with total assets. This lets you find interesting trends, such as whether the company is increasing its spending on research and development or the company's debt is rising. You just need to divide each item on the income statement by revenue and each item on the balance sheet by total assets to perform this analysis, called *common sizing*.

Figure 10-3: Comparing a company's sales and earnings growth rates is a valuable exercise.

Investopedia teaches you how to common size a balance sheet and an income statement. Go to the homepage (www.investopedia.com), select Dictionary and enter **common sizing** into the search window. Then select the appropriate items from the list. NetMBA (www.netmba.com) also explains why common sizing financial statements is a good idea. Select Finance from the menu bar at the top and scroll down to Common-Size Financial Statements.

Using financial statements to understand the company

Financial statements can help you understand the structure and objective of a company. Consider the following aspects of the company:

- **Value:** Some investors try to figure out how much a company is worth by using its financial statements. If the company is worth more than the stock price would suggest, that tells these *value investors* the stock may be undervalued. One way investors determine how much a company is worth is by examining book value. Book value is a complex accounting principle. Just know that *book value* generally measures the value of the company's tangible assets recorded in the financial statements minus liabilities. If the company's market value is less than the book value, some investors see it as being undervalued. The *market value*, the stock price multiplied by the number of shares outstanding, tells you how much the company is worth in investors' eyes. We show you how to use the price-to-book ratio to determine whether a stock is undervalued or overvalued in Chapter 11.

- **Growth prospects:** Some investors look for companies posting gigantic earnings or revenue growth, hoping to dig up the next market leaders. *Growth* companies generally don't pay large dividends and prefer to keep any extra cash to invest in new products. Rapidly rising revenue and earnings are signs that a company has morphed into a growth company.

- **Link to broader economic cycles:** Some companies' earnings and revenue rise and fall along with swings in the broader economy. These companies are called *cyclical* companies because they follow economic cycles. Typically, industrial companies like steelmakers belong to this category.

- **Protection from economic cycles:** Companies that don't follow the economy's ups and downs are often called *defensive* companies. These include companies, such as utilities and grocery stores, that tend to sell the same amount of goods no matter what the economy is doing.

✔ **Stability and sustainability:** Some companies generate steadily increasing revenue and earnings because they rely on several products with stable demand. Many large companies belong to this category. But companies involved in finding breakthroughs, such as biotech companies researching cures and oil companies looking for untapped reserves, have big ups and downs in their earnings, based on their luck. Companies with volatile earnings are called *speculative* companies.

✔ **Gearing:** The term simply refers to a company's debt, and the balance sheet shows you how much money the company is borrowing. You can compare a company's total debt with its total shareholders' equity to see how heavy the load is. We show you how to use online screening tools to find companies with low debt levels in Chapter 11.

Getting specific

Almost all companies will use the methods listed in the previous section to measure their own performance, but different industries have particular yardsticks that are important only to them. Here are some of the more regularly used examples:

✔ **Like-for-like sales** is a term used in the retail industry to compare year-to-year sales from existing stores as a group. In any given year they may open more stores so sales growth is more accurately measured using this metric.

✔ **Net earned premium** is the measure that insurance companies use to refer to the money they have taken for insurance coverage that has already been provided. For example, if you paid $600 car insurance last year and didn't make a claim, that would be counted as part of the company's net earned premium.

✔ **ARPU** is an acronym for average revenue per user and is used by telcos. This amounts to every customer's spend with the phone company averaged out over the number of customers. Bigger spending customers mean bigger profits!

✔ **Cost-to-income ratio** is a useful tool for watchers of banks and financial institutions to measure how costs are growing relative to income. What you're looking for is a number that is getting smaller.

✔ **Net interest margin** is another important measure for bank watchers. This measures the cost at which banks are charged for funds and the cost at which they then lend them out.

Looking for Clues

One of the more enjoyable aspects of investing can be stalking your prey. In addition to getting forensic with a company's financial statements, you can gather information on a company in plenty of other ways.

This section covers a few more examples of financial reconnaissance you can perform from your home office.

Getting the lowdown on company announcements

Company's listed on the ASX must abide by the group's many rules, and one of the most important is that of *continuous disclosure*. When a company has an important event — referred to by investment pros as a *material event* — the company is required to tell shareholders and potential shareholders about it. This is done in the form of a statement made to the ASX and posted on the ASX website. You find out how to view these statements in the section 'Understanding Financial Statements' earlier in the chapter. Other types of announcement include the following:

- **Discoveries:** These are one of the most anticipated announcements from mining companies. If a company strikes oil or finds gold, you can find an announcement regarding the discovery on the ASX website.

- **Substantial shareholder notices:** These notices are another type of announcement that are carefully read. When a person or company owns more than 5 per cent of a company, they're required to inform the ASX each time they buy or sell more stock. This ensures shareholders are kept informed if a key shareholder is bailing out or, conversely, another company is buying in. A big company buying a large stake in another company can be viewed as a prelude to a takeover bid, which generally increases a stock price significantly.

- **Profit forecasts:** These can be revised both up or down with predictable results. When new management is installed at a listed company, a popular approach is to 'clear the decks'. This usually includes getting all the company's bad news out of the way early on, in the form of revised profit downgrades.

- **Speeding tickets:** When a stock begins to make significant gains or losses in a single day without announcing any material events, the ASX steps in and issues what is known as a speeding ticket. This is essentially a 'please explain' on behalf of the regulator.

AGM surveillance

Some months after annual results, companies hold what's called an *annual general meeting (AGM)*, which is similar to when a university holds an open day. Generally speaking, the company will host a day-long event at a neutral location like a hotel or convention centre, where key executives give presentations on the company's performance and its future, and vote on a number of issues at the same time

Sound exciting? Well, not really. Most of the time you're getting the company 'spin' — they're telling you what you already know or what they want you to know about the company. Voting is performed well in advance with much lobbying done behind the scenes, so even that is usually a foregone conclusion.

Still, they're a good way to get to know a company. Key personnel like the chief executive and the chair are wheeled out for a bit of a song and dance, key issues the company faces are raised and there may even be free tea and coffee! These days a lot of AGMs are broadcast live on the internet, either from the company's homepage or a business news website, so you can watch all the fun from the comfort of your own home, but you will have to make your own beverages.

Keeping tabs on the trouble makers: Shareholder activists

Depending on who you speak to, shareholder activists can be either a necessary function of a democracy or serial pests. Shareholder activists use their stake in the company as a platform from which to take the company to task for infringements, both real and imagined. They often use the annual general meeting as their one opportunity of the year in which they can be heard.

Two well-known shareholder activists in Australia are Jack Tilburn and Stephen Mayne. Jack Tilburn is a retired schoolteacher who has attended more than 330 AGMs and is known for attacking companies with unbridled enthusiasm. Stephen Mayne is a former political media adviser, journalist and publisher who has stood for the boards of more than 31 listed companies (and failed). In particular, Mayne has had some success in drawing people's attention to what he sees as examples of bad governance and conflicts of interest.

In some circles (and at some AGMs) shareholder activists are jeered for their ego-driven antics, which often amount to little more than wasted time. However, the US also has a strong history of shareholder activism, and such people are household names. Billionaire US investor Carl Ichan has had some impact on the companies he's campaigned against and is famous for the quote, 'A lot of people die fighting tyranny. The least I can do is vote against it.'

The big pay-off: Executive salaries

Tucked away in the annual report is some of the most intriguing information you can find out about a company: What they pay the top dogs. Public companies are, by law, required to disclose the details of their packages, which typically include a salary, bonus, shares in the company and options linked to performance.

Most of these are pretty straightforward. But options, which we describe in more detail in Chapter 15, can radically turbo-charge an executive's salary. *Options* give someone the right (but not the obligation) to buy a stock at a particular date at a particular price. This is a common way for the board to reward executives for the performance of the company stock.

For example, when Mr X joined the EFG Widget Factory, the share price was in the doldrums, trading at around $1.02. In addition to his healthy package, which included salary and equities, he was also granted 100,000 options at $1 each with an excise price of $2 that expired in two years.

Just under two years later Mr X had done a remarkable job in turning around the company, net profit was up, sales were booming and free cash flow was making up serious ground. With the shares now trading for $2.17, Mr X could excise the options. The options are worth the difference between the $1 per share and the actual price, which is, in this case, $1.17 multiplied by the number of options — 100,000. After two years, Mr X has pocketed a tidy $117,000 on top of his existing salary.

Investment banks, in particular, have been fond of this method of remuneration, with the Australian investment bank Macquarie at one stage dubbed 'the millionaire's factory' because of the fabulous amounts of wealth generated by such schemes among its employees.

Executive salaries are a particular bugbear of shareholder activists and it's not unusual to see them foaming at the mouth about the absurd amounts paid to chief executives; however, the standard reply is that most companies need to pay salaries commensurate or in line with overseas packages. World-class companies need world-class talent and they aren't going to get them paying peanuts.

Chapter 11

Evaluating Stocks' Prospects

*W*hen investors say they bought a stock because 'it's a good company', you should automatically become sceptical. As you find out in this chapter, one of the biggest mistakes investors make is confusing a company and its stock. They're not the same thing.

A company's success is measured by its revenue and earnings growth — things that are discussed in Chapter 10. But a stock is a different animal. Stock prices are determined by how much investors are willing to pay. If too many people think a company is good, they may pay too much for the stock and drive up its *valuation*. And when a valuation rises, your potential return decreases. Valuations are the basis for one of the most frustrating realities in investing: Good companies can be bad stocks. If you overpay for a stock, even if the company delivers great earnings growth, you can still lose money. Switched-on investors know the price they pay for a stock is one of the biggest factors that determines how much they'll profit.

This chapter shows you how to find good stocks with reasonable valuations. Although measuring valuations can get maths-heavy, we spare your calculator by showing you online tools that do much of the work for you. You also discover the ins and outs of the price-to-earnings ratio, one of the most commonly used — and misunderstood — ways to measure a stock's valuation. We show you stock tools that step you through the process of picking stocks, and ways to compare a company's valuation with its peers.

Finding Out How to Not Overpay for Stocks

Even if you find a great company with a crack management team and popular products, it doesn't mean you should buy the stock. Why not? The sad truth is you're probably not the first or only person to know about the company's bright future. And, if other investors bought the stock already, they're likely to have pushed the stock price higher. When a stock price has already risen in anticipation of good news, the good news has been *priced in*. That could mean that, even if the good news you're expecting pans out, the stock price may not budge because it has already shot up in anticipation of the good news.

The difficulty of evaluating a stock's valuation is one reason why investing in individual stocks is more complex than buying and holding index managed funds and exchange-traded funds (refer to Chapters 8 and 9). Before we show you how to measure a stock's valuation, we run through the things you should ask yourself before you decide to buy a stock:

- **Does the stock fit into your asset allocation?** If your portfolio is already stuffed with small companies, you may not want to add another small company. Instead, you'll want to invest in different types of companies that better fit your asset-allocation plan. (We talk about asset-allocation plans in Chapter 7.)

- **Does the stock have solid fundamentals?** When you pick apart a company's financial statements, as described in Chapter 10, you're doing what's known as *fundamental analysis*. Essentially, you determine how fast the company's revenue and earnings are growing and examine the management. (Pretty much all you need to know about fundamental analysis can be found in Chapter 10.)

- **Does the stock stack up favourably against the competition?** Companies that have a defendable edge against rivals — typically thanks to a strong brand name — can remain more profitable.

- **Is the price for the stock reasonable?** You'll want to study how much other investors are paying for the stock before you jump in. Overpaying for a good company is just as bad as overpaying for a bad one. You may lose money in both cases. You see how to measure a stock's valuation in the section 'Quick ways to determine how pricey a stock is' later in this chapter.

A stock's price alone doesn't tell you how expensive or cheap a stock is. Just because one company's stock price is $100 and another company's stock is trading for $1 doesn't mean the $1-a-share company is cheaper. A company's share price on its own tells you nothing; it must be compared with something else, such as earnings or revenue, to determine its value.

Quick ways to determine how pricey a stock is

Determining whether a stock is cheap or overvalued is an arduous process that can be a full-time job even for investment pros. Luckily, there's one quick way you can get an idea of how pricey a stock is — valuation ratios. *Valuation ratios* give you a rough idea of a stock's value by comparing the stock price with a measure from the company's financial statements.

Most financial websites that provide stock quotes, including the ones discussed in Chapter 2, provide several valuation ratios. News.com.au (`www.news.com.au/business`), for example, provides you with a lot of the important valuation measures across a couple of screens, whereas others just display a handful of the most popular ones. Enter the stock code in the Stock Quotes text field on the right-hand side of the screen. Click the Earnings tab for some of the most frequently sought-after ratios and click the Ratios tab for some of the more exotic examples.

In search of low returns

Investors figure if they buy the stocks of 'good companies', they'll get great returns. But research has shown that's not true. Companies that are growing and have popular products, but are so trendy with investors that their shares have lofty valuations, tend to be poor investments.

It's not just theory. In Tom Peters' 1982 book *In Search of Excellence*, Peters, a management expert, extolled companies he determined to be the best. Had you bought $100 worth of stock in these excellent companies in 1981, your investment would have grown 82 per cent to $182 up to 1985, according to research by market strategist Michelle Clayman. But here's the funny part: Clayman created a portfolio of 'unexcellent' companies missing all the things that made the excellent companies great. The same $100 invested in these unexcellent companies out-performed the excellent ones by a wide margin. The same $100 invested in the unexcellent companies jumped 198 per cent and turned into $298. The counter-intuitive idea that the best companies are often not the best stocks is described at length at Damodaran Online (`http://pages.stern.nyu.edu/~adamodar`), a site dedicated to stock valuations maintained by Aswath Damodaran, Professor of Finance at New York University. Enter **In Search of Excellence** to the search window to access the article, listed under Investment Fables.

Table 11-1 lists a few valuation ratios you should pay the most attention to.

Table 11-1	Guide to Valuation Ratios That Matter
Valuation Ratio	*It Tells You How Much Investors . . .*
Price-to-earnings (PE)	Are willing to pay for each dollar in earnings the company generates. PE is measured by dividing stock price by the company's earnings per share. A high PE shows that some investors are prepared to pay many times its annual earnings, whereas a low PE shows that investors are not prepared to pay many times its annual earnings.
Dividend yield	Receive in dividends relative to the stock price. The dividend yield is the company's annual dividend payment divided by the stock price. If a $30 stock has a dividend yield of 5 per cent, that means it's paying $1.50 per share every year in dividends. Stocks with high dividend yields are seen as potentially being undervalued.
Earnings per share (EPS)	Could receive if the entire profit was paid out to shareholders before going into debt. EPS is the company's net profit divided by the number of ordinary shares on issue.
Price/earnings-to-growth (PEG)	Are willing to pay for the company's earnings growth. The PEG ratio compares a company's PE ratio to its expected growth rate. The PEG is calculated by dividing the stock's PE by its expected growth rate. A PEG of 2 or higher tells investors that the stock is either expected to grow very rapidly or the stock is overvalued.
Net tangible assets (NTA)	Would receive if the company was broken up and sold tomorrow. This is often expressed as NTA per share.
Return on equity (ROE)	Receive as profit generated on shareholder equity. The higher the ROE, the more efficiently management is using that equity to generate a profit.
Debt-to-equity	Hold as equity in relation to the debt the company carries. A ratio of less than 100 per cent is considered sound.
Interest cover	Allow (of their profit) to be at the company's disposal to service its debt. A number higher than 3 is usually considered acceptable.

The PE ratio is the golden child of valuation ratios and gets most of the attention. The PE is popular because it's easy to understand. Imagine a stock price is $30 a share, and the company earned $1.50 a share. That means investors are paying a price that's 20 times higher than the company's earnings. If the price of earnings, or PE, is high, it means the earnings are very valuable to other people, usually because they expect the company to grow rapidly.

Still confused about what a PE means? Imagine that a company put all the money it earned per share during the year in a box, promised to add more money if it was profitable in the future, and auctioned it off. Say the company earned $1 a share, so there was $1 in the box. If investors paid $1 for the box, the stock would have a PE of 1. But if a bidding war ensued and someone paid $20 for the box containing a dollar of earnings, the stock would have a PE of 20.

PEs can get more complicated because different people measure earnings differently. A *trailing* PE divides the stock price by the company's earnings over the past financial year. A *forward* PE divides the stock price by what the company is expected to earn over the next financial year. Both ways to measure PE are correct; just know which one you're talking about. Google Finance (http://finance.google.com) gives both the trailing PE and the forward PE. Just enter the stock's code into the Get Quotes search field and look for P/E (trailing) and F P/E (forward) on the new page that appears.

Ways to interpret valuations

If you took a look at Chapter 1 and figured out from our discussion there that you're a passive (as opposed to an active) investor, you're probably pretty sure that the stock price actually measures what one share of a stock is worth, or its fair value. If the market is willing to pay $20 for a stock, the stock is worth $20. Passive investors believe markets are *efficient* over the long term and set stock prices that reflect all available public information. But active investors (including bargain hunters known as *value investors*) believe the stock market is *inefficient* and tends to overpay or underpay for stocks from time to time. These investors try to find out whether a stock is too expensive or cheap by studying its valuation ratios and comparing them with the rest of the market, the sector or certain guidelines, explained next.

✔ **The rest of the market:** Some investors compare valuation ratios, such as the price-to-earnings ratio and dividend yield, with both the overall market and individual sectors to get an idea of whether the company might be undervalued. If the valuation ratios are lower than that of the market, that tells some investors the stock might be undervalued.

Yahoo!7 Finance (http://au.finance.yahoo.com) provides market data on its index's valuation, as shown in Figure 11-1. Enter the company code and click on Key Statistics under the Company heading on the left. Concentrate on finding out the following:

- **Dividend yield:** A higher dividend yield than the market may indicate that the company is undervalued, but it may also indicate a falling share price.

- **PE ratio:** When the market's PE ratio falls to around 7 it generally means that the market is undervalued and due for a rebound. When the market's value reaches 20 it can mean that it has been overvalued and due to be sold down.

✔ **The sector:** Comparing a stock's valuation ratios with other stocks in the same industry is also a good idea. Some industries tend to grow more slowly and almost always have a lower valuation than the stock market. That means the only way to know whether a stock's valuation is truly lower than average is to compare it with the ratios of similar companies.

Yahoo!7 Finance (http://au.finance.yahoo.com) also gives you the sector averages alongside company and market ratios.

Some investors completely ignore PE ratios. These investors figure that good companies are worth paying more for and deserve higher PEs. In these investors' minds, a high PE is justified just as wagyu steak at a high-end restaurant deserves a bigger price tag than a T-bone counter meal at your local pub. These investors tend to pay more attention to how fast a company is growing and patterns in its price movements. (We discuss such investors in Chapter 16.)

✔ **Guidelines:** Investors typically have a general idea of what they think makes a cheap or expensive stock. Some investors, for example, think a stock is reasonably priced if the PEG is less than 2. You can calculate a stock's PEG yourself by dividing the PE by the growth rate, or you can get it from Yahoo!7 Finance (http://au.finance.yahoo.com) by entering the stock symbol into the search field, clicking on Get Quotes and choosing Key Statistics on the left, where it is listed as P/E Growth Rate. MoneyChimp (www.moneychimp.com) provides more information about the PEG ratio. Enter **PEG Ratio** into the search window and choose PEG Ratio: How Accurate Is It?

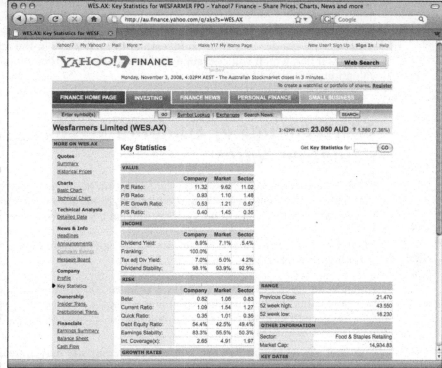

Figure 11-1:
Yahoo!7
Finance
provides
comprehen-
sive data on
valuation
ratios
across
sectors and
the entire
market.

Studying stocks using automated tools

Is your head spinning with all this talk of PEs and PEGs? Don't worry. Online tools are available that can hold your hand through the process of analysing a stock's valuation. Aspect Huntley is an excellent place to start to get you thinking about what goes into evaluating a company's stock price and whether it might fit in your portfolio.

Huntley's Newsletters (www.aspecthuntley.com.au) have been around for a long time and maintain a strong following. Bought by Morningstar in 2006, Huntley's continues to provide good analysis of ASX-listed companies. Visit the Huntley's homepage and click on the Huntley's Newsletters link on the right-hand side of the page. The site is a subscription-only site, but you can get a free four-week trial by clicking on the Free Trial link.

After you've registered, just type in the company's ASX code in the search field and you'll be presented with a broad overview. Don't get too interested in the simplistic Buy/Sell instruction printed at the top of the page in bright colours. Drill deeper and click on Investment Perspective in the left-hand navigation bar, which will contain a detailed analysis of the company's valuation, growth and profitability.

Shortcomings of studying stocks' valuation ratios

We don't want to leave you with a misconception many investors have: Just find 'cheap' stock with a low valuation, buy it, hold on to it forever and you'll make money. Unfortunately, investing isn't that easy.

Using valuation ratios alone to pick stocks has several inherent problems, including the following:

- **Cheap stocks may be cheap for a reason.** Sometimes a stock has a low valuation because the company is poorly run, it's in a slow- or no-growth industry or other companies or technologies are stealing away customers.

- **You get what you pay for.** Sometimes a company may appear to be overvalued and have a high PE. But, if the company's profits grow by a huge amount, the PE will fall and the stock price may skyrocket.

  If a company reports strong earnings, a stock's PE can suddenly go from looking high to looking low. The PE is the stock price divided by earnings. That means that, if earnings per share, the denominator of the fraction, rise rapidly, the PE plunges. Imagine a company trading for $40 a share that has posted earnings over the past financial year of $1 a share. That gives the stock a pricey-looking PE of 40. But, if the company's profit surges and pushes earnings to $2, the PE falls to a more reasonable 20.

- **Dividends aren't a contract.** Some investors target companies with high dividend yields. They figure these stocks' prices are temporarily depressed. And, as a bonus, even if the stock doesn't go up, they get paid their dividend.

  Watch out, though. Dividend payments aren't set in stone. Companies can cut or stop their dividend payments at any time up until the ex-dividend date.

The Four (headless) Horsemen of the Internet

Despite the problems with valuation ratios — problems described elsewhere in this chapter — they're still a good way to get a quick idea of how highly valued a stock is. When you start seeing stocks' PE ratios going above 60, though, you should get suspicious. Few stocks are able to maintain such lofty valuations before getting their comeuppance, as investors realise they've been too bullish. Even if the company can boost its earnings by 100 per cent for a year or two, eventually the industry or the company will stumble and bring its stock back to earth.

Internet stocks were a classic example of how valuations were inflated as investors got caught up in the dot-com mania. Many investors rightly viewed the internet as a huge phenomenon for society and business. Many of them were built on business models that weren't expected to generate any earnings at all for years to come. As a result, investors in these stocks began to ignore PE ratios. Many internet stocks have since vanished completely, and those that didn't have been very poor investments for anyone who invested at the peak.

The valuations of Cisco, EMC, Oracle and Sun, the leaders of the internet nicknamed the Four Horsemen of the Internet, soared in March 2000. Their stock prices have since plunged, though, erasing tremendous amounts of shareholder wealth on the way.

Sitting in on the armchair investor's way to not overpay

If you want to buy cheap stocks, but studying PE ratios and interest-cover ratios makes your head swim, there's an easy shortcut: Buy a managed fund or an exchange-traded fund (refer to Chapters 8 and 9) that owns value-priced stocks. That way, you own stocks that are in value indices. Morningstar (www.morningstar.com.au) offers a search tool that can help you identify those funds easily. From the homepage, click the Tools tab, then click on the Fund Screener link. Under Fund Type, change the category to either Australian Large Value or Australian Mid/Small Value. By adjusting the other inputs you should be able to find a fund that's right for you. When you've entered all the inputs you want, click the Show Result button.

Evaluating Stocks' Potential Return and Risk

If you're taking a gamble on a stock, you'd better get an ample return to make it worth your while. We tell you how to measure your portfolio's risk and return in Chapter 6. It turns out that you can apply the same techniques to individual stocks. We show you how.

Measuring a stock's total return

Past performance is no guarantee of future results, but studying how stocks have done in the past can help you get a very crude handle on what to expect. To find out how stocks have done previously, you need their total return in previous years. A stock's *total return* is the amount its price has gone up — its *price appreciation* — plus its dividend. You can get a stock's total return by the following methods:

✔ **Checking the company's website:** Some companies include total return calculators in the Investor Relations section of their websites.

✔ **Calculating it by using online stock price downloading services:** You can download a stock's annual stock price for different years using services described in Chapter 2. Add the company's stock price at the end of the year to the amount per share it paid in dividends during the year. Divide that sum by the stock's price at the end of the previous year and multiply by 100 and you get the total return for the year.

✔ **Using Huntley's:** The company profile feature at Aspect Huntley (www.aspecthuntley.com.au) provides information on total shareholder returns over one, three, five and ten years at the click of a mouse. Just enter the ASX code into the search field, click Enter and you find the total shareholder return figures halfway down the page.

After you get the stock's total returns for many years, enter them into Horton's Geometric Mean Calculator at www.graftacs.com/geomean.php3. (If you're not sure how to do that, refer to Chapter 6.) After doing that, Horton's Geometric Mean Calculator shows you how much you would have gained in the stock each year on average and also how risky it is. You can then compare the stock's returns and risk with popular indices, just as you do with your portfolio in Chapter 6. If the stock's returns are lower than the stock market's and the risk is higher, it may not be a good fit for your portfolio.

Before you decide that a stock is too risky or the returns are too low, you should compare its movements with those of the rest of your portfolio. If a stock rises when your portfolio goes down, it may actually reduce your portfolio's total risk by offering diversification.

Microsoft (http://office.microsoft.com) provides instructions on how to calculate correlations using Excel, the result known as *R-squared*. Load up the web address and click the Products tab. On the left-hand navigation bar, click on Excel. Enter the term **CORREL** in the search box and click the Search button. Select the first result, which should be Statistical Functions, scroll down to CORREL and click on the link provided.

Don't get bogged down with all the scary maths terms. Just know this: If R-squared is close to or equal to 1, then the stock and your portfolio are going to move in the same direction, which is the opposite of diversification and increases the risk of your portfolio.

Given that modern portfolio theory recommends an asset allocation based on diversification, what you're seeking is a value closer to –1, which means that, if your portfolio sinks, then this stock will rise, decreasing your overall risk and offsetting any losses you may incur over the long term.

Many online stock quote services let you compare several stocks by graphing them on the same chart. And there's no easier way to see which stock has done best than looking at a colourful chart! Yahoo!7 Finance (http://au.finance.yahoo.com) has an easy-to-use charting function that lets you compare stock movements with other stocks and indices. Visit the Yahoo!7 Finance website, enter the ASX code of the stock you're interested in and click Enter. When the page loads, click on Basic Chart and either enter the name of another stock or tick the boxes next to the indices provided. Then select One, Two, Five or Max to see how they pan out.

Finding out more about risk and return online

If you're interested in learning more about how a stock's risk and return are linked, you can consult several sites dedicated to the topic. The sites listed next are a good start.

- ✔ **Path to Investing** (www.pathtoinvesting.org)**:** This site provides an excellent primer for investors seeking to understand the correlation between the returns they're getting from stocks and the risk they're accepting. Click the Investment Choices tab, choose Stock and then scroll down to Risk & Return at the bottom of the page.

- ✔ **FIDO** (www.fido.gov.au)**:** This consumer-oriented website offers a more detailed look at the risk–reward trade-off. From the homepage click the Money Tips tab and select Risk and Returns from the dropdown menu.

Digging Even Deeper: Advanced Valuation Techniques

Valuation ratios are often the most popular ways to measure how pricey stocks are. But even proponents of valuation ratios acknowledge that such ratios *do* have problems. For example, a stock with a seemingly high PE, of 50 or more, going even higher isn't unheard of.

Investors use valuation ratios as general rules, but other more involved ways to try to figure out whether a stock is a good buy are available. Some investors try to use advanced mathematics to figure out what a company is truly worth, or what's sometimes called its *intrinsic value.*

Using the dividend discount model to see whether a stock is on sale

Sometimes investors get so wrapped up in the drama of online stock investing that they lose sight of what they're buying. As a stock investor, you're letting a company use your money to sell goods and services for a profit. If the company makes money, it will ultimately give back your fair share of the profits over time. Typically, that's done by paying a dividend. Even young companies that don't pay a dividend now eventually start to as their profits exceed their needs for cash.

And that's the basis of the *dividend discount model* approach to valuing stocks. The idea is that most companies pay a dividend, and those that don't will. The size of the dividend a company pays, and how quickly it grows, can help you figure out how much a company is worth. There's an ugly formula for a dividend discount model, but we'll spare you the agony. If you can't resist finding out how the calculation is done, Motley Fool (`www.fool.com`) provides a helpful description of the basic and more advanced versions of the models. Enter **Dividend Discount Model** to the search window and click on Search Site. Scroll down until you find the research article by John Del Vecchio.

Here's a link to another article that uses the dividend discount model to evaluate the popular large-cap conglomerate Wesfarmers. This article, by Scott Francis of *Eureka Report*, examines the case for investing in this stock based on the growth of its dividends, but it also highlights areas where the model could let you down. The website is subscription-based, but we've negotiated a special web link for readers to access the article for free (`www.eurekareport.com.au/iis/iis.nsf/ak/qKMDb2?opendocument`).

The dividend discount model is pretty clever and is used by many serious investment professionals. But the model does have some big problems, being extremely sensitive to your assumptions, especially the required rate of return or discount rate that you enter. The *discount rate* is the return you demand for investing your money in the company. If you enter a discount rate of 10 per cent, you get a wildly different answer than if you enter 12 per cent or 8 per cent. And good luck determining what a company's growth rate will be. Still, it's a useful tool to get a general understanding about a fair value for a stock.

The value hunter's favourite weapon: Discounted cash-flow analysis

Ask someone who the best investor ever is, and you'll probably hear the name Warren Buffett. Buffett doesn't publish a playbook that tells the world how he picks companies. He offers some pretty good clues, though, through his Berkshire Hathaway's annual reports. In a nutshell, Buffett tries to measure a company's intrinsic value and buy shares of the company only when it's trading for less than the intrinsic value.

Many speculate that Buffett and investors like him use what's called *discounted cash-flow (DCF)* analysis. The DCF method works on the assumption that successful companies generate cash flow every year and will hopefully generate more each year. The DCF model attempts to estimate how much cash the company will generate over its entire lifetime, and tells you how much that cash would be worth if you got it today. If the company's intrinsic value is greater than the stock price, the company is a good deal.

Time for a concrete example. Imagine that you're a lucky lottery player and have just won a million dollars. Say the government says you could either have the million now or wait 30 years for it. You don't even have to think about it: You take the money now. You didn't realise it, but you just did a discounted cash-flow analysis in your head. Because money received today is more valuable than the same amount received later, you know that a million dollars paid 30 years from now is worth less than a million paid today.

The discounted cash-flow analysis can get somewhat complicated. You must first estimate a company's free cash flow, as described in Chapter 10. Next, you have to determine how rapidly the company's free cash flow will grow over the years and how much it would be worth if paid to shareholders right now. If you're interested in the nitty-gritty of this analysis, Incademy Investor Education (www.incademy.com) offers a helpful and in-depth description of how the discounted cash-flow model is crunched. Scroll down the homepage until you find the heading Comment and choose Ten Great Investors. Buffett, of course, is number 1! Click on the link and then scroll down to the link for the DCF analysis example.

Luckily, you can use online resources and get the benefits of the DCF model without actually doing any calculations. Check out the following helpful sites:

✔ **MoneyChimp** (www.moneychimp.com): Click on Search in the top menu bar, enter **DCF Calculator** into the search window and click the Go button. Then choose Stock Valuation — DCF Theory and Calculators and select DCF Calculator from the list of articles on the right. Definitely one of the easier discounted cash-flow model sites to use. You need to enter only five pieces of information and the website will generate the stock's value. You must enter the following data:

• **Earnings per share over the past 12 months.**

• **Initial expected annual growth rate.**

• **Number of years earnings will grow at that pace.**

- **What the growth rate will fall to after the initial growth period.**

- **The return you can get on a similar investment.** If the stock is a large company stock, you would enter the 13.5 per cent average return of the S&P/ASX 200.

MoneyChimp does all the maths for you and tells you how much the stock is worth. If you're interested in the approach Buffett uses, MoneyChimp also provides a slightly different discounted cash-flow model believed to be closer to Buffett's approach. Repeat the previous steps from the homepage (www.moneychimp.com) and select Buffett Formula (?) from the list of articles on the right.

✔ **Valuation Technologies** (www.valtechs.com/r2.shtml): This site offers several different online worksheets that use discounted cash-flow and dividend discount models. The first worksheet lets you enter future cash flows and find out what they'd be worth if received today. The second one estimates a stock's value based on its dividend track record. And the last one measures the value of a company that slows down as it ages. It's an interesting site because it provides text that explains how the calculations are performed.

✔ **Numeraire DCF Valuator** (www.numeraire.com/value_wizard): A page from the Global Value Investing site offering all sorts of free valuation calculators. Read the Introduction and then click on the Portal link to find the model that fits your needs.

✔ **Expectations Investing** (www.expectationsinvesting.com): This site takes the discounted cash-flow analysis and turns it on its head. The site owners, Alfred Rappaport, a professor emeritus at Northwestern University, and Legg Mason Capital money manager Michael Mauboussin, say investors should examine a stock's price first and then work backwards. By dissecting the stock price, you can figure out what the majority of other investors expect the company's cash flow and growth to be. Then you can decide whether the market is expecting too much or too little. You can read about the approach in the tutorials section and also download all the spreadsheets you need to do the analysis yourself.

✔ **Damodaran Online** (http://pages.stern.nyu.edu/~adamodar): New York University finance professor Aswath Damodaran offers dozens of advanced valuation models that use variations of both the dividend discount model and the discounted cash-flow model. The site even has a 'right model' spreadsheet that tells you which valuation model to use.

Chapter 12

Finding Investment Ideas with Online Stock Screens

*O*ne of the most popular questions investors ask is, 'What stock should I buy?' These investors figure that, amid the pile of thousands of publicly traded stocks, a handful of stocks will be the big winners for the year. They're right. Some stocks will be big winners and some will be big losers each year. The problem, though, is that no-one knows ahead of time which ones.

No online tool can tell you what stocks will be next year's winners. But some online resources and databases can help you find stocks with traits you believe make them likely candidates.

This chapter shows you how online stock screens are your best friends when you're trying to sort through thousands of stocks for those you may want to own. Online screening tools scour the ASX for stocks that meet criteria you set. We show you a few of the top online stock-screening tools and give you some pointers on how to use them. You also find out about many ways you can filter stocks and how to pick criteria for your screen. We also cover methods to compare companies with their peers or other companies.

Getting Familiar with Stock Screens

No one person can do an in-depth analysis of each of the publicly traded stocks out there. There's just not enough time. Even large investment companies, with giant teams of researchers, can only study so many stocks. But that doesn't mean you want to miss out on stocks that may belong in your portfolio.

Stock-screening tools are the answer. Screening tools are systems that let you describe what kind of stock you're looking for, and then the screening tool returns a list of results to you. The screening tool searches through thousands of stocks in a database and finds the ones that match your parameters.

Stock-screening tools aren't all that different from online dating services. Say you're looking for a mate with dark brown hair and green eyes who likes to run and follow the stock market. You can enter those traits into an online dating service and get a list of people who match. Similarly, stock screens are excellent tools to help you come up with a list of stocks that may be attractive. You enter a list of traits for the stock, such as the industry, growth rate and valuation. Where you get a list of the companies that fit your criteria, you have a smaller and more manageable list of stocks you can study more closely.

Investors who use online stock-screening tools benefit in a number of ways:

- ✔ **Less time wasted:** Screening tools keep you from wasting time studying companies that aren't appropriate. You can design your stock screen to throw out companies that are undesirable to you for certain reasons, such as having too much debt or too little profit.

- ✔ **No stone unturned:** Screening tools can highlight stocks you may have overlooked. One of the best things about stock screens is that they're dispassionate and robotic. Screens don't get caught up in marketing hype — they look only at the numbers. That means screens may find stocks you've overlooked because you weren't familiar with the companies' products.

- ✔ **Great head-to-head comparisons:** Screening tools are great when it comes to comparing stocks. Stock screens are built using specific financial metrics and ratios, which are calculated for all stocks. Online screening tools allow you to rank companies against each other based on these objective measures.

The biggest gripe about stock screens is that they do only what they're told. If you filter stocks using meaningless variables, your results are only as good as the elements you're searching for.

Creating an online screen

Many stock-screening sites are available and they all work slightly differently. But the general procedure of getting into the screening game is essentially the same:

1. **Choose a screening site.**

   We discuss several websites that provide free or low-cost screening tools in the section 'Choosing an online screening site' later in this chapter.

2. **Decide what kind of stock you're looking for.**

   Perhaps you're trying to find a stock that fits your asset allocation. Are you looking for a company that's being ignored by other investors and should therefore be considered value-priced? Are you trying to find a fast-growing company that will blow away earnings forecasts? Are you looking for a stable stock that pays a large dividend? You can find all these types of stocks by using screens.

3. **Pick measurable traits shared by stocks and companies you're looking for.**

   We show you general traits you can include in your search, as well as pre-made screens where professionals have already created the search criteria so you don't have to spend your time doing it.

4. **Refine your screen.**

   Screening for stocks is a bit of a trial-and-error process. At first, the list of companies that meet your standards might be too large. You can make the criteria more stringent or add additional criteria to help narrow down the list even more.

Now that you've seen the screening process, the fun part begins. The best screens are carefully designed to pinpoint stocks that have the traits you're looking for. When building screens, it's best to be as specific as possible so you find stocks that are the perfect matches for your portfolio.

Understanding the general characteristics you can use to screen stocks

The number of characteristics you can use to screen stocks is virtually unlimited. If you can measure it, you can screen stocks for it. Even so, most investors use the following primary measures in screens:

- ✔ **Company information:** We're talking basic elements of companies' location, size or industry here. Common criteria you may use would include the industry the company is in and what stock market index the company is part of. How much money the company brings in — its *revenue*, in other words — is also important.

- ✔ **Price and performance:** This category deals with how the stock has been moving. You can search for stocks that tend to swing more or less than the general stock market, stocks that are close to their highs or lows and stocks that trade hands between investors more often or less often. You can also find companies that investors are betting against by *shorting* the stock. (For more on shorting stock, see Chapter 15.)

- ✔ **Market value:** This measures how much the company is worth. Market value is used to determine whether a company is small, mid-sized or large, which helps you select stocks that fit in with your asset allocation. (For more on asset allocation, refer to Chapter 7.)

- ✔ **Profitability:** The level of earnings and cash flow a company generates is of utmost importance to investors. Not surprisingly, you can search on both earnings and cash flow. You can drill down even further by looking for specific things about profits, including how quickly profit has grown over the most recent quarter or year, or over the longer term.

- ✔ **Valuation ratios:** Investors pay close attention to how much they're paying for companies, or what's called a stock *valuation*. Valuations are covered at length in Chapter 11.

- ✔ **Dividends:** These periodic cash payments made by companies to shareholders are important because they account for about a third of many large companies' total return. Dividends are also widely watched because they're an indication of a stock's valuation.

Some stock screens use the cryptic terms TTM and MRQ to describe the timeframe in which you'd like to base your search. *TTM* means *trailing 12 months*, which means the most recent 12 months. *MRQ* is the most recent quarter.

Choosing an online screening site

Before you can start screening, you need to pick an online screening site. Most investors are more than satisfied with the many free screening sites that are available, and we focus mostly on those sites. Some of these sites provide pre-made screens that you can call up immediately, without programming in specific criteria. If using pre-made screens seems like your speed, we provide more details on how to do that with some of the screening sites in the 'Getting Started with Pre-made "Canned" Screens' section later in this chapter. You may decide, though, that you want to go off the beaten path a bit and build a screen exactly to your taste. We show you how to design a screen from scratch using a few of the sites as examples in the 'Designing Your Own Custom Screens' section at the end of this chapter.

No matter if you decide to go with canned or custom screens, the screening sites you might consider are (in no particular order):

- **Australian Stock Screener** (www.australian-economy.com) is an excellent free resource for those just starting out. But don't let its no-frills layout fool you; this simple yet effective stock screen contains many of the most popular and important screening variables, including price-to-earnings (PE) ratio, market capitalisation, dividend yield and earnings per share (EPS). Simply tick the boxes of the characteristics you're looking for (you can tick as many as you like) and click Submit. You'll be presented with a list of appropriate stocks that you can sort by clicking on the relevant columns.

- **ninemsn Share Screener** (http://money.ninemsn.com.au) is for those who are getting a little more confident with stock screens. From the homepage, select Shares and Funds from the list at the left and then choose Find Shares (see Figure 12-1). From there you can find a selection of pre-made screens and a Custom Share Screener, which allows you to build on existing screens or start from scratch.

- **StockScan** (www.stockscan.com.au) focuses more on creating your own stock scanner, rather than on pre-made screens, although some example screens are included in this dedicated stock-scanning site. It provides a huge number of inputs to choose from and it can get overwhelming for first-time users. The site is subscription-based but, if you think you're up for it, you can test out its wares by signing up for a free trial. Users on a free trial, however, are limited to saving only one scan, which will run once a week only, instead of every day.

✔ **Brokerage websites** sometimes provide stock-screening tools. Many of the leading online brokers, especially those we refer to as *premium services* back in Chapter 3, such as CommSec (www.commsec.com.au) and E*TRADE (www.etrade.com.au), offer stock-screening tools on their websites, in order to differentiate their product offering.

If you're interested in stock screening, most online brokers' sites offer a tour or tutorial of the tools they can provide. If screens are important to you, you may consider checking out the tools on various online brokers' sites to see whether they're good enough for you to open an account.

Figure 12-1:
The share screener available at ninemsn's Money offers pre-made and customised screens, making it perfect for intermediate users.

Knowing What You're Looking For: Popular Screening Variables

Investors can search for countless criteria by using screens, but certain variables routinely show up in stock screens because they're so useful. If you know what these variables are and why they matter, you can build some very helpful screens. This section helps with identifying those variables.

Sussing out the basics: 'Cause you have to start somewhere

When you're first figuring out how to build a screen, you want to start with some of the more basic variables. That way you can get comfortable with the idea of building a screen first and then add more advanced variables as you narrow your search. In this 'basics' category we include the following:

- ✔ **Valuation ratios:** These ratios include the price-to-earnings (PE) ratio and debt-to-equity ratio. *Valuation ratios* are ways to compare a stock price with the company's value. If you're looking for potentially undervalued stocks, for example, search for stocks with low PE and debt-to-equity ratios.

  The PE ratio and other valuation ratios are discussed at length in Chapter 11.

- ✔ **Market cap:** This is a measure of the price tag the stock market puts on the whole company. The market value — often called *market capitalisation* — is measured by multiplying the stock price by its number of shares *outstanding* (the number in shareholders' hands). This measure determines whether a stock is large, mid-sized or small.

- ✔ **Earnings per share (EPS):** Earnings per share is the bottom line. It measures what portion of the company net income holders of each share of stock are entitled to.

- ✔ **Current ratio:** This ratio measures how prepared a company is to pay bills that are due in a year's time. You can calculate the current ratio by dividing current assets (assets that can be turned into cash in a year or faster) by current liabilities (bills due in a year or less). If the company's current ratio is 1, the company has enough assets to cover bills becoming due in a year. The higher the ratio, the more solid the company's financial condition.

Getting more particular: More-advanced variables to screen for

Just using the basic screening variables is somewhat limiting. If you want to carve the list of stock candidates up further, you can use some more-advanced variables. Good choices here include:

- **Gross margin:** One of many ways to measure a company's profitability, *gross profit* is how much revenue a company keeps after paying for things directly involved in the production of the goods or services sold. A cake stall's gross profit is the dollar value of the cakes sold minus the cost of things used to make the cakes, such as flour and sugar. This gross profit, divided by the company's revenue, or turnover, gives you gross margin. *Gross margin* tells you how much of every dollar in sales the company keeps after paying costs directly tied to making the goods or services. The higher the gross margin, the more profitable the company.

- **Operating margin:** This method of measuring a company's profit includes more costs than gross margin. *Operating profit* is gross profit minus indirect costs, such as overhead. Overhead might include the cost of hiring a company to promote the business. *Operating margin* is the company's operating profit divided by revenue. The higher the operating margin, the more profitable the company.

- **Net profit margin:** This particular margin compares the company's bottom line with its revenue. The *net profit margin* is measured by dividing a company's net income, which counts all company costs, by its revenue. It tells you how much of each dollar in revenue the company keeps as profit after paying all costs. The higher the net profit margin, the more profitable the company.

- **Return on equity:** A great way to see how efficiently the company's management is using the money invested in the company, *return on equity (ROE)* is measured by dividing net income by shareholders' equity. *Shareholders' equity* measures how much money shareholders have invested in the company. So, ROE shows you how much profit the company generates per dollar invested in the company.

- **Return on assets:** Shows you how much profit the company is able to squeeze out of its assets. The higher the number, the better the company is at making money from things it owns.

- **Dividend payout ratio:** Tells you what proportion of profit a company is paying out as dividends. You calculate this ratio by dividing a company's dividends by net income.

  If a company's dividend payout ratio gets high — paying 85 per cent or more of its profit out as earnings, for example — it might be paying more than it can afford, depending on what industry it's in.

- **Dividend yield:** Tells you what kind of return you're getting as a dividend from the money you've invested in a stock. The *dividend yield* is a company's annual dividend paid per share, divided by the stock price. A $100 stock that pays $2 a year in dividends has a 2 per cent dividend yield.

- **Institutional ownership:** This measure tries to show you whether the 'smart money' is buying a stock. The ratio shows you what percentage of shares are in the hands of large managed funds and institutions, which presumably have large research units. Some investors look for stocks with low institutional ownership, figuring the stock will rise rapidly as these big investors discover the stock and buy shares.

- **Debt-to-equity ratio:** Shows you how deeply in debt a company is. The ratio divides a company's liabilities by its shareholder equity. The higher the ratio, the more *leveraged*, or in debt, the company is. Remember, though, that different levels of debt are acceptable in various industries.

- **Beta:** Most online screening tools use a measure called *beta* to gauge volatility. The higher beta is, the more volatile the stock is compared with the rest of the stock market. If a stock has a beta greater than 1, that means it's more volatile than the S&P/ASX 200. If a stock's beta is less than 1, it's less volatile than the S&P/ASX 200. And if a stock's beta is equal to 1, it's equally as volatile as the S&P/ASX 200.

  If you can't stomach stocks that swing as wildly as the stock market, you want to add a beta filter to your screens. Just look for stocks that have betas of less than 1.

Finding stocks using trading-pattern variables

Some investors are interested more in a company's stock than the company itself. These investors, generally known as *technical analysts*, believe stocks follow certain patterns. And, if you detect the pattern fast enough, you can figure out where the stock is going and make money. Some screening variables are designed to find *technical stock patterns*, including:

✔ **Average daily volume:** Some investors think, if there's heavy trading in a stock when it rises or falls, that means more than if there's light trading volume. If a stock goes up, these investors look at trading volume to find out how many investors are buying. If the stock is rising and trading activity is strong, that tells these investors there's great demand for the stock and the uptrend might continue.

✔ **Proximity to moving averages:** This indicator tells you whether the current stock price is higher or lower than where it has been in the past. The 200-day moving average, for example, tells you what the stock's average price has been over the past trading year. If the stock falls below the 200-day moving average, some see that as a bad sign because it means everyone who bought the stock in the past year, on average, is losing money and may be eager to sell.

✔ **Proximity to a stock's price highs and lows:** You can use screens to find out whether a stock's price is close to its high price over the past year, called the *52-week high*, or its low price, the *52-week low*.

✔ **Stock performance:** This is a simple measure that shows you how much the stock has risen or fallen in a set period.

Getting Started with Pre-made 'Canned' Screens

If you've never built a stock screen before, you may want to first try out some of the pre-made screens available on various websites. The websites have done most of the work for you and entered in all the variables, saving you the hassle. The following list highlights some of the better known 'canned' stock screens:

✔ **StockScan** (www.stockscan.com.au)**:** Although StockScan isn't exactly aimed at the casual user, it does provide some information on how to run a couple of pre-made screens. Register by clicking the Create a Free Account tab on the homepage. When you receive a confirmation email, log in using the details provided, then from the Members Area scroll down the page to Helpful Links and click on Example Scans. Included among the pre-made screens are the 10-Week Low filter, which can be used as a way to identify cheaper entry points into quality Australian stocks.

- **ninemsn Money** (http://money.ninemsn.com.au): This site offers a good selection of pre-made screens that you can run endlessly or even adapt to your own specifications. Select Shares and Funds from the left-hand menu and click on Find Shares. Some of the screens that you may find useful to start include Top Income and Growth, Growth at a Reasonable Price and Low PE Bottom Trawlers. Select the screen you want and click the search button. Don't forget that these can all be altered to suit your own requirements by selecting Customise a Search at the top of the pre-made screen.

- **Aspect Huntley** (www.aspecthuntley.com.au): The scan provided by this site is one of the simplest around, although it should be used with caution. Aspect Huntley provides five different types of recommendations for stocks — buy, accumulate, hold, reduce and sell. The recommendations are based on companies with strong growth in EPS, growing dividend stream, strong returns on equity and free cash flow.

Visit the Aspect Huntley homepage and click on the link for Huntley's Newsletters on the right-hand side of the page. The site is a subscription-only site, but you can get a free four-week trial by clicking the Free Trial button at the top of the page. After you've registered, click on Search in the left-hand navigation bar and then select Simple Search. In Step 1, select Recommendation. In Step 4, select Buy and then click the Run Query button. That will give you a list of all the stocks with a buy recommendation.

Now that you know all the stocks Huntley's recommends, perhaps it's a good time to narrow down the list a little. Click the Advanced Search tab and repeat the same steps as before but click the Add Query button. This will add the previous search to the Query List. Now go back to where it says Select Category and choose Company Stats. In the second dropdown menu, select Industry and then, in the fourth, select Misc. Indus. Add the query to your query list and click Run Query to get a list of those industrial stocks that were among Huntley's buy recommendations.

Designing Your Own Custom Screens

After you begin dabbling with stock screens, you may start enjoying it! You can get a rush sifting through thousands of stocks for precise variables and getting a list of candidates in a matter of seconds. Many investors, when they realise what stock screening is and how easy it is to do, can get kind of addicted to building screens.

The pre-made screens described in the preceding section cover most of the main searches investors would want to do. But, sometimes, a canned screen isn't good enough. Many of the same sites that offer canned screens also let you create a screen from scratch. You may consider building a screen from the ground up if you encounter the following issues with a pre-made screen:

✓ **The screen is too lenient.** A pre-made screen may not be as restrictive as you want. That's especially true when searching for value-priced stocks, because investors' opinions on what makes a cheap stock varies. A canned screen may consider a PE of 10 to be cheap, but you may want to limit the list to stocks with a PE of less than 8 or even 5.

✓ **The screen isn't aggressive enough.** If you're looking for a company that's expanding very rapidly, you may want to ratchet up what it takes to get into your screen. Many screens consider 20 per cent annual earnings growth to be rapid, but you may want 30 per cent or more.

✓ **The screen isn't to your taste.** Some investors go after stocks that defy characterisation. You may want to find stocks with high PE ratios and a low beta, which are unusual things to look for at the same time. You need to build these personalised screens yourself.

Finding different industries' best companies using ninemsn Money

If you're trying to figure out which companies in an industry are performing the best or worst, ninemsn Money's screening tool makes it easy:

1. **Point your browser to ninemsn Money's Share Screener.**

   We show you how to get there in the section 'Choosing an online screening site' earlier in this chapter, or you can visit (`http://money.ninemsn.com.au/shares-and-funds/share-screener.aspx`) directly.

2. **Under Custom Share Screener, select Create Your Own Search.**

   The first dropdown menu, named Category, will display Company Statistics. In the second dropdown menu, named Indicator, change your selection to Industry. The third dropdown menu will display Define Criteria; change your selection to Equal To. Now a fourth dropdown menu appears, named Value; use this to select the industry you're interested in. If you're interested in diversified resource stocks, select Div. Resources.

3. **Now click the Add Criteria button.**

4. **Now that you've selected the industry you're interested in, define what you mean by a 'best company'.**

   The definition of a 'best company' is in the eyes of the beholder. You may, for example, want companies with an industry-leading return on equity. To find companies with an industry-leading return on equity, from the Category menu you select Performance Measures, and from the Indicator menu you select Return on Equity. From the Define Criteria menu, select Show Highest and then click the Add Criteria button. Now click the Run Search button. Your screen should look something like that in Figure 12-2.

5. **Add more variables.**

   If you want to continue refining your screen, click the Add Criteria button. This again brings up the three dropdown menus, so you can add different criteria if you choose. You can add criteria that finds stocks with the smallest or largest price-to-earnings ratios, earnings-per-share growth, free cash flow or debt-to-equity ratio. You're only limited by your imagination and what you think makes a great company.

6. **Again click the Run Search button.**

   Your search results appear on a new page, displaying the leading companies that beat the industry, based on the additional criteria you've added.

Figure 12-2: ninemsn Money's screening tool allows you to see how companies and their stocks compare with industry peers.

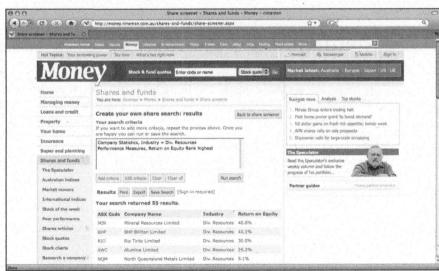

Finding growth and value companies using ninemsn Money's share screener

You could design a convoluted set of criteria to find value and growth stocks. But why go to the trouble when ninemsn Money's stock screener has done the work for you? The site helps you design a custom screen, but with some helpful handholding. Here's how:

1. **Point your browser to ninemsn Money's share screener.**

   We show you how to get there in the section 'Choosing an online screening site' earlier in this chapter, or you can visit (`http://money.ninemsn.com.au/shares-and-funds/share-screener.aspx`) directly.

2. **Under Custom Share Screener, click on Customise a Search.**

3. **Select the pre-made screen Growth at a Reasonable Price, then click the Customise This Search button.**

   You can narrow your search further, based on growth or profitability grades and other items. Select Add Criteria and refine your screen even further like you did with Step 5, for the search for industries' best companies.

4. **When you're done, click the Run Search button.**

   You get a lovely list of results. You can save your searches if you want, but you'll need to register to access this feature.

Getting help from the best

You can identify investment opportunities online in many different ways, and screens are certainly one of the most powerful. But, if you're alert, you can also collect tips from industry insiders. Although nothing is better than your own fundamental analysis skills, sometimes it pays to see where the 'smart money' is going before seeing if a stock stacks up against your own rigorous requirements. We can already hear you say, 'But I don't know any industry insiders,' and, although that may be true, it shouldn't stop you from finding out just where their money goes.

Top performers

Sometimes top performers in the listed-managed-investment sector stand head and shoulders above the crowd. By then, it's often too late to pile in with everyone else, but it can be a good time to start watching their investments. As we explain in Chapter 9, these investment vehicles are required to report what their holdings are at regular intervals. When they add a new company to their portfolio may be a good time to see if they measure up to your own exacting standards.

Listed managed investments report their NTA at the end of each month and often put out an additional statement detailing their top 20 holdings, which you can find under Company Announcements on the ASX site at www.asx.com.au. If you see a new company creeping into the list, it may be time to 'run the ruler' over it and consider adding it to your portfolio.

Following the money

Stocks fall when more people are selling than buying, and they rise when more people are buying than selling, but wouldn't it be great to know just who is doing the buying and selling? Well you can. Whenever two very important groups of people are trading a particular stock, they're required to release a statement to the exchange that can contain interesting clues about the direction of the company.

Directors in listed companies are required by law to inform the ASX whenever their holdings in the company change. These are clearly marked as a Change of Directors Notice in the Company Announcement section of the ASX website. In the document, you need to look at three rows. The first two are Number Acquired and Number Disposed, which tell you simply whether shares were bought or sold as part of the transaction.

The third row you need to look at is marked Nature of Change. What you're looking for here is the phrase 'on market trade'. If you see that on the site with no further explanation, then it's very likely that the company director bought or sold shares in the company. And, if anyone is going to have a clear picture on what the company is doing, it's a director!

But be careful. Sometimes trades appear here that are part of a salary package, an exercise of options or part of a share buyback. Shares may have been bought or sold but the trade isn't really a true indication of what the director feels about the company. It's also true that sometimes a director may sell for reasons unrelated to company performance — he may need to free up some capital for some other reason. A common excuse for director sales is 'tax considerations'; however, a director is not required to give any reason for a sale.

Used wisely, a change of Directors Notice can be a good way to keep tabs on sentiment surrounding the company from people who should know. If you can't be bothered keeping up with each individual company announcement, then Business Spectator keeps a handy summary of all the most recent trades made. Just visit the homepage at www.businessspectator.com. au, follow the left-hand navigation bar all the way to the bottom and select Director Dealings. You'll have to scroll through the long list of articles to find those you may be interested in.

Another group of investors required to inform the ASX when they buy or sell shares in a company are known as *substantial shareholders*. The term refers to anyone who owns more than 5 per cent of a company. Most of the time it refers to institutions like managed funds, banks and other companies but, occasionally, it can refer to specific individuals who have big stakes in a company. Again, you need to pay close attention to the detail of the statement, as we outline earlier, to ensure you understand the nature of the transaction.

Chapter 13

Analysing the Analysts and Stock Pickers

*W*hen you're looking to make a big purchase, such as a car, house or big-screen TV, you probably ask other people questions before making your decision. You might ask a friend or family member for their recommendation, or consult with a magazine or website that ranks products.

Recommendations play an important role for some investors when picking stocks too. Traditional brokers have long made it their business to recommend stocks for their clients to buy. Many business news channels feature guests who can fire off stock tips as rapidly as weather reports. And friends and colleagues play their role here as well. Even before you've been offered a drink, a friendly BBQ can start sounding like an investment club meeting as everyone brags about their winners (and, occasionally, their losers).

Stock recommendations are impossible to avoid, and that makes them important to think about. There are smart ways, though, to handle recommendations. In this chapter, we show you various online resources for stock recommendations, as well as how to interpret them. You get a chance to read about different stock-picking newsletters and sites and how to evaluate them. And we show you some new online sites that reveal how other individual investors rate stocks.

Picking Apart Professional Analyst Reports

Nearly all the major brokerage firms have teams of research *sell-side* analysts. The sell-side analyst's job is to study companies and tell investors who are clients of the brokerage firm which stocks are attractive. You can also find *independent* research firms — research groups not connected with a brokerage firm that analyse stocks and sell their research.

Blindly following buy or sell recommendations is generally a bad idea. Smart investors know how to scan through research reports to pick out important insights on the company or industry. Later in this section, we show you how to quickly pull the most important information out of analyst reports.

Knowing how to access analyst reports online

Before you can analyse research reports, you have to get your hands on them. You can use several techniques to do this online — some will cost you money, but many won't. The following list highlights a few resources of both the free and not-so-free types:

- **Online brokers:** You don't have to be a client of the full-service brokerage firms to get good research. Some online brokers provide research free of charge. CommSec customers, for example, get access to the suite of regularly updated reports from its in-house research team that cover popular companies and sectors. E*TRADE customers can access reports from Aspect Huntley and optionsXpress customers can access research from Standard & Poor's.

  Many online brokers also offer access to independent research, including reports from Morningstar. Getting research from your online broker is generally the best route because there's usually no charge.

- **Research providers:** Some independent research providers sell their reports directly to investors. The reports include a forecast of what the stock's future price could be in 12 months, called a *target price*, in addition to an analysis of the company's earnings. Research firm Aegis, through its shareAnalysis website (www.shareanalysis.com), provides unlimited access to more than 200 regularly updated reports via a subscription for $699 a year. If you think that's a bit rich you can sign up for a month for just $69. Alternatively, you can buy individual

Aegis reports from InvestSMART (www.investsmart.com.au) for as little as $16. Just visit the homepage, register your details and, from the Shares tab, select Research Reports. You can also take out a week-long free trial of the reports from the shareAnalysis site. Go to the homepage, select the link for Premium Web-based Investor Service — Free Trial and then click on the Register link on the right of the screen. Personally, we like the last option!

Don't assume that, just because stock research comes from an independent research firm, it's more accurate or better. Sometimes research from brokerage firms is very good. The quality of research varies greatly, and largely depends on the strength of the specific analyst covering the stock. We show you how to track down the best analysts on various stocks in the section 'Determining which analysts are worth listening to' later in this chapter.

✔ **Summary sites:** If you want just the bottom-line recommendations from analysts, several sites summarise the data. Nearly all the websites that provide stock quotes also compile analyst recommendations. Some examples include:

- *The Australian* **Business** (www.theaustralian.news.com.au/business) provides a good summary of broker recommendations on its feature-rich stock quote page. Simply enter a company code into the Stock Quote field in the top right-hand corner of the page and click Go. When the following page loads, click the Company Profile tab underneath the price information and scroll down to the Consensus Recommendation Summary to check the broker positions collected by Aegis.

- **ninemsn Money** (http://money.ninemsn.com.au) also provides a good overview of broker opinion, but you'll need to register before you can access the information. And don't worry; it won't cost you a cent! Load up the homepage, enter the company code in the Stock & Fund Quotes field at the top of the screen and then click Go. From the dropdown menu to the right of the search field, select Buy/Sell/Hold and click Go again. Here, you'll be prompted to either register (which we strongly recommend!) or, if you're already registered, it will provide you with a chart of current analyst recommendations collected by Aspect Huntley.

Most summary sites convert stock ratings into numbers on a 1–5 scale, where 1 is a 'strong buy', or 'out-perform', and 5 is a 'strong sell', or 'under-perform'.

- **FN Arena** (www.fnarena.com) has an excellent financial news service provided by Rudi Filapek-Vandyck. This service has a real edge: He reports on the recommendations from brokers as they happen, in a segment of the website called 'Australian Broker Call'. So, unlike the previous two summary sites, where you can just find out consensus figures, Rudi names the brokers and relays their calls and their reasons for them. Covering all the major brokers and some of the smaller ones too, it really is quite a unique service. If you're interested, you can subscribe for $39 a month or $300 for a whole year.

When 'hold' really means 'sell'

Research reports issued by Wall Street investment banks got a bad rap in 2002. That's when New York's attorney general began investigating a number of internal emails sent within several large Wall Street brokerage firms. The emails allegedly indicated that sell-side analysts routinely issued glowing 'strong buy' and 'buy' ratings on stocks they had serious reservations about. During the internet boom, for example, for every stock with a sell rating, there were 100 stocks with a buy rating, according to the University of Pennsylvania (www.upenn.edu/researchatpenn/article.php?76&bus). Those ratings proved to be overly optimistic in many cases, and some investors who followed the research suffered large losses as a result. The regulators alleged that analysts promoted stocks of companies that the brokerage firms hoped to sell lucrative investment-banking services to. The analysts, in turn, would receive bonuses resulting from the business that came from the companies they wrote positively about. The investigation resulted in dramatic reforms in the way investment banks handled stock research.

In 2003, ten investment-banking firms agreed to a settlement with regulators in which they would pay roughly US$1.4 billion in various penalties and fees in connection with issuing allegedly misleading research reports. (See the US Securities and Exchange Commission page at www.sec.gov/news/press/2003-54.htm for more about the case.)

The settlement resulted in several research changes that affect online investors. One of the significant outcomes of the settlement included the requirement that Wall Street investment firms make their analysts' ratings and price targets available to the public. By giving investors access to analysts' track records, investors gained the ability, thanks to several websites, to see which analysts might be worth listening to and which ones to ignore. Following the reforms, perhaps due to the greater accountability, analyst ratings improved in accuracy.

Determining which analysts are worth listening to

Don't just assume research from an independent analyst is better than research from a sell-side analyst. What really matters is performance. If an analyst is always wrong, independent or not, you probably don't want to listen to his advice. But how do you find out which analysts are the best?

✔ **You can take somebody else's word for it:** StarMine is a US operation aimed at professional money managers and Wall Street brokerages. StarMine lets investors view lists that rank the top analysts. You can find the best overall analysts and firms and also find the ones that are the most accurate in specific industry sectors, such as financial, industrial or utilities. What StarMine does is rank analysts by building a portfolio based on their recommendations.

In November of each year, StarMine, in conjunction with the *Australian Financial Review*, publishes a list of Australia's top 10 analysts. To find a list of Australia's top 20 analysts, as ranked by StarMine, visit the website at www.starmine.com and, from the Awards tab at the top, select Analyst Awards. Scroll down to Region and click on Australia/ New Zealand.

✔ **You can develop your own opinion:** After you've been reading analyst reports for a while, you'll begin to develop your own internal 'ranking system' for analysts. The pool of analysts in Australia isn't anywhere near the size of that in the US, so you may not need the assistance of performance-tracking websites like StarMine or Investars (www.investars.com), another popular analyst-tracking website.

One thing that StarMine doesn't take into account is experience. Some of the most astute and influential analysts in the business have never won a StarMine award because they didn't out-perform within the awards' terms of reference. When business is going well, time in the market is a quality often overlooked but, when things take a turn for the worse, most investors look for seasoned hands. Table 13-1 lists some of James' favourite analysts.

Table 13-1	Good Analysts May Not Be Regular Award Winners	
Name	*Sector*	*Brokerage*
John Kim	A-REITs	Merrill Lynch
Brian Johnson	Banks	J.P. Morgan
Christian Guerra	Telcos and media	Goldman Sachs JBWere
Tim Smeallie	Telstra	Citigroup

What to look for in an analyst report

Many investors who read analyst reports tend to concentrate on the analyst's rating. These investors want to know instantly whether the stock is rated as a buy, hold or sell.

Savvy investors often skip past the analyst's rating on a stock. Much of the worthwhile information in an analyst report isn't in the rating, but in the insights about the company, management and industry. Investopedia (www.investopedia.com) provides a useful guide in how to read analysts' research reports. Choose Articles from the left-hand menu, type **Analyst Recommendations** into the search window and scroll down to Articles.

One of the most important components of an analyst's report is the industry comparison. Most analysts are assigned to cover companies in a specific industry. As a result, these analysts spend time going to industry conferences to meet with employees, customers and suppliers, and build deep knowledge of industry trends. Industry information is one of the top things you should look for. Pay special attention to any signs that one company is taking market share from other competitors.

Another key component is the *price-to-target justification*. Analysts often use a variety of stock valuation techniques (explained in more detail in Chapter 11) to put a price target on a stock. A *price target* is the analyst's best guess at how much the stock may be worth in the future, usually one year from now. The most interesting part of the price target is often analysts' explanations of how they arrived at the number.

Pssst ... understanding the 'whisper number'

Many analysts put their MBAs to good use and pick apart the financial statements of companies to determine how much the stocks are truly worth. But some analysts take the lazy way out by blindly following the forecast given to them by the company. This presents a problem for online investors because companies can steer some analysts to lower their expectations for growth. And, if the company is successful in lowering the earnings bar, it's easier for the company to beat the results. The opposite can happen too. A company might convince analysts to go along with an overly optimistic view of the future, setting investors up for a disappointment.

That's where the earnings whisper number comes in. The *whisper number*, in theory, is the unofficial earnings number most investors honestly expect the company to report.

Whisper numbers gain even more prominence during strong bull markets, when investors' expectations begin to soar. For example, in April 2000, Yahoo!'s stock fell 9 per cent in the two trading days after reporting a profit of ten cents a share, which topped official earnings estimates, but missed the whisper by two cents a share.

Accessing and understanding credit ratings

Research analysts who study companies and their stocks get the most attention from many investors. But a second type of company analyst exists out there — the debt-rating analyst, or bond analyst. *Debt-rating analysts* study companies to determine how creditworthy they are. Debt-rating analysts are important because, if they determine a company is stable and trustworthy, the company can borrow money at lower interest rates. Debt-rating analysts give companies letter grades to measure their financial strength, with A being high and either C or D being the lowest grade possible.

The two major debt-rating firms are Moody's and Standard & Poor's. The ratings used by Moody's vary slightly from the ratings used by Standard & Poor's. The debt-rating firms employ armies of analysts trained to pick apart a company's financial statements looking for trouble. Although they miss problems from time to time, they're still a helpful source of information for investors.

Even if you're buying a company's stock, not its debt, credit agencies' ratings are very important because they give you an idea of how solid the company's financials are. Three leading credit agencies exist, but only the following two agencies make their ratings available for free online:

- ✔ **Moody's Australia (**www.moodys.com.au**):** Moody's provides easy online access to its credit ratings for free, but you need to register first. Then just enter the company's symbol or name in the Search field and click Go. Scroll down until you see the company's name. To find the company's rating, either hover your cursor over the gold icon or click on the company's name and scroll to the bottom of the new page. You may see several ratings for each company, but the rating of most importance to investors is the one called Senior Unsecured.

- ✔ **Standard & Poor's (**www.standardandpoors.com**):** S&P lets you view its credit ratings for the thousands of stocks it covers without having to register. When the page loads, make sure you select the Australia/New Zealand website (see Figure 13-1). It displays the country at the top of the page in the centre; if it displays United States, click on Change. In the left-hand navigation bar, click on Ratings, then click on Corporates in the left-hand navigation bar. When the page loads, click the Credit Ratings List tab at the top. This presents you with a list of more than 100 company ratings provided by Standard and Poor's.

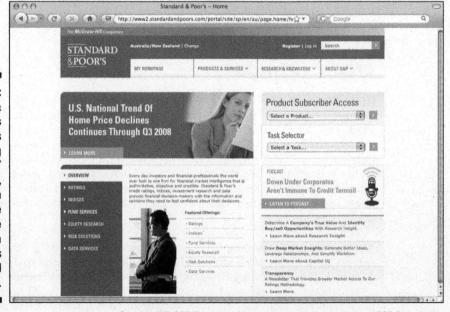

Figure 13-1:
Standard & Poor's lets you see its debt-rating analysts' ratings, which measure how secure they think a company's financial standing is.

Copyright 2008 S&P. This material is reproduced with the permission of S&P. Reproduction of this S&P information in any form is prohibited without S&P's prior written permission.

Connecting with Online Stock Ratings

Big broking houses aren't the only sources for ratings on stocks. A handful of online stock-rating services allow either a computer or other investors to rate a stock. Rating services that are based on computer models, sometimes called *quantitative* (or *quant*) *models*, analyse companies' financial statements and key ratios to decide whether the stock is a good buy. Other stock-rating services allow investors to share their ratings on stocks, with the idea that, as a whole, the average of the crowd's opinions will be close to accurate. We cover both types of stock-rating services in the following sections.

The black box: Using quant models

Research reports issued by Wall Street analysts and debt-rating analysts can be helpful, but they're not perfect. These analysts are human too, and often fail to sound the bell before financial catastrophes occur — think the collapse of dot-com stocks as well as the implosion of Enron and companies caught up in the sub-prime collapse. These missteps by human analysts have led some investors to think that it would be great if you could get ratings and recommendations on stocks, yet somehow eliminate the potential of human error or lapses in judgement. That's where quant models come in. These models are programmed by market experts to analyse stocks by using a series of criteria and to rate them. Most of these systems are untouched by human hands after they're designed. Instead, they follow very strict preset guidelines.

Often the variables that are used won't be disclosed, in which case they're referred to as *black box* quant models. This means that you have no idea what is generating the recommendation and are effectively pulling results out of a box. Although quant models are often complicated and back-tested against many years of data, they're really just a more robust version of the stock-screening models we show you how to use in Chapter 12.

Many newsletters — too many to list here — use quant models to pick stocks for a fee, without disclosing their methodology. Our advice to anybody thinking of paying for a black-box quant model or newsletter service is don't. You're much better off with a system or screen that you can control and modify rather than blindly following the advice of a computer program. After all, the number-one rule of investing is: 'If you don't understand it, don't invest in it.'

Sharing stock ratings with other investors online

In his book *The Wisdom of Crowds*, journalist James Surowiecki argues that a crowd of regular people making decisions, on average, will get closer to the right answer as a whole than just a few experts. Collectively, a group of diverse and independent-thinking people will, on average, come up with an accurate guess.

Several online sites are trying to harness this wisdom of crowds and turn the masses' guess into information you can use to boost your returns. Although no Australian-specific sites are around yet, we're sure there will be soon. In the meantime, the US sites are still helpful for identifying trends and overall sentiment. If you're really keen to follow some of their recommendations, then read Chapter 18 to find out how to go about buying stocks listed overseas. Some good sources for this kind of collective intelligence are listed here:

✔ **Motley Fool CAPS (**`http://caps.fool.com`**):** This particular corner of the Motley Fool website allows members to enter their ratings on thousands of stocks. The ratings are then compiled into a single average rating that's available to all users of the website. Just enter a stock's code into the search field and click Get Quote — you see how other CAPS users rate the stock, based on a star rating. A stock with five stars is a strong buy, and a stock with a one-star rating is a strong sell.

But CAPS gets more interesting when you dig a little deeper into the website. For example, you can read why certain CAPS members rated a stock the way they did by scrolling down the page and looking under the heading CAPS Members. And even these blurbs are rated by members, so you can read the most highly rated comments on a stock. And, if you click the Chart tab underneath the stock name, you can see how the CAPS rating has changed over the past few months. Anyone can view most CAPS ratings and information but, to rate stocks yourself, you'll need to register with the site, which is free.

And what does CAPS stand for? You're going to be sorry you asked. CAPS doesn't appear to stand for anything, but rather seems to be a play on the word cap, since the Motley Fool's founders are known for wearing jester hats. Participants in the CAPS system are assigned a colour-coded hat, or cap, icon to signal how good they've been at picking stocks.

✔ **PredictWallStreet** (www.predictwallstreet.com): PredictWallStreet lets you start sharing recommendations with others pretty quickly and easily. From the homepage, just enter a stock code into the search field and click the Up button if you recommend the stock and the Down button if you think the stock will fall. You can see the average recommendations of other users for other popular stock market indices or popular stocks. One of the nice things about this site is that you can use it without registering.

✔ **Consensus View** (www.consensusview.com): At Consensus View, you get to rate just about every stock, foreign market or investment you can think of as bullish or bearish. All the users' predictions are compiled and averaged, and you can see what other members think and how their opinions have changed over the months. You must sign up for a free membership to use the site.

Following the crowd when it comes to investing is often a bad idea. During periods of market manias, when investors become overly bullish about particular types of stocks, they often bid stock prices up too high and set themselves up for disappointment. Some investors, who call themselves *contrarians*, instead figure out what the crowd is doing and then do the opposite. If the crowd is bullish about a stock, a contrarian would assume the group is wrong and be bearish about the stock.

Evaluating the Stock-Tipping Industry

Whenever a crowd is trying to make quick money, there's no shortage of people happy to offer their expertise and skill . . . for a fee. Stock investing is no different. You can find dozens of stock- and managed-fund-picking newsletters, websites, books and seminars. They all make great pitches for why you need to pay to subscribe to their wonderful services.

By and large, many of the pitches you see for stock-picking newsletters aren't worth much, and you should be very sceptical before paying money for 'systems' and 'programs' that claim to be able to beat the market. A 1998 study by Jeffrey Jaffe and James Mahoney — available at http://papers. ssrn.com (enter **The Performance of Investment Newsletters** to the search field and click Search) — found that stocks recommended by newsletters don't out-perform the market. The study also found that newsletters tend to pile onto yesterday's winning stocks by recommending stocks that had done well in the recent past.

Before you sign up for a stock-picking service ...

Try before you buy! Almost all stock-picking services and investment newsletters offer new customers a free trial of anything from a week to a month. Sign up when you know you have enough time to read what they publish and don't sign up for several all at once or you'll never have enough time to read them all and evaluate them carefully. And, if you're still seriously considering forking out for a newsletter, make use of the free-trial period by accessing material they published one, two and three years ago through their website archives and looking at their longer term predictions.

Another good place to visit would be Mark Hulbert's column at MarketWatch (www.marketwatch.com/news/newsletters). Hulbert is a well-known tracker of newsletter performance and has built his own indicator, the Hulbert Stock Newsletter Sentiment Index, or HSNSI, which measures newsletter sentiment. Hulbert's theory is that newsletters become most enthusiastic about investing when the market nears its top. Conversely, when newsletter sentiment turns bearish, or against investing in equity markets, then markets are at their bottom.

Using newsletters to your advantage

You may be wondering, if stock-picking newsletters are often so wrong, how can they help you? Again, the contrarian approach may make sense, and it's a strategy used by many professional money managers.

The simplest way to see what newsletters are saying about stocks (and doing the opposite) is by determining how many newsletter writers are bullish and how many are bearish. When newsletter writers are nervous about the market and selling stocks, that's a signal to contrarian investors that now is a good time to buy stocks. And, when newsletter writers are bullish and buying stocks, these contrarian investors start to take money off the table by selling stocks.

Although focused on the US market, Schaeffer's Investment Research (www. schaeffersresearch.com) provides some of the information you need to be a contrarian. Click on the Market Tools link under the Quotes & Tools tab and scroll down to Other Related Tools. Select the Investor's Intelligence link. Doing so brings up the Investor's Intelligence newsletter indicator in both tabular and chart form, which tells you what percentage of newsletters are bullish and what percentage are bearish.

Don't let reading newsletters bring on a junk-mail and telemarketing deluge

One potential peril of signing up for stock-picking services and newsletters is that some sell your name and address to other companies for profit. This may fill your mailbox with ads you don't want, including pitches for shady penny stock shams, and have your phone running hot from telemarketing time-wasters.

Here are two strategies to prevent you from getting slammed by junk mail and telemarketers:

✔ Use a slightly different name when you sign up for the stock-picking service. Instead of signing up as Joe Smith, use JoeD Smith or something like that. If junk mail starts showing up to that unique name, you'll know it's the stock-picking service that's selling your information. You can call the service up and tell them to stop.

✔ Sign up for the Australian Communication and Media Authority's Do Not Call Register. This service will take you off the list from being hassled by direct marketers of all persuasions, not just stock-tipping news-letters, so don't blame us if your phone stops ringing! For more information about the register, visit the ACMA homepage at www.acma.gov.au and click on the Do Not Call Register link on the right of the screen. Or, to register, go to www.donot call.gov.au and click on the link.

Chapter 14

Researching and Buying Bonds and Other Fixed-Interest Securities

*B*onds don't make very good cocktail party chatter. Just try to brag about your 5 per cent annual bond return at a party. The only heads you'll turn will be the ones running away from you yawning. Bonds just aren't as exciting or glamorous as stocks, which can often gain more value in an hour than you'll collect from bonds all year.

But don't let the fact bonds are, well, often boring discourage you from owning them. *Bonds*, which are part of an investment class called *fixed-interest securities*, are essentially IOUs issued by governments and corporates, or companies. These IOUs come with a promise to repay the lender by a specific time at a specific interest rate that may or may not be tied to the official interest rate. These stable streams of cash flow can be very valuable if you choose bonds wisely. Bonds can help smooth out the ups and downs in your portfolio and help you reach your financial goals. Most of the time when people talk about bonds they mean government bonds and when they talk about fixed-interest securities they mean corporate bonds.

In this chapter, we explain what a bond is and how it differs from other investments, including stocks. We also show you ways to find out more about bonds and get up with the lingo. You get a chance to discover websites that let you research bonds to find the ones that might fit your portfolio the best. And we show you ways to buy bonds online, as well as a few alternatives to bonds you may want to consider.

Getting Acquainted with Bonds

If you've ever lent money to someone and set up a repayment program, you already know what a bond is. A bond is an IOU that entitles you to a stream of payments from the borrower. Bonds come in two different flavours, government bonds and corporate bonds.

Cities and government agencies often sell bonds so they can raise money to build facilities, build bridges or finance their operations. The money that was borrowed must be repaid at a predetermined interest rate (often called the *coupon rate*) and by a set time in the future (called the *maturity date*), along with the money borrowed (called the *principal*).

Bonds, by their nature, offer investors several benefits:

- **Generally stable and predictable cash payments:** Investors who aren't looking for any big surprises tend to appreciate bonds' preset rate of return. When you buy a bond and hold it until maturity, you know ahead of time what your return will be. This can be useful for meeting financial obligations.

- **Repayment of principal:** When you buy a bond, you receive back interest payments in addition to the money you lent, as long as the borrower can afford the payments and doesn't default. Investors who want to preserve their initial investment like bonds for this very reason.

- **Liquidity:** You may be familiar with term deposits, which also pay interest and return the original investments. But, unlike term deposits, which you must hold for a set period or pay a penalty, you can sell your bonds to other investors, in most cases, at any time, just like you'd sell a stock. This characteristic of bonds means you can raise cash if you need to.

You have two ways to make money from a bond. You can hold it until it matures. That way, you collect the interest as it's paid. Your other option is to sell the bond to someone else before it matures on what is called the *secondary market*. Just remember, though, when you sell a bond, you may not get back what you paid. The bond's price may fall if the bond becomes less desirable, for reasons discussed in the section 'Knowing the common traits of bonds' later in the chapter.

✔ **Diversification:** Bond prices tend to move up and down in a different pattern than stock prices. By owning stocks and bonds, you can smooth out the bumps in your portfolio. Bonds may not go up as much as stocks, but they don't usually fall as much either.

Typically, investors who need a more stable portfolio place most of their investments in bonds. But, even if you're terrified of the thought of losing money, putting your entire portfolio in bonds usually isn't a good idea. Mixing some stocks in your portfolio can reduce your risk and increase your returns because bonds and stocks usually don't rise and fall at the same time or by the same degree.

Knowing who issues debt

Before you can buy or sell bonds, you must understand there are several types of bonds, based on who sells them. Each type of bond has unique traits and can be bought or sold online differently. The following is a quick rundown of the major issuers of bonds:

✔ **Governments:** Bonds sold by the government are among the most popular, because they're backed by the balance sheet of the government that issues them. That greatly reduces, if not eliminates, the risk you won't get paid. In Australia, you can buy bonds from the Reserve Bank of Australia (www.rba.gov.au), which offers fixed-coupon bonds, where the interest rate is fixed for the term of the security, and capital-indexed bonds, where the return is adjusted for inflation.

However, most of the time when you hear people talking about government bonds, they're referring to US government bonds. These are also called *treasuries*, and come in three main varieties: Treasury bills that mature in one year or less; treasury notes that mature in more than a year and up to ten years; and treasury bonds that mature in more than ten years.

Even if you're not interested in buying bonds, it's still important to keep an eye on bond yields. Yields tell you how much return you can get for taking little to no risk. If a risk-free bond pays 5 per cent, you probably wouldn't be willing to buy a risky stock unless it promises to return considerably more than 5 per cent.

Bonds are often called risk-free investments, but that's not really true. Even bonds face *interest-rate risk*. Say you buy a bond that pays 5 per cent interest. If inflation rises, and interest rates rise to 6 per cent as a result, your 5 per cent rate of return isn't looking so hot anymore.

If you sell the bond, you'll get less for it than you paid. And if you hold on to the bond, your 5 per cent interest rate is lacklustre.

✔ **State governments:** Bonds issued by Australian state governments are considered investment grade but not as safe as bonds issued by the federal government. Because of that, they pay a slightly higher rate of return. Examples of this include the Tasmanian Public Finance Corporation, New South Wales Treasury Corporation and the South Australian Finance Authority. In the US, the ability to issue bonds has been extended to municipalities, like local government, and individual government departments. These bonds carry significantly more risk than those issued by Australian state governments.

✔ **Banks:** Banks also issue debt in the form of bank bills or bank bonds. Bank bills are short-term investments of between 30 and 180 days. They are non-transferable, which means you can't trade them on the secondary market. Bank bonds are longer term investments but have the added feature of being able to be traded before maturity.

✔ **Companies:** Bonds issued by companies, sometimes called *corporates*, allow them to pay for equipment and services they need in order to expand or grow. Companies pay higher interest rates than the government because the chance they'll default is higher. Companies may also hit hard times and have trouble paying back the money they borrowed. Bonds sold by rock-solid companies are called *investment grade*. Small companies or companies with shaky finances issue what's called *high-yield* or *junk-bond* debt. Investment-grade bonds pay lower interest rates than junk bonds because investors are more certain they'll get their money back.

The ASX gets in on the action

In 1999, the ASX decided to get in on the action, offering a range of tradable fixed-interest securities, including corporate bonds, floating-rate notes and hybrid securities. You already know about corporate bonds from the section 'Knowing who issues debt', but floating rate notes and hybrid securities? *Floating-rate notes* do not offer a fixed rate of return; they usually offer a return 1 or 2 per cent above the official cash rate. For this reason, they're popular with income-seeking investors who know that interest rate movements can adversely affect the value of a bond.

Hybrid securities, on the other hand, contain characteristics of both debt and equity. They include convertible notes and convertible preference shares. *Convertible notes* convert into shares at maturity, whereas *convertible preference shares* have a set value at maturity and are then used to buy securities in the company at a discount. Although bonds and floating-rate notes usually are relatively steady, the value of hybrid securities tends to mirror the performance of the company's equity.

Using online resources to find out more about bonds

One of the toughest things about bonds is just figuring out the vocabulary. Investors who focus on buying and selling stocks often struggle with the different terms when they enter the brave new world of bonds. It's critical, though, for you to understand the lexicon of bonds before jumping in. Several websites step you through the bond world and can get you up to speed in no time. Here's the (relatively) short list:

- **Investopedia's Bond Basics** (www.investopedia.com/university/bonds): This corner of Investopedia runs through everything you need to know to get started with bonds. The site covers the terminology and shows you how to calculate how much bonds are worth.

- **Business Spectator** (www.businessspectator.com.au): This site runs a daily overview of the international bond markets each weekday morning between 8 am and 9 am under the heading SCOREBOARD. You can find it by logging on to the website and browsing the right-hand column of the homepage.

- **ASX** (www.asx.com.au): The ASX website contains a great primer on the world of exchange-traded fixed-interest securities, including a tutorial. Visit the homepage and then select Products from the left-hand menu before clicking on Interest Rate and Hybrid Securities.

- **Reserve Bank of Australia** (www.rba.gov.au): The RBA is the issuer of federal government bonds in Australia so it stands to reason that it offers plenty of information about bonds on its website. And it does! To find yield information and current prices of bonds on the secondary market, visit the homepage and select Financial Services from the left-hand navigation bar, click on the last option, Commonwealth Government Bond Facility for Small Investors, and then, under Prices, click on Today's Indicative Buying/Selling Prices. You'll then receive a warning that the RBA does not provide investment advice. Click the OK button and at that point you'll be prompted to open up an Excel spreadsheet. Click OK again and then OK once more to view the data.

- **Bloomberg** (www.bloomberg.com): From the News dropdown menu, select Markets and then click on Bonds. This corner of Bloomberg gives you all the latest breaking news on the bond market.

- **Investing in Bonds** (www.investinginbonds.com): The name says it all. Check out the site for several well-written checklists and guides for beginning bond investors and be sure to look on the right side of the page for the Learn More column. There you can find articles that cover bond basics and things you should know.

Knowing the common traits of bonds

Bond investors have their own language — and the Investing in Bonds website (www.investinginbonds.com) provides a comprehensive glossary of terms. Just click on Glossary in the navigation bar at the top. Before you get overwhelmed by all the terms, the following list offers a quick description of the most important ones you need to know. Nearly all bonds have the following characteristics:

- **Face (or par) value:** The face value is the amount of money you'll get back when the bond matures. For many bonds, the face value is the *principal*, or amount that you've lent.

- **Interest rate:** The interest rate measures how much you'll receive as a payment in exchange for lending the money. Generally, the interest rate is a percentage of the money lent (the face value). Interest, also called the *coupon rate*, is often paid twice a year.

  Example: If you buy a $1,000 bond that pays 5 per cent interest, you'll be paid $50 a year in interest, or $25 twice a year. You'll get your $1,000 back when the bond matures.

  Interest rates can be *fixed*, meaning the same rate of interest is paid to the investor for the life of the bond. Interest rates can also be *floating* and move up or down based on the direction of interest rates paid by other bonds. Bank securities are often floating. Some bonds don't pay interest until the bond matures. These bonds, called *zero-coupon bonds*, are bought for less than their face value. Instead of receiving an interest payment twice a year, as with many bonds, a zero-coupon bond pays nothing until it matures. When the zero-coupon bond matures, the investor receives the face value, which includes the interest.

  Another example: Say you pay $600 for a zero-coupon bond that matures in ten years, when it will pay $1,000. At the end of the ten years, you get your $600 principal back plus $400. That $400 is the interest, which in this case amounts to an interest rate of more than 5 per cent a year.

- **Maturity:** A bond's maturity is the date by which it must be paid off. Debt maturities can range from just days to 20 or more years.

- **Maturity schedule:** A timeline featuring details of when and how much the bond holder gets paid.

- **Special provisions:** Bonds can be customised by the borrowers and contain unique privileges for either the seller or the buyer of the bonds. A *call* provision is especially important if you're interested in buying bonds. If a bond can be called, that means the borrower can repay the loan before the maturity date. You can expect a bond to be called if current interest rates fall below the interest rate on the bond.

✔ **Price:** You can buy bonds directly from the issuers and, when you do, you often pay the face value. But you can also buy bonds from previous owners in the secondary market and, when you do, you'll pay the current price. A bond's price is determined by many variables, such as the current interest rates on similar bonds.

When a bond's price is less than its face value, it's said to trade at a *discount*. Bonds trade at a discount when interest rates rise (say, to 6 per cent), making the bond's interest rate (say, just 5 per cent) less attractive. When a bond's price is greater than its face value, it's said to trade at a *premium*. This happens when interest rates fall (perhaps to 4 per cent), making this bond's interest rate (still at 5 per cent) look more attractive and the bond worth more.

✔ **Credit ratings:** When you buy a bond from a company, one of the biggest dangers you face is the chance the company won't be able to pay you back, or will *default*. *Credit-rating agencies* study companies' financial statements and rate them based on their ability to pay. The shakier the company, the more it will need to pay in interest to attract investors. Table 14-1 shows the ratings used by the credit-rating agencies recognised by ASIC.

✔ **Current yield:** The current yield tells you how much interest you'll receive from the bond, based on the bond's price. You can calculate a bond's current yield by dividing the annual interest payment by the purchase price.

Example: You pay $900 for a bond with a $1,000 face value that pays 5 per cent, or $50 a year, in interest. The current yield is 5.6 per cent, which is calculated by dividing $50 by $900 and multiplying by 100 to convert the answer into a percentage.

✔ **Yield to maturity:** Tells you how much interest you'll gain as a percentage of the price you paid for the bond if you hold the bond until it matures. Yield to maturity is one of the best ways to measure the true return of a bond.

Remember that bond prices fall when yields rise, almost like a seesaw. Many beginning investors get hung up on this concept. Just think of it this way: If you own a bond that yields 5 per cent, but yields on similar bonds rise to 6 per cent, your 5 per cent looks pretty paltry. If you try to sell your bond, you have to cut the price to find a buyer. If someone tells you bonds are down, make sure you know if they're talking about bond yields or bond prices.

✔ **Duration:** A bond's *duration* measures the time it takes, on average, for the bond buyer to get her money back. Duration differs from maturity in that it counts the interest payments made before the bond comes due. Duration is very handy because it can help you compare different bonds and determine which ones are more volatile. The larger the duration, the longer it takes for investors to get their money back, which makes them more volatile. Investopedia's Bond Duration Calculator will tell you a bond's duration. Visit www.investopedia.com, click on Calculators in the left-hand column and then select Duration on Coupon Price. Enter the bond's details, including face value, yield to maturity, interest rate, current maturity and the schedule for payments.

Table 14-1		Credit Ratings	
Investment Grade			
Fitch	Moody's	Standard & Poor's	
AAA	Aaa	AAA	Highest credit quality
AA	Aa	AA	High credit quality
A	A	A	Good credit quality
BBB	Baa	BBB	Moderate credit quality
Non-Investment Grade			
Fitch	Moody's	Standard & Poor's	
BB	Ba	BB	Speculative
B	B	B	Highly speculative
CCC	Caa	CCC	High default risk
CC	Ca	CC	High default risk
C		C	High default risk
DDD	C	D	Default
DD			Default

Source: ASIC.

Understanding the yield curve

Whenever you read about or investigate bonds, you'll inevitably hear someone mention the yield curve. The yield curve is a chart that shows you how yields on short-term fixed-interest securities (with maturities of three months or less) compare with long-term bonds (with maturities of 30 years or so). Generally, yield curves come in four shapes:

✔ **Normal:** Most of the time, investors demand higher interest rates on long-term bonds than they do on short-term notes. That's natural. If you let someone borrow money for 30 years, you'll want more interest because there's a greater chance you'll never see your money again. That's why yields (most of the time) will be at their lowest point for the short-term fixed-interest securities and gradually move higher.

✔ **Steep:** Most of the time, investors demand two or more percentage points in extra yield when lending money for 30 years compared with lending money for a short time. If the interest rate on a three-month note is 4 per cent, investors will demand 6 per cent or higher on a comparable long-term bond in normal times. But, if the difference between the short-term and long-term rates gets even wider, that creates a steep yield curve. A steep yield curve often indicates investors expect economic growth to speed up.

✔ **Inverted:** When investors are willing to lend money for the long term and accept lower interest rates than they'd take for a short-term loan, the yield curve is inverted. Inverted yield curves can indicate that investors are worried the economy is about to slow down for a prolonged period. If the economy slows down, interest rates in the future may also fall. That means investors want to lock in current interest rates for the long term before they decline.

✔ **Flat:** When the interest rates on short-term loans equal long-term rates, you have a flat yield curve. A flat yield curve indicates investors aren't all too sure about where the economy is headed.

Understanding Other Types of Fixed-Interest Securities

Although we've outlined the four main types of bonds earlier in this chapter, the many varieties of fixed-interest securities offered by corporations deserve further explanation. With the exception of capital-guaranteed products, they all entail more risk than your garden-variety government bond; as a result, they also provide greater returns. ASIC advises investors that banks, building societies, credit unions, super funds and life insurance companies are the only institutions specially overseen by the regulator to ensure that they can meet their obligations. Securities issued by any other institution are just as risky, if not more so, than shares. Here are the main types:

- **Debentures:** These are a type of corporate bond, but the term is generally used to describe lower quality or junk corporate bonds. Corporate bonds of AA-rated entities like a blue-chip mining company are a long way from those of unlisted investment companies, which means they should be viewed cautiously. The funds themselves are used to finance a range of business activities, including lending the funds to other businesses. Because they're mostly unlisted, they're vastly illiquid, and ascertaining their face value is virtually impossible.

- **Mortgage trusts:** Money you invest in a mortgage trust is then lent on to residential or commercial property developers in exchange for quarterly or twice-yearly payments known as *distributions*. Neither your distributions nor your capital are guaranteed. Mortgage trusts are often extremely *illiquid*, which means they're difficult to change into cash at short notice. Mortgage trusts mainly exist to lend money to property developers who can't get a line of credit from a bank. And, if a bank isn't prepared to lend money to them, why are you?

- **Promissory notes:** These securities are almost exactly what they sound like, a promise to pay you an agreed sum of money at a fixed time in the future. Because promissory notes with a face value of less than $50,000 fall outside the Corporations Act, which the regulator can use to protect investors, they're often used to raise short-term finance for companies with less than stellar credit ratings (and we're being very kind!).

- **Capital-guaranteed products:** In periods of sharemarket volatility, you often see a rash of products that are marketed as *capital guaranteed*. These are mostly complicated fixed-term investments based on derivatives that promise to, at worst, return your capital at the end of the term. Although this might sound attractive, these products are frequently loaded up with fees and your upside is cut off at the knees. Regardless of the performance of the underlying securities, your return will be capped at the *headline* rate; that is, the rate that's advertised as the biggest return you can hope for.

You also need to consider the time value of money. If the investment goes belly up and your stake of $10,000 is returned to you after three years, and inflation has been running at 3 per cent, then your capital is now worth only $9,126.

Finding and Buying Bonds Online

Just as with stocks, there's no one way to buy bonds. You can buy individual bonds using a mainstream online broker, you can buy directly from the borrowers or you can deal with brokers that specialise in bonds. But you can also buy bonds through a managed fund or exchange-traded fund. In the following sections, we show you how to buy bonds using these major methods.

Doing the legwork: Finding individual bonds online

Finding bonds and other fixed-interest securities is a similar process to that of finding stocks or units in a managed fund, but slightly more difficult. Because they're not quite as sexy as stocks in the world of high finance, the breadth of whiz-bang tools available for other financial instruments isn't readily on offer, but don't let that stop you. Here are a few places to start your search:

- ✔ **Bloomberg** (www.bloomberg.com.au) is a global financial service that has a dedicated section for government bonds. Load up the homepage, place your cursor over Market Data and select Rates and Bonds. From there, click the Australia tab underneath the heading Government Bonds (see Figure 14-1).

- ✔ **The ASX** (www.asx.com.au) offers prices of all exchange-traded fixed-interest securities online, delayed by 20 minutes. Visit the homepage and select Products from the left-hand menu before clicking on Interest Rate and Hybrid Securities. Then, under the heading Statistics and News, click on Prices and Specifications for a full list of securities alongside current prices in the secondary market, coupon rate, maturity date and payment frequency.

- ✔ **AFR Smart Investor** (www.afrsmartinvestor.com.au/tools/tables/ Fixed_interest.pdf) produces a table of both exchange-tradeable fixed-interest securities and government bonds, shown in Figure 14-2. Go to the homepage, click on Shares Tables in the top menu bar and scroll down to Fixed Interest Securities at the bottom of the list of monthly tables. As an added bonus, you can print out the sheet for further reference; however, be warned, it's only updated once a month so it should be used as a rough guide only.

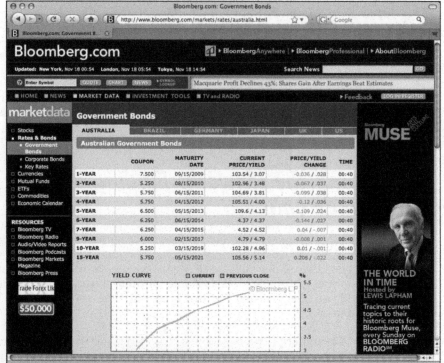

Figure 14-1: Bloomberg offers an overview of the market for Australian government bonds.

FIXED INTEREST LOAN SECURITIES

Authority AASE code	Rate %	Maturity date	Next payable	Paid p.a.
ABN AMRO BANK N.V.				
ABOHE	6.250	24/03/2010	24/03/2009	2
ABOHF	0.000	24/03/2010	24/12/2008	4
ABOHG	6.500	17/05/2018	17/11/2008	2
ABOHH	0.000	17/05/2018	17/11/2008	4
A.B.C. LEARNING CENTRES LIMITED				
ABSG	9.968	13/06/2016	13/12/2008	2
AUSTRALIAN CENTRAL CREDIT UNION LIMITED				
ACDHC	9.000	31/07/2015	1/10/2008	4
ADELAIDE BANK LIMITED				
ADBHB	8.290	0/00/0000	1/12/2008	4
ADBHC	6.250	22/05/2009	22/11/2008	2
ADBHD	0.000	22/05/2009	22/11/2008	4
ADBHE	0.000	28/03/2012	28/09/2008	4
ALLCO FINANCE GROUP LIMITED				
AFGHA	10.040	15/11/2017	17/11/2008	2
ALPHA FINANCIAL PRODUCTS LIMITED				
AFPHA	10.443	20/03/2012	22/03/2009	2
AINSWORTH GAME TECHNOLOGY LIMITED				
AGIG	8.000	17/12/2009	31/12/2008	2
ALLCO HYBRID INVESTMENT TRUST				
AHUG	10.290	17/08/2009	18/02/2009	2
AUSTRALIA AND NEW ZEALAND BANKING GROUP LIMITED				
ANZHC	6.000	2/03/2009	2/03/2009	2
ANZHD	0.000	2/03/2009	2/12/2008	4
ANZHE	6.500	21/05/2014	21/11/2008	2
ANZHF	0.000	21/05/2014	21/11/2008	4
ANZHI	0.000	1/03/2010	1/12/2008	4
ANZHJ	6.000	1/03/2010	1/03/2009	2
ANZHK	0.000	17/08/2015	17/11/2008	4
ANZHL	6.000	17/08/2015	17/02/2009	2
ANZHM	6.000	1/03/2011	1/03/2009	2
ANZHN	0.000	1/03/2011	1/12/2008	4
ANZHO	6.250	23/05/2016	23/11/2008	2
ANZHP	0.000	23/05/2016	23/11/2008	4
ANZHQ	6.500	8/11/2011	8/11/2008	2
ANZHR	0.000	8/11/2011	8/11/2008	4

Authority AASE code	Rate %	Maturity date	Next payable	Paid p.a.
COMMONWEALTH BANK OF AUSTRALIA				
CBAHD	6.000	24/06/2009	24/12/2008	2
CBAHE	0.000	24/06/2009	24/12/2008	4
CBAHJ	6.250	12/03/2010	12/03/2009	2
CBAHK	0.000	12/03/2010	12/12/2008	4
CBAHL	7.750	21/01/2011	21/01/2009	2
CBAHM	0.000	21/01/2011	21/10/2008	4
CBAHN	8.500	24/06/2011	24/12/2008	2
CBAHO	0.000	24/06/2011	24/12/2008	4
CHINA CENTURY CAPITAL LIMITED				
CCYG	12.000	30/09/2010	7/10/2008	2
COMPAGNIE DE FINANCEMENT FONCIER				
CFFHA	5.750	17/02/2010	17/02/2009	2
CFFHB	5.500	22/09/2015	22/03/2009	2
CFFHC	6.250	30/01/2017	30/01/2009	2
CHALLENGER MILLENIUM SERIES 2007-1E TRUST				
CHJHA	0.000	7/04/2038	7/10/2008	4
CHJHB	0.000	7/04/2038	7/10/2008	4
CHJHC	0.000	7/04/2038	7/10/2008	4
CHJHD	0.000	7/04/2038	7/10/2008	4
CHJHE	0.000	7/04/2038	7/10/2008	4
CHALLENGER MILLENNIUM SERIES 2007-2L TRUST				
CHUHA	0.000	7/12/2038	7/10/2008	12
CHUHB	0.000	7/12/2038	7/10/2008	12
CHUHC	0.000	7/12/2038	7/10/2008	12
CENTRO SHOPPING CENTRE SECURITIES LIMITED.CMBS SERIES 2006-1				
CMBHA	0.000	20/06/2013	20/12/2008	4
CMBHB	0.000	20/06/2013	20/12/2008	4
CMBHC	0.000	20/06/2013	20/12/2008	4
CRUSADE EURO TRUST NO.1E OF 2007				
CSNHA	0.000	13/09/2038	15/12/2008	4
CSNHB	0.000	13/09/2038	13/10/2008	12
CRUSADE ABS SERIES 2008-1 TRUST				

Authority AASE code	Rate %	Maturity date	Next payable	Paid p.a.
GREAT SOUTHERN LIMITED				
GTPGA	6.400	31/12/2036	31/10/2008	2
GTPGB	7.750	31/12/2050	31/10/2008	2
HYPOTHEKENBANK IN ESSEN AKTIENGESELLSCHAFT				
HESHA	6.000	30/11/2016	30/11/2008	2
HALCYON SECURITIES LIMITED				
HLCHA	11.193	3/08/2010	5/11/2008	4
HEEMSKIRK CONSOLIDATED LIMITED				
HSKG	8.000	29/04/2011	30/09/2008	2
HARVEY TRUST 2006-1				
HTRHA	0.000	11/09/2037	11/10/2008	12
SERIES 2007-1 HARVEY TRUST				
HTVHA	0.000	11/07/2038	11/10/2008	12
HY-FI SECURITIES LIMITED				
HYFHA	9.092	8/10/2008	8/10/2008	4
HYFHB	10.742	8/10/2008	8/10/2008	4
HYPO REAL ESTATE BANK INTERNATIONAL AKTIENGESELLSCHAFT				
HYPHA	0.000	22/02/2011	22/11/2008	4
HYPHB	5.750	7/03/2016	7/03/2009	2
HYPHC	6.250	16/08/2011	16/02/2009	2
IAG FINANCE (NEW ZEALAND) LIMITED				
IANG	6.340	31/12/2036	15/12/2008	4
INSTITUTO DE CREDITO OFICIAL				
ICFHB	5.500	11/10/2012	11/10/2008	2
ICFHC	5.500	8/03/2011	8/03/2009	2
ICFHD	6.000	19/10/2009	19/10/2008	2
ICFHE	6.125	27/02/2014	27/02/2009	2
INTER-AMERICAN DEVELOPMENT BANK				
IDBHB	5.750	15/06/2011	15/12/2008	2
ILLAWARRA SERIES 2006-1 RMBS TRUST				
ILAHA	0.000	14/10/2037	14/10/2008	12
ILLAWARRA SERIES 2005-1 RMBS TRUST				
ILWHA	0.000	14/10/2036	14/10/2008	12

Figure 14-2: AFR Smart Investor provides a handy table of bonds and fixed-interest securities that you can print out.

Sealing the deal: Buying individual bonds online

When you've found the bond that's right for you, you'll want to seal the deal. There are about as many different ways to buy bonds as there are types of bonds themselves. Following are the main ways you can go about it.

Government and semi-government bonds

If you want to save on fees and charges (and we assume you do because you're reading this book), then you can go straight to the source and buy directly from the government. For federal government bonds, visit the RBA website (www.rba.gov.au), click on Financial Services in the left-hand navigation bar and then click on the last option, Commonwealth Government Bond Facility for Small Investors, where you can find all the information you need for buying and selling federal government bonds. If you want to buy state government bonds, see Table 14-2 for the respective web addresses.

Table 14-2	Issuers of State Government Bonds
Issuer	*Web Address*
New South Wales Treasury Corporation	www.tcorp.nsw.gov.au
Queensland Treasury Corporation	www.qtc.com.au
South Australian Government Financing Authority	www.safa.sa.gov.au
Tasmanian Public Finance Corporation	www.tascorp.com.au
Treasury Corporation of Victoria	www.tcv.vic.gov.au
Western Australian Treasury Corporation	www.watc.wa.gov.au

On the other hand, if you want to talk turkey before you buy bonds (and perhaps get some advice about their different features) then going through a broker is perhaps the best way. Alternatively, you can go through one of the many mainstream financial institutions that sell bonds and fixed-interest securities, usually starting at $5,000. You can find a comprehensive list of brokers at the ASX website (www.asx.com.au). Visit the homepage and then select Products from the left-hand menu before clicking on Interest Rate and Hybrid Securities. Under the heading How Interest Rate Securities Work, click on the link for a list of advisers, where you'll find a list of all the big names.

Some brokers charge so-called *mark-up* fees for bonds. Mark-up fees are added to the price of the bond. For example, you might buy a bond for $1,000 but later see that you actually paid $1,045, where $1,000 is the price of the bond and $45 is the mark-up. Mark-up fees aren't illegal, and they're a common way for brokers to charge commissions for buying bonds. You just want to find out ahead of time how much the mark-up fee will be and make sure you weren't overcharged by reviewing the confirmation of your order.

Corporate bonds and fixed-interest securities

Much like government bonds, you can cut out the middleman and approach the issuer directly. You need to visit the website of the company issuing the bonds, print out an application form and send it off with your details and a cheque.

You can also buy many corporate bonds and fixed-interest securities through a broker. The best thing about this is that you can get advice if you need it, but you'll be charged for the privilege. The ASX provides a list of brokers at its website (www.asx.com.au). Select Products from the left-hand menu and then click on Interest Rate and Hybrid Securities. Under the heading How Interest Rate Securities Work, click on the link for a list of advisers.

Exchange-traded fixed-interest securities

The beauty of exchange-traded securities is that they perform just like shares, and they can be bought just like shares as well (refer to Chapter 4 if you need to refresh your memory). Although they tend to be more liquid than other bonds, they aren't anywhere near as liquid as shares, so keep that in mind.

Considering Bond Alternatives

The relative safety of bonds, as well as their lower volatility, make them well suited for many investors' portfolios. But don't make the mistake of thinking bonds are without risk. The Investing in Bonds site (www.investinginbonds.com) describes the risks of bonds in detail. From the Learn More list on the right of the page, under the heading What You Should Know, click on Learn More and then scroll down to Risks of Investing in Bonds.

These are the risks you should be most aware of:

- **Default risk:** Unless you're buying government bonds, you're taking a chance the borrower won't pay you back.

- **Market risk:** If bonds go out of favour because investors are seeking higher returns, the price of your bonds may decline.

- **Liquidity risk:** From time to time, investors get nervous about the economy or about bonds, and they simply refuse to buy bonds. This is generally more of a problem with unusual or rare bonds, and it isn't a worry with government or investment-grade bonds.

- **Interest rate risk:** The threat of higher interest rates is one of the biggest risks you face when you buy a bond. If rates rise, the interest rate you locked in suddenly isn't so lucrative, which decreases the value of your bond.

Some investors have an aversion to bonds for these reasons and others. These investors don't like the fact that bond values can fall, because bonds are supposed to be safer investments. If you're a bond hater, keep reading. The rest of this section explores a few bond alternatives.

- **Bond funds:** Buying individual bonds can be somewhat complex. You need to understand yields, prices, duration and other cryptic measures of value. You can find bond funds with the same managed-fund screening tools discussed in Chapter 8. But think twice before buying a long-term government bond managed fund. You'll pay an annual fee for the fund, sometimes 1 per cent a year. That's probably not a good idea considering you can buy them direct.

- **ETFs:** Another option for buying bonds is through exchange-traded funds. ETFs, explained in depth in Chapter 11, are baskets of investments that trade like stocks. A bond ETF is ideal for investors who primarily buy stocks but want to easily add bonds to their portfolio and keep fees down. It's easy to get started. Just pick the bond ETF you want and buy it through your online broker just as you'd buy a stock. You can read how to buy and sell stocks in Chapter 4.

- **Online transaction accounts and term deposits:** For some investors, bonds can be a lot of work for just 1 or 2 per cent over the cash rate. If you're happy with the kinds of returns available to you on an at-call or term basis, then visit www.infochoice.com.au and click the Savings Account tab to make sure you're getting the best deal.

Taking On More Risk: Is It Worth It?

An unfortunate feature of the last few years has been the collapse of various schemes that utilised debentures, promissory notes, mortgage trusts or sometimes a collection of all three to gather capital from investors. One of the reasons these schemes were allowed to flourish was the relatively low levels of supervision that some of these types of investments are subject to in comparison with listed companies and financial institutions.

The schemes were pitched mainly to unsophisticated investors by taking out big colourful ads in mainstream media and sometimes using well-known sports personalities in their promotion. The rates of return were generally only a few per cent over what you get from an online savings account but the companies were involved in highly speculative property developments and paying exorbitant kickbacks to the planners who recommended the investments.

When the money ran out, close to a billion dollars was lost by investors in the Westpoint, Fincorp and Australian Capital Reserve collapses of 2006–07. Ask yourself if you're prepared to take the chance of losing everything for just a few dollars more.

Part IV
Expanding Your Investment Opportunities

Glenn Lumsden

'But how can I sleep when I know that, somewhere out there, a foreign stock exchange is open for trading?'

In this part ...

Fancy a taste of adventure? This part takes your online investing another step further, dealing with some of the offerings that more confident investors choose from time to time. We look at different trading techniques and technical analysis, and we delve into derivatives like going short and buying options. We also take a careful look at buying international stocks online.

Chapter 15

Going off the Beaten Path with Different Trading Techniques

*I*f all you could do was buy and sell investments, traders would get awfully bored. Investors looking for a little more excitement can dabble with some more-advanced ways to enter online trades that go beyond these 'vanilla' investing strategies. The most common ways to get a little fancier with your trades are:

✔ **Selling stock short:** A way to make money even if a stock declines in value.

✔ **Buying stock on margin:** This method lets you bet big on a stock you think will go up. You borrow money to buy stock, which will magnify your returns if it rises.

✔ **Examining your options:** Use a small stake to build a large position with derivatives like options and warrants.

Cashing In When Stocks Fall: Selling Stock Short

Most investors are pretty optimistic. When they go to a hotel with great fittings, get great service and see plenty of other people having a great time, they rush home to buy stock in the listed company that owns the hotel. This type of investor, who hopes to profit from a company's good times and rising profits, takes what is called a *long position*.

But a whole other class of investment is out there also, called *short positions*, where investors do just the opposite. They might visit a hotel that's rundown, unfriendly and serving bad food, for example, and look for ways to cash in on the stock falling.

Investors looking to *short a stock* do it through four steps:

1. **They borrow the stock they want to bet against.**

   Short-sellers contact their brokers to find shares of the stock they think will go down and they request to borrow the shares. The broker then locates another investor who owns the shares and borrows them, with a promise to return the shares at a prearranged later date. The shares are then given to the short-seller.

2. **Short-sellers immediately sell the shares they've borrowed.**

   They then pocket the cash from the sale.

3. **Short-sellers wait for the stock to fall and then buy the shares back at the new, lower price.**

4. **They return the shares to the brokerage they borrowed them from and pocket the difference.**

Here's an example: Shares of XYZ are trading for $40 a share, which you think is way too high. You contact your broker, who finds 100 shares from another investor and lets you borrow them. You sell the shares and pocket $4,000. Two weeks later, the company reports its CEO has been stealing money and the stock falls to $25 a share. You buy 100 shares of XYZ for $2,500, give the shares back to the brokerage you borrowed them from and pocket a $1,500 profit.

When you short a stock, you should be aware of some extra costs. Most brokerages, for example, charge fees or interest to borrow the stock. Also, if the company pays a dividend between the time you borrowed the stock and when you returned it, you must pay the dividend out of your pocket. You're responsible for the dividend payment, even if you've already sold the stock and didn't receive it.

Tracking the short-sellers

You may be interested to find out how many investors are shorting a stock you own, a statistic known as *short interest*. Some investors even incorporate tracking short interest in their strategies by seeking stocks that are heavily shorted, on the theory that, if the shorts are wrong, the stock may surge higher in a *short squeeze*, or a *bear trap*. This is what happens when the short-sellers get nervous that a stock they're betting against will rise and they rush out and buy the stock back so they can return it to the brokers they borrowed from.

The Australian Securities Exchange (ASX) requires brokers to disclose their net short positions at 9 am each morning. The ASX has approved around 250 stocks and ETFs for shorting, and updates the short interest on these lists every morning. Although the frequency that this information is updated is commendable (the NASDAQ, for example, only updates this information once every month), the ASX has been criticised for significantly underestimating the volume of short-selling by excluding much of the trading done by hedge funds because it doesn't meet the definition of short-selling set by the ASX. With that in mind, the ASX list of net short-sale positions should be taken with a grain of salt and used as a rough guide only.

To check out the ASX list of net short-sale positions, go to the homepage (www.asx.com.au), click on Sitemap and then select Detailed View. Click on Education & Resources and select Short Sales. From here, scroll to the bottom of the page and click on Download the Report. If this is information you might be regularly interested in, you may want to bookmark this link for later use.

Here you see a detailed list of all the ASX-approved short-sale products and exchange-traded funds, and three columns of numbers (see Figure 15-1). The first column of figures lists the number of shares that have been reported by brokers as borrowed for the purposes of shorting. In the next column is the total number of shares issued by the company. In the final column the number of shares being shorted is expressed as a percentage. In this case, the higher the percentage, the higher the number of investors who are hoping for the share price to go down.

Understanding what you can and can't short-sell

There are rules about what you can and can't short-sell ... and then there are even more rules! Short-selling has always been very carefully monitored by the regulators but, following the financial crisis of 2007–08, the regulators moved to suspend short-selling while the sharemarket regained stability. Various exceptions were made to the rule, however, and whether or not the suspension had any effect on the overall market is debatable.

But let's start with the basics first. Short-selling is only allowed of 'approved' securities, which we note in the previous section, 'Tracking the short-sellers'. In addition, you can't short a stock that is under a takeover offer. If you know enough about a stock to want to short it, we presume you also know whether it's under a takeover offer or not, but you can check by seeing if it has 'NS' after its name on the ASX website or your online broker's site. The third rule you need to keep in mind is the *up-tick rule*. This means that you can't short-sell your stock at a lower price than the previous sale.

Living On Borrowed Time: Buying Stock on Margin

The standard brokerage account is called a *cash-management account*. That's where you deposit cold hard cash with the broker and use that pooled money to buy stocks. But when you set up your account, as we describe in Chapter 3, you can also request a *margin account*. This is an account type that lets you borrow money you can use to buy stocks.

Buying stock on margin isn't for the faint of heart. Remember, if you borrow money, you must not only pay interest on that cash but also eventually pay back the money you borrowed, even if the stock goes down. Buying on margin is generally a good idea *only* if you're a highly risk-tolerant investor. You can determine your taste for risk by reading Chapter 1.

Calculating returns when buying on margin

As is the case anytime you borrow to invest, buying stock on margin can boost your profit when you're right and sting badly when you're wrong. When you buy a stock that goes up, using margin, you can boost your returns. But, if your bet is wrong and you buy one that goes down, margin magnifies your loss. To understand why, take a look at the following example:

Imagine buying 50 shares of a stock that goes from $40 a share to $50 a share. Your investment of $2,000 turns into $2,500. Assuming you paid a $30 commission both when you buy and when you sell the stock, your rate of return, as we explain in Chapter 1, is 21.6 per cent and your profit is $440.

It's calculated like this:

1. **Subtract the commission of $30 from the sale proceeds of $2,500. Write this down.**

2. **Add the commission of $30 to the amount paid of $2,000. Write this down.**

3. **Subtract the answer to Step 2 from the answer to Step 1 and divide that answer by the answer to Step 2. Multiply by 100.**

That $440 profit represents a pretty good return, but, if you bought on margin, then your return would be even bigger. Here's how it works. Brokers allow you to borrow money to invest in certain stocks, providing you can meet the *loan-to-value ratio*, or *LVR*. Big online broking houses routinely require an LVR of 70 per cent for most blue-chip stocks. This means that you can borrow 70 per cent of the purchase price, but you'll need to put up 30 cents for every dollar you invest. In this case, you put up $600 of your own cash — that's 30 per cent of the $2,000 purchase price. You then borrow the remaining $1,400 at 10 per cent interest. Thanks to margin lending, your rate of return goes from 21.6 per cent to 47.6 per cent.

Here's how your rate of return when using margin is calculated, using the facts above as the example:

1. **Subtract the commission of $30 from the sale proceeds of $2,500.**

   Write this down, $2,470.

2. **Add the commission of $30 to the amount paid of $2,000.**

   Write this down, $2,030.

3. **Multiply the amount you borrowed, $1,400, by 10 per cent to calculate the interest you owe.**

4. **Subtract the answer to Step 2 from the answer to Step 1.**

   Subtract the answer to Step 3, $140, from that difference, $440. You get $300.

5. **Divide the answer to Step 4 by $630, which is the amount of your own money you put up plus the commission you paid to buy the stock.**

   Multiply by 100. The answer is 47.6 per cent.

If the preceding is too much maths for you, do it online. Most online brokers' sites calculate your margin requirements. If you're interested in buying on margin, make sure the broker has margin-tracking capabilities. Figure 15-2 shows AFR Smart Investor's free gearing simulator. To access the application, visit www.afrsmartinvestor.com.au and click on the Tools tab. Then scroll down to Investment and click on the link Margin Lending Calculator — Gearing Simulator.

The call you don't want to get: The margin call

Most online brokers require investors to maintain a certain percentage of ownership of stocks relative to what has been borrowed. This is called the *maintenance margin*, and it's typically 30 per cent at most firms. If a stock rises, this isn't a problem because the value of the loan becomes a smaller slice of the position. But, if the stock falls in value, the shareholder's stake shrinks. If it falls below 30 per cent, the broker requires the investor to put up more cash, or the shares will be sold.

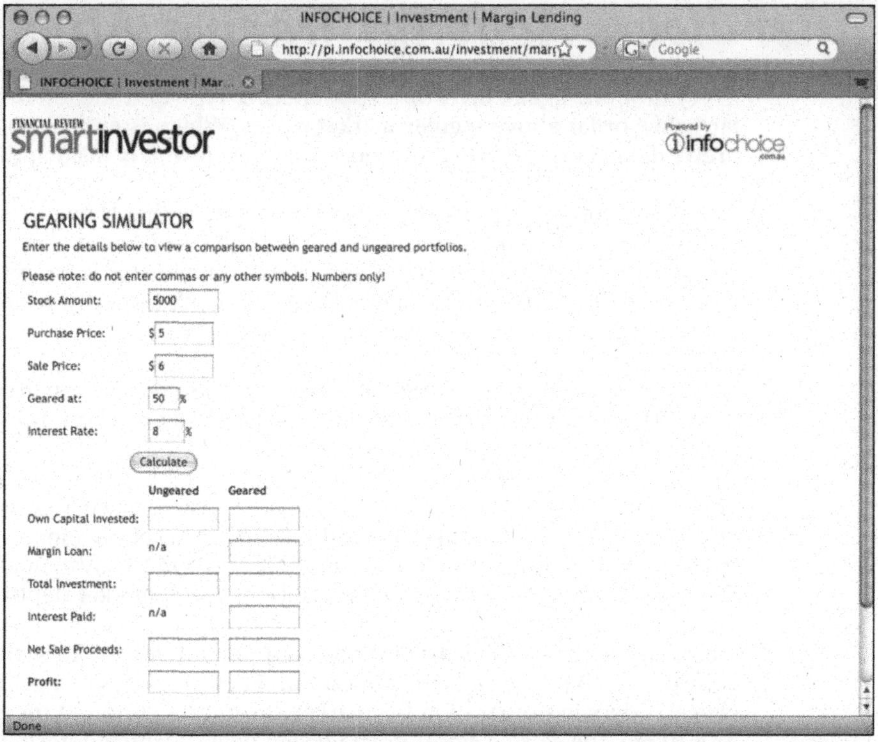

Figure 15-2:
AFR Smart
Investor's
Gearing
Simulator
helps you
measure
how much
stock
you can
buy with
borrowed
money and
estimate the
costs.

Imagine that, when you bought the $40-a-share stock from the example in the preceding section, you borrowed 70 per cent, or $28 a share, meaning your ownership stake is $12 a share, or 30 per cent. But say the stock falls to $35 a share. Because you borrowed $12 a share, you own only $7 of the $35 share price. That means you own just 20 per cent of the stock, violating the 30 per cent margin requirement.

If you still have questions about investing on margin, Citibank provides an easy-to-follow description of margin. Go to the homepage (`www.citibank.com`) and click on Planning. Select Investment Planning from the options on the left, scroll down through the list of articles to All About Stocks and select Buying on Margin.

Some online brokers will crunch down the numbers for you automatically and let you know when margin calls will kick in. And you can be certain online brokers won't waste any time contacting you for a margin call. But if the preceding calculations seem too complicated to do yourself, you may want to steer clear of using margin.

After-Hours Activity: Trading After Dark

Every now and again, investors spot another type of trade, often at prices far below or far above regular market prices. Which is enough to make you pretty damn curious! What are these trades and who is making them?

One of the great things about stocks and bonds is that they're easy to sell. Unlike real estate, which usually requires hiring a real estate agent who sprinkles air freshener through the house and invites prospective buyers to an open house, you can sell stocks pretty much instantly, as long as it's between the hours of 10 am and 4 pm, Monday to Friday.

So, if you're viewing the course of sales or market depth, you may come across these unusual records of sale (you can find out about these records of sale and dissecting stock quotes in Chapter 16).

From 7 am to 10 am the market is in *pre-open*, when brokers enter orders into ITS (refer to Chapter 4) to prepare for the market opening. Overseas trades and off-market transfers are also recorded in the system at this time, which often accounts for any movement you see in market depth.

For most investors, the market closes at 4 pm but, for brokers, the market goes back into pre-open, which allows brokers to enter, change and cancel orders in preparation for market close for a period of ten minutes. At 4.10 pm, the *closing single price auction* begins, which determines the closing price. In most markets, a spread exists between the bid and the ask, and in this case the closing price is taken from the last trade executed. But, in the case of the spread disappearing and prices overlapping, a complicated series of equations determines the closing price.

Between 4.11 pm and 5.00 pm, the ASX allows brokers to trade under a number of circumstances. Errors, off-market transfers and orders received before the closing single price auction may take place at this point. ITS does not execute trades and new orders can't be entered. At 5.00 pm the market goes into *after-hours adjust*, when brokers can cancel unwanted orders, amend orders and otherwise tidy up their order books. So, although some action seems to be taking place outside the regular trading hours, rest assured that it's all part of the administrative process.

Three codes that pop up frequently in after-hours trading are XT, EP and EC. *XT* refers to a *cross trade*, which is when a single broker is behind both the buying and the selling of shares, and can often happen between clients of a broker, for example. They can't just swap the paper between accounts, however; the transaction needs to be recorded. *EP* and *EC* are *exercised puts* and *exercised calls*, which we explain in more detail in the next section.

Knowing Your Options: Basic Ways to Best Use Options

If you've ever put down a deposit so someone would hold something for you, you know what an option is. For example, you may pay someone a $100 non-refundable deposit to hold a car so that it'll be available for you if you decide to buy it. If you don't buy the car, you lose the $100.

Options are the financial version of that idea. If you own an option, you have the right, but not the obligation, to buy or sell an investment, including shares of stock by a certain preset time in the future. Options can be extremely powerful in the right hands, and they can either help you boost your returns or reduce your risk, depending on how you use them.

We often describe options as the financial version of dynamite. If used prudently and safely, options can remove perils in the way of your financial goals. But, if abused, misunderstood or used recklessly, options can blow your financial plan to smithereens.

Buying trouble by buying calls

Buying calls is the best way to maximise returns if a stock is about to go up. And that's why they're perfect tools for investors who use *illegal insider information* about stocks for personal gain. Illegal insider information is important information the public doesn't know yet but will move the stock when the news gets out. It's illegal to trade using important and confidential information you get from working for a company or being connected to people with such secret information. For just a little cash, these investors can post giant gains when the *market-moving news* — news they already know about — hits the market.

A classic example involved the News Corporation takeover bid for Dow Jones in 2007. News Corporation proprietor Rupert Murdoch had made a formal approach to the Dow Jones board with a written offer of $60 a share on 17 April — a premium of roughly 45 per cent to its trading price at the time. But the offer was not made public until 1 May, which opened a large window for insider trading to occur. As it turned out, on 25 April an investor bought an option to buy 280,000 Dow Jones shares for $40 each. Each option cost a mere 85c each, or a total of around $238,000. But, when the takeover offer was announced, the shares jumped to $56 and each option was instantly *in the money* to the tune of $16 each, or a paper profit of $4.5 million. In this case, however, the volume of options in the company rarely exceeded 100,000 a day, let alone 280,000 in a single order, which gave the game away. The Securities and Exchange Commission (the US regulator) has since fined the four people involved more than $24 million for insider trading.

When you own an option, you have the power to make someone follow through on a trade for an *underlying asset*, such as a stock, no matter what happens to the price. Depending on their length, options expire on the Thursday before the last business Friday in the month.

Need an example? Say XYZ stock is currently trading for $30 a share, and you own an option to buy it for $20 a share on its *expiration date* in one month. That option is worth $10 a share, the difference between $30 and $20, which is its *intrinsic value*. If you own an option like this that lets you buy a stock for less than its current value, it's *in the money*. But, if the price you can buy the stock at, known as the *exercise price*, is higher than the current price, the option is *out of the money*.

The different types of options

Options strategies can get pretty complex. If you're serious about trading them, you can find out all the gory details in *Futures & Options For Dummies*, by Joe Duarte (Wiley Publishing Inc.). But we're perfectly willing to give you the basics.

Two types of options exist:

- **Calls** give their owners the right, but not the obligation, to buy a stock at a certain price (called the *exercise* or *strike price*) at a certain time (called the *expiration date*) in the future. One call contract gives you the right to buy 1,000 shares of the underlying stock.

- **Puts** give their owners the right, but not the obligation, to sell a stock at a certain price at a certain time in the future. One put contract gives you the right to sell 1,000 shares of the underlying stock.

Basic options strategies

The real beauty of both call and put options kicks in because you can either buy or sell them to other investors. That gives you four distinct strategies, summarised in Table 15-1:

- **Buying a call:** When you buy a call, you have the right to force someone to sell you the stock at the exercise price you agreed on ahead of time. You make money on a call when the stock price rises above the exercise price. This strategy is for investors who are convinced a stock will rise and want to bet big. Buying a call isn't free. You must pay the seller for the option, in what's called the *premium*.

Nothing says you must exercise an option. But not exercising an option that's worth something would be foolish. So foolish, in fact, that most online brokers automatically exercise options that are worth something, or in the money.

✔ **Selling a call:** When you sell a call, you're on the other side of the option strategy of buying a call. You get paid the premium and pocket the money. And it gets better; if the stock falls, you keep that money free and clear. But, if the stock rises, you're in trouble because you've agreed to sell the stock for the lower price. If you don't already own the stock, you're what's called *naked*. That means you'll have to go out and buy the stock you've already sold, no matter the price. A seller *always* has to deliver.

You should never sell a call unless you know what you're doing. If you sell a call and don't own the underlying stock, that's called *writing a naked call*. If the stock rises, your losses are unlimited because in theory the stock could rise hundreds of points.

If a call sounds like something you'd like to trade, you can check two ASX (www.asx.com.au) resources to find out more:

- **Getting Started with Options class:** Visit the ASX website and click on Education & Resources in the left-hand navigation bar before clicking on Education. Then click on the link Browse the Full List of Online Classes before clicking on Options. You'll need to register to access the class but it's well worth it!

- **ASX Options Booklets:** The ASX also provides a number of booklets to help you familiarise yourself with options and strategies. They're designed for printing, so you can read them from the comfort of your favourite chair! Go to the homepage, click on Sitemap and select Detailed View. Then click on ASX Products and scroll down below Futures & Options. You'll find Options Booklets underneath the Equities heading.

✔ **Buying a put:** When you buy a put, you have the right to make someone buy a stock from you for a prearranged price. You're betting that the price of the underlying stock will fall. And, like buying a call, it lets you make a big gamble with little up-front money. It's another way to bet against a stock, similar to shorting a stock, as described in the section 'Cashing In When Stocks Fall: Selling Stock Short' earlier in this chapter.

✔ **Selling a put:** This strategy places you on the other side of the person who is buying the put. When you sell a put, you're usually betting the price of the underlying stock will rise. But you might also sell a put if you're willing to buy the stock at the current price but think it might go lower in the short term. That way, if the stock does fall, you must buy the stock at the higher exercise price but get to keep the premium.

Selling a put can be extremely risky. If the stock falls, you keep losing money until it hits $0. Don't sell a put unless you know exactly what you're doing.

Insurance to protect you from losing money investing online

You can buy insurance to cover you in case your house burns down or your car is stolen. But what about your online stock portfolio? Can you buy insurance to protect yourself from losing a catastrophic amount of money from investing online? Yes, you can but, instead of buying a policy from an insurance company, you can buy a put option.

Buying a put is normally a way to bet against a stock. But if you buy a put for a stock you already own, you have what's called a *protective put*. Say you own 100 shares of XYZ. The stock is trading for $30 a share, and you're worried about a market meltdown. You can buy a put that would give you the right to sell ABC for $30. Even if the stock crashes and falls to $15 a share, you can still sell it for $30. You've essentially bought catastrophe insurance. You can do this as long as there is a *counter party* out there who is prepared to sell you the option at the desired price. This isn't always the case.

Table 15-1	The Four Basic Option Strategies	
	Calls	*Puts*
Buy	A bet that the stock will go higher. If you're right, you can make a large profit with little investment.	A bet that the stock will fall. If you're right, you can make a large profit with little investment.
Sell (or write)	A bet that the stock will fall. It's very risky, because your loss is unlimited if you're wrong.	A bet that the stock will rise. It's risky, but your losses are limited because a stock can fall only as far as $0.

How to get options prices online

Most online brokers provide options prices, usually called *options chains* because they show data on options for many exercise prices and for different expiration dates. Another helpful place to get options chains is the ASX website (www.asx.com.au). Just click on Futures & Options underneath ASX Products in the left-hand navigation bar. If you're a client of optionsXpress, you can just visit its homepage (www.optionsxpress.com.au), click on the Quotes tab and choose Chains.

No matter where you look up options chains online, most providers will give you a chart with the same basic information, including:

- **Premiums (or prices) of both call and put options at all price levels:** The bid is how much you'll get for selling the option, and the ask is how much you'd pay to buy one.

- **Volume:** This shows you how many contracts are being bought and sold.

- **In the money and out of the money:** You can see which options are in the money and which are out of the money. Remember, a call option is *in the money* if the stock price is higher than the option's strike price. A call option is *out of the money* if the strike price is higher than the stock's price.

- **Open interest:** shows you how many contracts that haven't been exercised, expired or delivered. Open interest is a good indication of liquidity; the higher the open interest, the better chance you have of disposing of your contract.

- **Prices for different dates:** You can see how much options with different expiration dates are trading for.

- **The security code of the option:** Options have five-letter codes. The first three letters represent the stock. The next two letters represent the month the option expires and the series. Nearly all the options sites described in this chapter have a feature that will look up a code for you.

How to buy options online

Most of the mainstream online brokers allow you to buy and sell options. Some of the brokers are specialists with options and can help you calculate your gains and losses. Those specialty firms are listed in Chapter 3. You also need to pay a commission to buy or sell options, just as you pay to buy or sell stocks. The fees vary by broker. Table 15-2 lists a few examples.

Table 15-2	Some Online Brokers' Options Commissions
Broker	*Commission per Contract*
optionsXpress	$2.80 per contract, minimum $27.95 a trade
CommSec	0.35% of total, minimum $34.95 a trade
E*TRADE	0.55% of total, minimum $44.95 a trade
Westpac	0.35% of total, minimum $38.95 a trade

Entering an option order is very similar to placing a trade for a stock. You must follow these steps:

1. **Go to the option-trading section of the online broker's site.**

2. **Enter an order to buy or sell a call or put option.**

3. **Enter the number of contracts you want to trade.**

   One options contract controls 1,000 shares of the stock.

4. **Enter the option security code.**

5. **Select an order type, such as a limit or market order.**

   For more on limit and market orders, refer to Chapter 4.

Discovering more about options online

Options aren't complicated, but they can be a little bewildering to novices. You need to make absolutely certain you know what you're doing before trying to play with options. These online resources can help:

✔ **Your broker's website:** Most brokers have an education section, where options are explained in detail. Brokerages that specialise in options, like optionsXpress (www.optionsxpress.com.au), have very comprehensive tutorial information.

✔ **The ASX:** Three online classes in options trading are offered, two for those just starting out and another for those with a little more confidence. Register at www.asx.com.au and get clicking! Click on Education & Resources from the list at the left, select Education, click on the link to browse the full list of online classes and scroll down to Options.

Warrants: Turbo-charged options

Warrants are very similar to options in that they derive their value from an underlying security. One of the key differences between options and warrants is that warrants *can* have a longer lifespan, lasting for as little as three months or as long as 15 years. Whereas options are issued by the ASX, warrants are products issued by investment banks. Here are some of the most popular warrants you may come cross:

✔ **Trading warrants** are often called vanilla warrants and represent the right to buy or sell a share at a point in the future at a particular price. The difference between trading warrants and options is that, whereas an option contract accounts for 1,000 shares, warrants are more flexible. Warrants can remain open for up to 15 years, whereas most options are only open for up to 3 years.

✔ **Instalment warrants** are a type of lay-by for share investing. Investors pay a proportion of the shares' value up-front and the remainder at a fixed point in the future. These types of warrants were a popular way into the three Telstra floats, but with varying results for investors. The first payment also requires the investor to prepay interest on the outstanding sum. Investors are free to sell the warrant on the exchange at any time. The risk for investors is that, if the share price doesn't move or falls, then the value of the share will be less than what you paid. Fortunately, you're under no obligation to make the final payment.

✔ **Index warrants** are similar to trading warrants except that they give you the right to buy or sell a basket of shares based on either an index or a group of shares selected by the issuer. These include the S&P/ASX 200, the S&P Share Price Index, the Dow Jones Industrial Average, the NASDAQ Composite or the S&P 500. Because indices are measured in points rather than dollar amounts, the exercise price will be set as points. So an index warrant tracking the S&P/ASX 200 might have an exercise price of 6,000. Index warrants are settled by cash, rather than exchanged for the index itself.

✔ **Barrier warrants** (or knockout warrants) operate much like trading warrants except that, if the warrant rises or falls through a predetermined level, then the warrant terminates. Barrier warrants contain an additional element of risk.

Many variations of the humble warrant exist. Over the years, more and more warrants have emerged to cater to investors' different needs. Some promise high returns, whereas others are capital-guaranteed. However, the golden rule should always remain, don't invest in what you don't understand.

Discovering more about warrants online

And you thought options were complicated! Thankfully, the ASX has produced a number of resources designed to help investors wade through the wonderful world of warrants. For general information about warrants go to www.asx.com.au/warrants. For a more detailed tutorial on how to read warrant codes, visit the same address and then scroll down to the FAQ under How Warrants Work. Under the list in the right-hand navigation bar, click on Understanding Warrant Codes.

Chapter 16

Taking It Further: Technical Analysis

*1*f you can't help but stare at flashing stock quotes on your computer screen, this chapter is for you. This chapter is dedicated to traders who think asset allocation and diversification are for wimps and are confident they can beat the stock market by studying the movements of stock prices.

In this chapter, you find out about *technical analysis*, which is the method of selecting stocks by looking for patterns in stock charts. You also get a crash course in reading stock quotes and understanding what different technical indicators can tell you about a stock. We then show you different websites that can provide you with advanced charting information.

Understanding Technical Analysis

You can usually spot technical analysts by just looking at their desks. Rather than having annual reports and industry profiles strewn all over them, a technical analyst's desk is covered with printouts of stock charts. If you ask technical analysts what the companies they've invested in actually do, they likely won't know or care. To them, such fundamental details are meaningless because, generally, technical analysts believe

- ✔ **Everything you need to know about a stock is reflected in the stock's price.** In the minds of technical analysts, the buying and selling of stocks yanks the prices up and down in patterns that give clues about the future. There's no sense wasting time reading financial statements, these investors figure. Other investors with more experience have already read the reports and made the proper adjustments to the stock price.

- ✔ **Stocks follow predictable patterns.** Like astronomers who find patterns of stars in the sky and name them, technical analysts look for patterns in stock price movements. The analysts look at 'double-tops', 'head and shoulders' and other patterns. These chart patterns, if identified early enough, can tip investors off about future price movements. Technical analysts believe this gives them an edge to buy and sell stocks at the right times.

- ✔ **Trends in stock prices continue long enough to profit from.** Many technical analysts invest based on momentum. Momentum investors believe that short-term price movements tend to continue, and that you can make money by piling on. For example, momentum investors like to find and buy stocks that are soaring, hoping the momentum will keep going. Similarly, momentum investors will avoid or short stocks (refer to Chapter 15) that are falling, betting they'll only decline more.

When you're at a dinner party and don't want to stoke controversy, you probably know to avoid certain topics like religion and politics. Believe it or not, technical analysis is a similar lightning rod among investors.

The topic of technical analysis can turn usually cool-headed investment managers red in the face. Fans of technical analysis say everything you need to know about a stock is reflected in its stock chart. Technicians also believe human nature causes investors to follow patterns, which, when spotted early, can make them money.

Fundamental analysts, who study financial reports to determine whether a stock is undervalued or overvalued, vehemently disagree. Fundamental analysts believe stock prices aren't a good measure of a company's true or *intrinsic value*. Fundamental analysts think investors can be successful only by studying financial statements and determining how much a company and its stock is worth.

Passive investors, who believe markets correctly price stocks over time, think both technical and fundamental analyses are a waste of time. Passive investors figure it's practically impossible for investors to consistently beat the market over the long term. These investors buy passive index managed funds (refer to Chapter 8), hold them and let other investors lose money buying and selling stocks, usually at the wrong times. Passive investors not only save time and effort but also tend to do better than more aggressive investors; considerable evidence suggests that beating the market is really quite difficult.

If you're new to investing and are in it for the long haul, passive investing is likely your best bet. Technical analysis often requires subscribing to expensive websites or installing complicated software on your computer. That's a lot of hard work for questionable returns. Most investors will be better off buying index managed funds or exchange-traded funds (refer to Chapters 8 and 9), and profiting that way.

Getting Started with Technical Analysis

Just as a palm reader claims to glean insights by studying the lines in your hand, technical analysts can look at a stock quote and tell you *something* about a stock. In the following sections, we dissect a stock quote, available from nearly all online-investing websites, and show you the things that may stick out for a technical investor.

Dissecting an online stock quote

Basic financial news services can provide you with the bare bones of a stock quote for free. Long-term investors, for whom small fluctuations are irrelevant, find this form of quote more than satisfactory. Table 16-1 shows you the information you'll get from a basic quote.

Table 16-1   Picking Apart the Data You Get from a Basic Quote

Data Point	What It Means
Company code	The abbreviation or code used to designate the stock
Previous close	The price the stock closed at in the last trading session
+/–	Tells you the dollar amount the stock has moved up or down since the previous close
%	Tells you the percentage the stock has moved up or down
Last sale (delayed)	The price at which the last shares of the stock traded hands

When you're looking at online stock quotes, pay close attention to the time of the quote. Most free online stock websites provide *delayed quotes*, which are usually delayed by at least 20 minutes. The ASX charges news services for real-time information. If you need a real-time current quote, most online brokers provide them for free from their sites; if your broker doesn't provide them you may need to pay separately.

Traders interested in technical analysis are unlikely to be satisfied with this basic level of quote. They'll be keen to seek out an advanced quote that provides them with the kinds of information they need to profit from miniscule changes in a stock's valuation. Much of this information can be gleaned for free but, again, in order to access real-time information, you'll have to pay for it one way or another. Table 16-2 lists the type of data contained in an advance quote.

Investors looking to dig even deeper will be interested in viewing the market depth. *Market depth* lets you view a list of all the orders waiting on ITS for a particular stock. Market depth information is available for free with most of the premium online broking services.

Figure 16-1 shows you market depth for Woodside Petroleum (WPL). On the left-hand side is the list of *bids*, or buy orders. These are expressed as an aggregate, grouped together by the value of the offer. In this case, all the bids at $43.13 are shown collectively, with the best offer at the top. At the same time, all the *asks*, or sell orders, are on the right-hand side, displayed in the same way, with the cheapest offer at the top.

Table 16-2	The Type of Data Prepared in an Advanced Quote
Data Point	*What It Means*
Bid	The price a buyer will pay for a share of the stock
Ask	The price a seller will accept for a share of the stock
Volume	The number of shares that trade hands during the day
Average daily volume	The number of shares that trade hands between investors, on average, over a period of time (such as a quarter)
Today's high	The highest level the stock trades at during the day
Today's low	The lowest level the stock trades at during the day
52-week high	The highest the stock's price has been over the past year
52-week low	The lowest the stock's price has been over the past year
Market capitalisation	The total value of the company based on the current stock price
PE ratio	The price-to-earnings ratio — a way to determine whether a stock is cheap or expensive (refer to Chapter 11)

Share Quote as at 1:06 PM Sydney Time, Tuesday, 31 July 2007

▲ WOODSIDE PETROLEUM FPO ▲ CommSec Margin Lending LVR: 70%

Code	Bid	Offer	Last	Change'	Open	High	Low	Volume	News
WPL	43.130	43.140	43.140	+0.390	43.150	43.210	42.960	912,917	🖙

Buy | Sell | Add to Watchlist | Research | Chart | Print | Help

Market Depth

	BUY				SELL		
Number	Quantity	Price	#	Price	Quantity	Number
4	1,428	43.130	1	43.140	1,152	4
1	587	43.120	2	43.150	1,414	1
1	225	43.110	3	43.180	2,220	5
3	4,097	43.100	4	43.190	6,857	3
1	291	43.070	5	43.200	10,384	3
3	1,623	43.060	6	43.220	1,100	1
2	3,844	43.050	7	43.230	1,500	1
1	958	43.030	8	43.240	476	1
1	1,747	43.020	9	43.320	933	1
5	2,941	43.010	10	43.330	700	2

Figure 16-1: Market depth helps investors gauge the level of demand for a particular stock.

The difference between the top bid and ask prices is what is known as the *spread*. In a fast-moving market the spread will widen, indicating a discrepancy in what the market is prepared to pay and what the seller wants. When orders are expressed in this format, you see how big the market for a particular stock is at a particular price.

Investors who want to examine the market for a particular stock but don't have access to market depth are advised to look up the *course of sales*, shown in Figure 16-2. This is simply a list of all the transactions that took place on a particular day in a particular stock. Course of sales has the advantage of showing you just how many sales have taken place at a particular price (therefore giving you a better idea of the market value) but it's also displayed in real-time. Most premium brokers offer this as part of the package but course-of-sales data is available for free at www.tradingroom.com.au, although you'll need to register your name and email address to access it. Enter the company code into the search field and click Go. At the bottom of the left-hand navigation bar, click the Course of Sales tab for the data; if you haven't registered yet, you'll be prompted to at this stage.

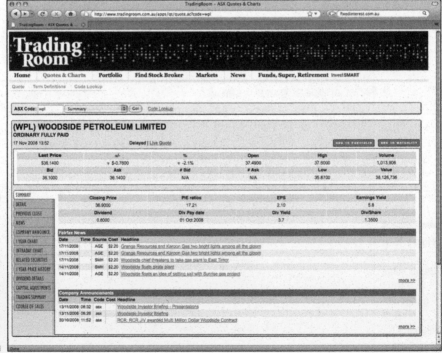

Figure 16-2: Course-of-sales data displays each on-market sale to investors as it happens.

Unless you're a serious daytrader trying to profit from small or split-second moves in stock prices, paying to get access to market depth probably isn't necessary.

How technical analysts interpret quote data and charts

The first thing technical analysts do when they're analysing a stock is bring up a stock chart. A *stock chart* is a graph that plots a stock's price on different days. Most financial websites provide charts, but some sites are more geared for technical investors, including Paritech (www.paritech.com.au). Paritech develops and distributes technical software packages but it also offers free charting tools. To access the charts, load up the homepage and then click on Support on the top navigation bar. Next, place your cursor over Corporate on the top navigation bar and select Web Based Products. Under the heading Paritech Charts Online, select the link for the basic html version.

Using Paritech's free service as a guide, we show you a few of the hundreds of indicators that technicians look for and how to interpret them. A stock chart allows analysts to quickly spot indicators that matter most to them. The following sections detail the most important indicators. Investors are frequently charting stock prices so, if you like the Paritech charting service, we suggest you bookmark it for easy access.

Price trends

Technical analysts pay close attention to stocks that are rapidly rising or falling because they think trends like these can continue. Moving averages are the tools commonly used to find stocks on the move. A *moving average* is calculated by adding up the stock's daily prices over a series of days and dividing by the total number of days.

The moving averages measure a stock's average price over a specific period of time. Generally, investors pay most attention to a stock's average price over a month (30-day moving average), three months (90-day moving average) or just over six months (200-day moving average).

To get a stock's moving average, go to Paritech's free charting service, as described in the introduction to this section. The page will display a default line chart of BHP's share price, but you can change it to any stock you like. A *line chart* is a simple chart of the stock's price. Enter the company code for the stock you're interested in to the search field with the black border, below the Help button. Below that are three pulldown menus; select Chart Type and change the type to OHLC Bar and then click the yellow Chart button. These types of charts are sometimes called OHLC and sometimes called bar charts; here they've used both names to avoid confusion. OHLC stands for open-high-low-close. *OHLC charts* are designed to show you a stock's range, which is where the stock started trading (the open price), how high it got, how low it got and where it closed. Figure 16-3 is a magnified view of the vertical bar used in the chart to help you understand how to read an OHLC chart.

And no, we haven't forgotten about the moving averages. That's next. Just below the Chart Type window is a section labelled Price Indicator Selector. Choose Simple Moving Average from the dropdown list. Below that are two fields. Enter 30 in the left window and 200 in the centred window before clicking the yellow Chart button. The line chart gets redrawn, this time including the 30-day average and the 200-day average.

Technical analysts generally evaluate moving averages in one of two ways:

- ✔ **Stock price is above the moving average: Good, or bullish, news.** Technical analysts think when a stock price is higher than its moving average, the stock has momentum in its favour.

- ✔ **Stock price is below the moving average: Bad, or bearish, news.** The stock is beginning to break down, and technical analysts would avoid the stock.

If you're looking for short-term trends in a stock, consider using the 30-day moving average. Longer term traders pay close attention to the 200-day moving average. Even if you're not a trader, the 200-day moving average is worth watching because sometimes it explains why a stock might act strangely at or around a certain price.

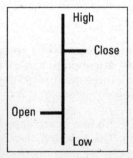

Figure 16-3:
A close-up view of an OHLC stock chart bar.

High

Close

Open

Low

Volume

Volume is the number of shares trading hands in a day. Technical analysts pay close attention to volume as an indication of how much conviction is behind stock price movements. It makes sense, right? Imagine you advertise your old golf clubs online for $200. If no-one calls, you know the price was too high. Conviction for the clubs at that price is low. But when you drop the price to $100, your phone rings off the hook. Conviction is now high.

Trading volume kind of works the same way. You can see how many investors are trading a stock when it rises or falls to find out how anxious investors are to sell or buy.

Using the same Paritech chart example from the previous section, check out the second chart — the one beneath the OHLC stock chart. You'll notice that it sports a bunch of vertical lines and is labelled Volume (millions). Those lines show you how much trading volume occurred on each day. The higher the line, the more volume there was.

Technical analysts generally compare a stock's volume with its average daily volume. Average daily volume is available on the main quote pages of most financial websites.

Table 16-3 gives you some general rules technical analysts use to interpret a stock's trading volume.

Table 16-3	How Chart Readers Interpret Trading Volume	
Stock Moves	*. . . And Trading Volume Is Lower than Average*	*. . . And Trading Volume Is Higher than Average*
Up	Move can't be trusted. There aren't many buyers supporting the rise.	The rally is for real. Indicates investors are eager to buy the stock.
Down	Sell-off may be temporary. Most investors are holding on as a few investors bail out.	A bad sign. Indicates investors are breaking the door down to get out of the stock.

Patterns

Technical analysts look for all sorts of patterns in stock charts. One pattern you may hear about is a *channel*, a low and high price that a stock tends to stick between. Think of an inner tube floating down a river. If it floats too far one way, it hits the riverbank and, if it goes too far the other, it bumps the other bank. Similarly, technical analysts believe stocks tend to float between a high and low point.

Technical analysts find stocks' channels by literally drawing a line that connects several high points and another line that connects several low points in the stock price. If the stock price breaks higher than the upper channel, that's considered bullish because it has busted through resistance to the upside. If the stock price breaks lower than the lower channel, that's considered bearish because the stock has fallen below the downside.

You can use the low and high prices to draw channel lines. When you have an OHLC chart on your screen, print the table by clicking on File from within your browser window and then selecting Print. Using a pen and a ruler, you can draw lines on the chart to help you find channels.

Finding out more about technical analysis online

Technical investors pay attention to hundreds of patterns, most of which have funny-sounding names. There are so many indicators, in fact, that covering them all could be the topic of a book itself. Fortunately, the following online resources describe the other indicators in detail if you're interested:

- ✔ **Investopedia** (www.investopedia.com): To access Investopedia's own Technical Analysis Chart School, click on Tutorials from the list at the left, scroll down to More Advanced Topics and select Technical Analysis. The tutorial offers 12 topics, including sample diagrams of different patterns at Topic 9.

- ✔ **Yahoo! Finance** (http://biz.yahoo.com): Yahoo! Finance offers video tutorials that cover both basic and advanced chart-reading techniques. Click the Investing tab at the top and select Education from the dropdown menu. Then, from the left-hand navigation bar, select Charts under the Investing 101 heading. Yahoo! Finance's charts are easy to use and let you examine long-term stock charts and easily compare stocks with competitors and indices.

✔ **StockCharts.com's ChartSchool (**http://stockcharts.com**):** Just click the Chart School tab at the top to explore this site. It covers basic technical analysis philosophy and uses examples to help you understand how to read charts.

✔ **InvestorGuide.com (**www.investorguide.com**):** Choose University from the list at the left, scroll down to Investing and click on More Articles. Now scroll down to Investing Strategies and select Technical Analysis. This article on the InvestorGuide site outlines the main techniques used by technical analysts.

Finding a Charting Service that Suits You

There's no shortage of websites that promise to help you read the message of the markets buried inside stock charts. If you're looking for another charting service that perhaps also includes editorial content or other features, try some of these sites to see what is the best match for your needs:

✔ **Yahoo!7 Finance (**http://au.finance.yahoo.com**):** Yahoo!7 Finance is one of the best sources of free information for investors (see Figure 16-4). It allows you to produce line or OHLC charts across a number of variables when you use its technical chart. It also offers a detailed financial summary, moving averages, volume data and too many other features to list here. In order to gain access to its full functionality, you'll need to register your details with the site.

✔ **ASX (**www.asx.com.au**):** The ASX is a fantastic free resource for any investor. In addition to the mounds of other information it provides, it's free charting feature is as good as any of the remaining free services listed here. As an added bonus for privacy-conscious investors, you can use the ASX's charting tools without registering or logging on. You are, however, limited to producing a basic six-month line chart with a 20-day moving average and volume data.

✔ **ninemsn Money (**www.ninemsn.com.au/money**):** This website is worth a look because it also contains a great deal of editorial content in addition to its charting features. It includes a popular column by small-cap mining specialist David Haselhurst called 'The Speculator'. In addition to the charting and editorial content, it also features a broad range of data on other financial services but, again, you'll need to register with the site to gain full access.

✔ **Netquote (**www.netquote.com.au**):** Like all financial software developers, Netquote exists to make a profit. But it also offers a basic level of access to its services for free. This includes access to its online portfolio manager, ASX announcements and a charting tool. The charting feature will generate 30-day, six-month, one-year, five-year and ten-year charts for you automatically, as well as moving averages and volume data.

Figure 16-4: Yahoo!7's Finance portal is among the best, with a raft of useful information sitting alongside a comprehensive charting tool.

Chapter 17

Getting In Early: Initial Public Offerings

Most investors are always looking for their pot of gold, and that's typically the elusive 'next CSL' or the 'next Google'. Investors aim to get in on the ground floor of a new company that's destined to grow exponentially and become one of the most valuable in the world.

That's why many individual investors are very interested in *initial public offerings*, or *IPOs*. In an IPO, companies sell pieces of themselves to public investors. Shares are first snapped up by large institutions and high-net-worth individuals at the offering price, which is the price a company's investment bank guesses the shares will sell at. This initial sale of stock is the only time the company itself makes money from the IPO. In 2007, Australian companies raised $10.4 billion selling shares through 260 IPOs, according to research performed by Deloitte Touche Tohmatsu.

Those initial investors who bought shares at the offer price, though, are free to do whatever they choose with their shares, including selling them to you. Large investors can sell their shares on the stock market, which is when most regular investors can buy them. When you buy IPO shares after they begin trading, it's called buying shares in the *aftermarket*.

Understanding IPOs

You may not believe this, but there are actually more IPOs in Australia each year than there are in the US. And, because the number of investors is smaller in Australia, that means more chances for Australian investors to get involved. As we explain in Chapter 5, the two main indices in the US have stringent rules about the size of a company that can list.

To list on the NYSE a company needs to be valued at more than US$100 million, and to list on the NASDAQ a company needs more than US$70 million. By comparison, to list on the ASX a company needs to be valued at only A$10 million. But, regardless of the size, the mechanics involved in becoming a *public company*, or one that is listed on the stock exchange, are the same.

When a company decides to go public, shares are usually offered to both institutions (like banks, managed funds and super funds) and retail investors like you. But first, in the early stages of an IPO, underwriters and company representatives may perform what is called a 'roadshow', which involves flying around from city to city doing presentations for the big institutions in order to drum up interest. When they have an indication of the level of interest and kind of prices the institutions are prepared to pay, the 'bookbuild' occurs.

The *bookbuild* is the process that sets the price. Institutions are given a price range (say $2.20 to $2.60) and asked to nominate how many shares they want for themselves and at what price. Or, if they don't like the offer, they won't apply at all. This is how the underwriter eventually sets the price for the retail offer. Shares obtained through the bookbuild are usually priced at a discount to the retail offer.

Getting access to an IPO

After the price of shares in an IPO has been set, individual investors have three entry points to the IPO:

- **Broker-sponsored bids** is the way that high-net-worth individuals (or as most people know them, millionaires) access shares in an IPO at the same price as the bookbuild. Investors approach a broking house directly with their request, and then the broker gathers all the requests of this type and presents them as a single bid, alongside his own, in the bookbuild.

✔ **The broker firm stage** is another possibility for wealthy investors. In the lead-up to the offer opening, brokers contact their best clients to ascertain whether they require an offer document (which contains offer details and an application form) and how many shares they want. The broker then commits to taking an amount of shares on behalf of their clients. When we mention a broker's 'best clients', we really mean it. When T2 (Telstra's second offering) was floated in 1999, the number of shares requested by broker firms exceeded the total value of the $16.6 billion float by $332 million. This request, of course, just couldn't be filled so brokers looked after their best customers first.

✔ **The retail offer** is what most investors have to settle for. So, if you don't have a relationship with a broker, like many people, don't despair. After the offer has been launched, there'll be a period of about two weeks in which you'll be able to register your interest in the float and apply for a prospectus. A prospectus is a requirement of all companies who plan to list on the exchange. The document is intended to provide investors with all the information they need about a company to make an informed choice. The prospectus also contains an application form, which is the only way to apply for shares in a float.

IPOs are generally pretty risky and regular investors who try to buy them are often disappointed. Making money from IPOs is still possible, though, and it's mostly about choosing the right one. According to studies by Deloitte Touche Tohmatsu, 52 per cent of IPOs in 2007 were trading above the issue price at the end of the year. So roughly half were trading at levels below the issue price. This included seven of the ten largest IPOs — which is important, because these are the offers that you're most likely to access. The average share price movement of the ten largest IPOs was −10 per cent. Table 17-1 shows how Australian IPOs performed in 2005, 2006 and 2007.

Table 17-1	IPOs Can Be Profitable, or Not		
	2005	*2006*	*2007*
Total number of IPOs	172	184	260
IPOs trading above the issue price at year end	109	141	135
IPOs above the issue price at year end	63%	77%	52%
Average price performance	30%	53%	30%
Median price performance	5%	18%	0%
S&P/ASX 200 stock market return	17.9%	18.7%	11.8%

Source: Deloitte Touche Tohmatsu 2007 IPO Activity Report.

Well, what's so good about IPOs then?

After looking at the numbers in Table 17-1 you'd be right to be at least a little hesitant about getting involved in IPOs. However, IPOs have their good points. To start with, no commission fees apply to an IPO. Your initial outlay for the investment is all you'll pay.

One group of people who love IPOs are called *stags*. These people are essentially speculators who buy into IPOs through the prospectus hoping to sell them on the first day for a tidy profit.

On the first day of trading, it's not unusual for IPOs to trade above the offer price. This is a simple function of demand as investors who missed out the first time around drive up the cost of the stock as they pile into the stock at their first opportunity.

Because of this, it's not unusual for IPOs to begin trading at 10 per cent above the offer price. So, if a stag can buy and sell, say, five such IPOs over 12 months, then they can potentially book a 50 per cent profit over the year.

Beware of the risks of IPOs

The idea of IPOs is alluring and irresistible to many investors. Companies that go public are often in industries of great interest to investors at the time. IPO companies also tend to sell products that have become household names to investors in a short period of time. These companies turn to IPOs as a way to raise cash to sustain their rapid growth. But, despite their allure, IPOs are highly speculative because they

- **Lack a stock-trading history.** It's impossible to see how the stock has behaved over the years because an IPO isn't trading yet.

- **Are usually young companies.** Smaller and fast-growing companies are often the ones that go public. These companies tend to have limited operating histories, immature management teams and only a few products or customers.

- **Sell their shares first to large institutional investors.** IPOs are usually first sold to large investors. When the stock begins trading, investors are free to bid those shares above or below that offering price. Much-anticipated IPOs often attract so much interest from the general public that the shares get driven to unreasonably high levels. Investors who buy in at the height of the mania are often disappointed with their returns.

How IPO hype can cost you

Platinum Asset Management's 2007 IPO was one of the most anticipated of the year. A high-profile fund-management business with a reputation for going against the flow, 20 per cent of the fund was floated for $560 million at $5 a share. Such is the reputation of managing director Kerr Nielsen that the float was over-subscribed by a factor of seven — that is, investors applied for almost $4 billion worth of shares. As a direct result, many investors who didn't receive an allocation sought to buy them in the aftermarket.

When the stock made its ASX debut on 27 May 2007, the first sale took place at $8.70 a share, or a gain of 74 per cent. An excellent result by anyone's standards. On 30 May, Nielsen sold approximately 3 million shares, pocketing roughly $25 million. Just a few months later, world equity markets began to weaken in response to the sub-prime crisis. One year to the day that Platinum was floated, its shares were trading for $4.03, or a 20 per cent discount to the offer price. Investors who jumped at the first chance to pick up Platinum in the aftermarket took a capital loss of 54 per cent.

Accessing Online Sources of Information about IPOs

Given just how risky investing in IPOs can be, knowing exactly what you're doing is that much more important. If you're going to dabble with IPOs — which you should do only if you're willing to take on large risk — you should check out a number of online resources, including the following:

✔ **The ASX** (www.asx.com.au) is an extremely helpful site for investors interested in IPOs. To find general information about IPOs, go to the homepage, select For Professionals & Companies from the list at the left and click on Listing Your Company. For an up-to-date list of upcoming floats, click on the link under Looking for a Listed Company? on the right-hand side.

Of course, you'll also find on the ASX site the prospectus of each and every company listing on the ASX by performing a search on the company code and looking under Announcements. If the company is about to list, then you'll find the prospectus here but, if the company listed some time ago, you may have to click on Search for Past Company Announcements to track it down.

The *prospectus* is the document that must be filed by a company going public. It outlines its business and the risks it faces, as well as details about its management and other information. The prospectus is the best and only source of information you'll get from the company.

✔ **Online newsletters** are pitched directly at retail investors so their coverage of IPOs is produced with your needs in mind. However, they won't cover every single IPO; most likely just the larger ones. As we cover in Chapter 13, a number of popular newsletters exist in Australia, such as Eureka Report (www.eurekareport.com.au), Intelligent Investor (www.intelligentinvestor.com.au) and Huntley's Your Money Weekly (www.huntleys.com.au). Most of these require a subscription but often you can take advantage of a free-trial period in the weeks leading up to the opening of an offer to read their views on a particular float.

✔ **The financial media** is another good source of information. Large floats, those worth billions of dollars, are big events in the finance world and create a great deal of coverage, although much of it is aimed squarely at finance professionals. Online publication Business Spectator (www.businessspectator.com.au) provides free news and analysis 24 hours a day, daily newspaper the *Australian Financial Review* is an excellent general source of financial news, particularly for the smaller IPOs, and stock-watching column 'Criterion', published in the *Australian*, is another good source of information.

Picking the Good IPOs from the Not So Good

The websites listed in the preceding section provide data and commentary about IPOs to help you find the ones with the best prospects. Even so, IPO investing is tricky. Pros look at many things when evaluating an IPO's potential, but a few things you should ask yourself include:

✔ **How stable is the company?** The company's prospectus shows you how much revenue and earnings the company has generated over the last couple of years. You should look to see whether the company is profitable and growing. In Chapter 10, we provide tips on how to analyse companies' financial statements and compare companies with their industry peers.

✔ **How expensive is the stock?** A company will constantly revise its prospectus as the IPO nears. One thing a company will disclose is the *expected price range* for the stock, which is how much it expects to sell the shares for. Take the time to evaluate the price and determine the company's valuation, using the techniques we describe in Chapter 10.

✔ **Does the management have a stake?** Scanning through the prospectus to see how the company's management is paid is a good idea. Some professional IPO investors prefer companies whose management team holds a large position of stock. That can be a sign that the top management still believes in the company's future.

✔ **What is the company planning to do with IPO cash?** The prospectus must state what the company is going to do with the money it raises from the IPO. The best answer here is if the money is being used to expand the business, rather than to pay off large investors who want to cash in their stakes.

Other Ways to Invest in IPOs

If you've read the warnings in this chapter and still think you're ready to dabble in the speculative world of IPOs, you need to now figure out how you're going to do it. If you choose not to go to a broker or take up the retail offer, several other ways to acquire stocks in a newly floated company are still available:

✔ **Managed funds:** Investing in IPOs through an actively managed fund provides several advantages. Most importantly, you'll invest in a variety of stocks, including IPOs, reducing your exposure to losses if any one newly public company runs into trouble. These funds also have analysts trained to study IPOs, which hopefully means they'll be able to sidestep the bad or especially risky IPOs.

✔ **Index funds:** As we cover in Chapter 8, index funds need to replicate an index, the entire index. So, when a new multi-billion-dollar float hits the market they'll be obliged to *re-weight* their portfolio to accommodate the new listing, which means they have to buy the stock. You won't get the same exposure to the stock that you would if you bought directly, but you'll get some.

✔ **Aftermarket:** Buying in the aftermarket shouldn't be ignored. In many cases, astute buyers wait for the hype to die down around an IPO and buy on the cheap. This was a particularly sound strategy for buyers of the second instalment of Telstra shares.

Chapter 18

Broadening Your Horizons: International Stocks

*T*hanks to the internet, it's just as easy to invest in a small company in the US as it is to buy shares of a giant Australian company like BHP or Telstra. Efficient trading systems plug you into global stock markets and let you pick and choose international stocks that can instantly broaden your portfolio.

The internet has cracked open global investment opportunities to online investors. The change is truly a breakthrough. International investments offer the ultimate in *diversification*, allowing you to spread your money around the globe and reduce your risk. By diversifying with foreign stocks, you can protect your portfolio in case a problem hits Australian markets. Although most markets are interconnected and big problems ripple through economies worldwide, most of the time international stocks tend to ebb when Australian stocks flow.

In this chapter, we show you the benefits and unique risks of international investing. You also find out the different ways to add international stocks to your portfolio. And we point you to online resources to find international managed funds and exchange-traded funds, which are very good ways to go global.

Knowing Why Investing in Foreign Stocks Is a Good Idea

Good old-fashioned domestic stocks are the cornerstone of a diversified portfolio. A mix of value-priced small- and large-company stocks, easily available by buying an index fund or exchange-traded fund (ETF), is a great place for beginning investors to start. But, as you refine your portfolio and look to make it really sing, it's time to start adding different international and emerging-market stocks to the mix.

What are international and emerging markets?

To make sure we're talking about the same thing, we want to define what we mean by international stocks. The emerging-market definition comes shortly after.

International stocks: Shares of companies based in nations in the developed world that have advanced economies. That includes nations such as the United States, United Kingdom, Japan, France, Germany, Korea, Spain, Italy, Sweden, Hong Kong and others.

International stocks are tracked using *international market indices*. Just as the S&P/ASX 200 index tracks large Australian stocks, international market indices track international stocks.

One of the most popular international market indices used by Australians to track growth is the Morgan Stanley Capital International (MSCI) World (ex-Australia) Index. This index tracks stocks of companies from all over the world, excluding Australia. One of the advantages of this is that it includes a sizeable exposure to industries like information technology, which is under-represented in Australia. It also rebalances the Australian bias towards finance and resource companies, providing access to companies like Toyota (automotive), Microsoft (IT) and Proctor & Gamble (consumer goods).

Okay, time for the emerging-markets definition.

Emerging markets: The up-and-coming nations that are rapidly expanding and experiencing robust economic growth. Generally, investors think of nations such as Brazil, Russia, India and China as examples of emerging markets. In fact, these four are also known as the *BRIC nations* for short. Others, like Mexico, South America and Taiwan, are also available, but the BRIC countries are the largest.

So, if Australian and international stocks have an index, guess what? So do emerging markets. One of the most popular indices of emerging-market stocks is the MSCI BRIC Index, which tracks stocks of companies hailing from Brazil, Russia, India and China. MSCI Barra's website (www.mscibarra.com) contains more information about its other emerging-market indices.

Advantages of investing overseas

Trust us, figuring out these new market indices and international stocks is worth the hassle. Adding a bit of foreign market exposure to your portfolio gives you two major advantages:

✔ **Turbo-charged growth:** If you're invested internationally and the economy sputters in Australia, you still have a chance to enjoy growth overseas. This is especially true with stocks in emerging markets. Developing nations like China and Brazil are so early in their development that they're growing much faster than a mature market like the United States.

Greater growth in emerging markets translates into the potential for greater returns. Emerging-market stocks can deliver huge returns over time. Over the period from 2004 to 2008 the S&P/ASX 200 produced an annualised return of just 10 per cent, compared with the annualised return of 38 per cent from the MSCI BRIC Index (we show you how to compare returns in Chapter 6). Table 18-1 shows the returns of both indicies for each of those years.

Don't let the rapid economic and recent stock price growth of emerging markets intoxicate you. Emerging-market stocks are very risky. Some academics consider emerging-market stocks to be some of the riskiest stocks you can buy. Putting all your money in emerging markets is a bad idea, just as putting your whole portfolio in Australian stocks isn't the optimum way of allocating your capital. Emerging markets can enjoy large returns, but they can swing wildly. Emerging-market stocks, for example, fell 31.8 per cent in 2000. Remember to keep your portfolio balanced and stick with your asset-allocation plan.

✔ **Diversification:** It might seem crazy to load up on stocks of companies you've never heard of, in countries you can barely find on a map. But the irony is that adding foreign stocks actually reduces your portfolio's risk.

Here's why: Foreign stocks don't move in lockstep with Australian stocks. Sometimes when Australian stocks are falling, foreign stocks don't fall as much, holding steady or even rising. You can find out how much foreign exposure is right for you by designing an asset allocation. You can read how to build the perfect asset allocation in Chapter 7.

Nearly all investors should have at least 10 per cent exposure to international and emerging-market stocks. Many investors should have even more. Use the online tools in Chapter 7 to find out what percentage is right for you.

Table 18-1	The Merits of Going International		
S&P/ASX 200 Returns		**MSCI BRIC Returns**	
2004–05	19.7%	2004–05	38.52%
2005–06	20.0%	2005–06	54.64%
2006–07	23.8%	2006–07	48.36%
2007–08	−16.9%	2007–08	16.49%

Source: Compiled from Bourse data and MSCI Barra.

Where to find out more about international investing online

By now, you're probably ready to sign up for this international stock thing. But wait a second. Before you go any further, we want to give you the downside of being fully diversified. Just as foreign stocks can beat US stocks, sometimes the opposite also can happen. Foreign stocks falling or lagging behind domestic stocks in some years isn't unusual.

During times when foreign stocks are under-performing, they can drag down your overall portfolio. This is especially hard to take in years in which the major Australian stock indices like the S&P/ASX 200 are doing well. During those times, though, you'll have to resist the temptation to dump your foreign stocks. That's why using online resources to fully understand international investing is the best bet. The following websites provide excellent global business and investing insights:

✔ **Yahoo!7 Finance** (http://au.finance.yahoo.com): Yes, Yahoo!7 Finance has its eye on what's happening overseas too. Just visit the homepage and click on ASX Indices under Investing on the left and then select the Major World Indices tab. This part of the site lets you closely monitor daily movements of most international stock markets.

You can check out daily closing values of major market indices around the globe, including the Americas, Asia–Pacific, Europe and Africa–Middle East. Just click on the region you're interested in. Figure 18-1 gives you an idea of what the screen looks like.

In this area of Yahoo!7 Finance, you can see the names of different countries' stock market indices and find out how much they rose or fell that day. To track long-term performances of these indices takes only a couple of clicks. Just click on the index's symbol in the list, such as ^GDAXI for the German DAX index. Next, click on the Historical Prices link on the left side of the page. The index's closing values going back for years pops up on your screen.

✔ **Historicalstatistics.org** (www.historicalstatistics.org): This site houses a massive directory of market and economic resources for international investors. Just click on the name of the country you're interested in on the left side of the page to call up a giant list of links to other websites with data and information about that country.

✔ **Economist Intelligence Unit** (www.eiu.com): A research firm affiliated with the *Economist* business magazine, the Economist Intelligence Unit provides data and information about the economies of more than 200 countries. You must pay for most of the content on the site, but you can get some free insights if you click on the Press Releases link on the left side of the screen. Here you can find summaries of international business studies the Economist Intelligence Unit has done.

✔ **International Monetary Fund** (www.imf.org): The IMF offers detailed economic data about countries and provides comprehensive global data and statistics.

✔ **World Bank** (www.worldbank.org): The World Bank provides in-depth information not only about countries' economies, but also their political and social environments. These are also important considerations for investors, as we discuss in the section 'Understanding the Unique Risks of Investing Internationally' at the end of this chapter.

✔ **Global Financial Data** (www.globalfinancialdata.com): An invaluable source if you're looking for very long term historical data for investments in any country you can imagine, but you must pay for most of the data.

✔ **Bloomberg (**www.bloomberg.com/news/worldwide**):** Bloomberg doesn't skimp when it comes to covering economic developments around the world. You can find numerous stories explaining how global market events can affect stock markets around the world, and Bloomberg's World Indexes section lists daily performances of the world's major indices. Click on Market Data in the top menu bar and select Stocks from the dropdown menu. Then click on World Indexes from the list on the left.

✔ **Economagic (**www.economagic.com**):** Economagic collects economic data on most major countries. Economagic is also a helpful site when you're looking for information about the US economy.

If you're relatively new to international markets, you may not be familiar with all the market indices that track foreign markets. Table 18-2 gives you an idea of some of the more popular foreign market indices.

Figure 18-1:
Yahoo!7
Finance lets
you quickly
scan foreign
markets
and see
how stocks
around the
globe are
doing.

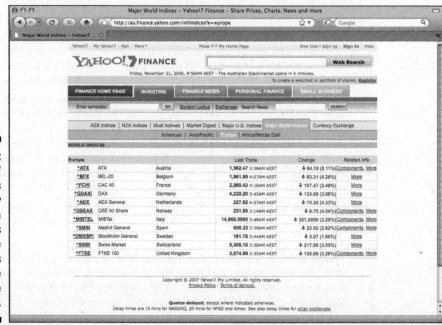

Table 18-2	Guide to Some Foreign Stock Markets
Foreign Market Index	*Tracks Stocks In*
Bovespa	Brazil
CAC 40	France
DAX	Germany
FTSE 100	United Kingdom
Hang Seng	Hong Kong
Madrid General	Spain
MerVal	Buenos Aires
Nikkei 225	Japan
Seoul Composite	Korea
Shanghai Composite	China
S&P/TSX Composite	Canada

Taking the Plunge: How to Trade Foreign Stocks

Are you ready to add a little international flair to your portfolio? Now's the time to get the trades done online. We step you through the following three main ways to buy foreign stocks:

✔ **Investing directly through the foreign exchange:** If you want, you can instruct your online broker to buy the foreign stock directly from the foreign exchange that particular stock trades on. This might seem like the most direct way to buy international stocks, but buying stock directly like this comes with serious headaches, including the need to convert your Aussie dollars into the local currency before the trade.

✔ **Buying an international managed fund:** You can buy shares of an actively managed fund. Active portfolio managers try to buy foreign stocks that they expect will out-perform those in a fund that simply tries to replicate an index. If you'd like to find out about how managed funds work, check out Chapter 8.

✔ **Buying an international index managed fund or exchange-traded fund (ETF):** ETFs are baskets of stocks that track a particular market index like the MSCI BRIC Index. Several ETFs that are available can track international and emerging markets. Refer to Chapters 8 and 9 to find out more about index managed funds and ETFs.

Going direct: Buying foreign stocks from an online broker

If you're interested in buying Japanese stocks directly from the Tokyo Stock Exchange or British stocks from the London Stock Exchange, some online brokers let you do so. Generally, you need to add what are called *global trading privileges* to your existing account. For example, CommSec lets you trade just about anywhere, including the US, Japan, Hong Kong, Indonesia, Singapore, Germany and Israel. Not all brokers will allow you to trade in international markets, but Table 18-3 shows a selection of those that will, and the prices they charge for buying US stocks.

Table 18-3	Buying International Shares Direct
Broker	*Commission*
CommSec	US$65 or 0.75%, whichever is greater
Interactive Brokers	0.5c a share
optionsXpress	$14.95 up to 1,000 shares 1.5c a share for 1,000-plus

Buying foreign stocks directly from the local exchanges isn't usually a good idea. You may need to convert your dollars into the local currency, a transaction that will cost you fees from the start. And you won't receive any franking credits. So make sure you factor these considerations into your assumptions.

Opting for an international managed fund

In many ways, managed funds were created for investing in things like international and emerging-market stocks. Buying a managed fund that owns international stocks lets you bypass many of the hassles in dealing with foreign currencies. You won't even have to worry about locating sometimes hard-to-find information about foreign companies.

You can buy an actively managed international managed fund and hope the portfolio manager is able to find the best foreign stocks. The other option is to invest in an international index fund that owns a basket of foreign stocks as directed by an international index such as the MSCI BRIC Index or the MSCI EM Europe, Middle East and Africa Index.

You can find international managed funds using the managed-fund screening tools discussed in depth in Chapter 8.

If you're looking for a low-cost index managed fund that will expose you to international stocks, you might consider Vanguard's Index International Shares Fund, which invests in around 1,700 shares across 22 economies and attempts to match the return of the MSCI World (ex-Australia) Index. With annual fees of just 0.9 per cent up to $50,000 and just 0.6 per cent above $50,000, it might offer the low-cost exposure to international stocks that you're looking for. Go to the homepage (www.vanguard.com.au) and click the Our Products tab. Select Investment Funds from the list at the left, scroll down to Sector Investor Index Funds and click on the link for International Shares Fund Profile. Click on Download Fact Sheet for more information, as shown in Figure 18-2.

VANGUARD INVESTOR FUNDS FACT SHEET - 31 OCTOBER 2008   **Vanguard** INVESTMENTS

International Shares

Fund Name:	Vanguard Index International Shares Fund *(Retail)*
Commencement:	26 October 1998
Investment Objective:	Seeks to match the total return of the MSCI World ex-Australia Index (with net dividends reinvested) on an unhedged basis before taking into account Fund fees and expenses.
Minimum Investment:	$5,000
Total Fund Size:	$140.2 Million
Management Costs:	0.90% pa - for that portion up to $50,000
	0.60% pa - for that portion from $50,001 to $100,000
	0.35% pa - for that portion over $100,000
APIR Code:	VAN0011AU
Buy/Sell Spread:	+0.30% reflected in Purchase price and -0.10% in Withdrawal price.

Performance*:

	Fund Return Before Fees and Expenses	Benchmark Return	Fund Return less Benchmark Return	Fund Return After Fees and Expenses
1 Month	-2.78%	-2.88%	+0.10%	-2.85%
3 Months	+1.17%	+0.90%	+0.27%	+0.94%
6 Months	-7.43%	-7.80%	+0.37%	-7.85%
9 Months	-9.04%	-9.55%	+0.51%	-9.66%
Calendar YTD	-17.25%	-17.76%	+0.51%	-17.88%
Financial YTD	+0.90%	+0.59%	+0.31%	+0.59%
1 Year	-17.06%	-17.66%	+0.60%	-17.81%
3 Years (pa)	-0.85%	-1.33%	+0.48%	-1.75%
5 Years (pa)	+3.57%	+3.11%	+0.46%	+2.65%
7 Years (pa)	-1.52%	-2.01%	+0.49%	-2.41%
Since Inception (pa)	+0.75%	+0.18%	+0.57%	-0.15%

* Fund returns assume the reinvestment of income distributions. Past performance is not an indicator of future performance.

Figure 18-2:
Vanguard's International Shares Fund offers exposure to some of the biggest companies in the world.

International funds often charge higher fees than most stock funds. Management-expense ratios of 1 per cent or more are fairly common with actively managed international funds. International index funds often charge between 0.5 and 1 per cent.

Going international with ETFs

Exchange-traded funds are extremely popular with investors who already have an account set up with an online broker. ETFs are like the baskets of stocks that you buy in a managed fund, just like you'd buy an individual stock. You can find out more about ETFs and how they can add instant diversification to your portfolio in Chapter 9.

ETFs really shine when it comes to international diversification. Many international managed funds have pricey expense ratios or strict restrictions. Even many of Vanguard's international managed funds require a $5,000 initial investment and charge fees if you sell the fund in less than two months.

ETFs are a great way to avoid these issues. You have many international and emerging-market ETFs to choose from, most with very low fees. And, if you choose an online broker with no minimum deposit and low commissions, as described in Chapter 3, you can start building an international portfolio with very little up-front cash.

All the ETF screening tools discussed in Chapter 9 can help you find the international ETF that's right for you.

If you're looking for diversified international ETFs, look for ETFs with names that include 'international' or 'emerging markets'. You can slice your international investment into finer pieces by investing in specific countries' companies, if that appeals to you.

Because you have so many choices, Table 18-4 shows you some of the largest international and emerging-market ETFs.

Table 18-4	Selected International and Emerging-Market ETFs	
ETF Name	*Symbol*	*Expense Ratio*
iShares MSCI Emerging Markets	IEM	0.74%
iShares MSCI BRIC Index Fund	IBK	0.75%
iShares MSCI Hong Kong	IHK	0.52%
iShares MSCI Japan	IJP	0.52%
iShares FTSE Xinhua China 25	IZZ	0.74%
iShares Singapore	ISG	0.51%
iShares S&P Global 100	IOO	0.40%
iShares S&P 500	IVV	0.09%
iShares Russell 2000	IRU	0.20%
iShares S&P Europe 350	IEU	0.60%

Source: Compiled from iShares data (http://au.ishares.com).

A-REITs with an international focus

Australia's A-REIT (Australian real estate investment trust) sector is acknowledged as one of the most innovative in the world. The name itself can be misleading, because today A-REITs account for around 12 per cent of the world's listed real estate.

One of the most attractive elements of A-REITs is the way they give you access to a notoriously difficult asset class — property — with the same kind of liquidity you can expect from shares. One of the more popular and well-run A-REITs is Westfield (WES). Westfield is not only the biggest in the sector, with a market cap of around $30 billion, it's a pioneer of the business model widely used around the world today.

But, importantly, Westfield is exposed to property around the world, with assets under management in the UK (16 per cent), the US (35 per cent) and New Zealand (5 per cent), giving it a truly international flavour.

A-REITs, like any other investment, come with their own set of risks. Most recently, extremely high levels of debt in the sector has seen some decimated by the credit crunch of 2007–08, as the sector slid into one of the biggest slumps seen in its history. But, by sticking to the fundamentals of good management, good assets and serviceable debt, you may be able to identify a real bargain.

Understanding the Unique Risks of Investing Internationally

By now, you can probably see why international investing is such a good idea. And, thanks to managed funds and ETFs, adding international exposure to your portfolio is as easy as buying an Australian stock. We want to impress upon you, though, that foreign investing comes with some unique risks. None of the risks are deal killers, but they're still important for you to be aware of, including the following:

- **Currency risk:** When you invest in foreign countries, you're taking on a hidden risk — exposure to rising and falling values of foreign money. When you invest in a company in a foreign country and the value of that country's currency rises, that makes your investment worth more. Why? When you sell the investment or get dividends, you receive money in the foreign currency. But you can't buy food or pay the rent with the foreign currency. You need to turn those dividends and payments back into Aussie dollars. To get dollars back, you must use the foreign currency to buy dollars. If that foreign currency rises in value compared with the dollar, you can buy more dollars, which boosts your return. Unfortunately, though, the opposite can happen, too. If the foreign currency declines in value, your returns take a hit when you buy dollars.

  OANDA.com (www.oanda.com) is a helpful online resource to find out more about currencies and exchange rates. Under the Currency Tools heading on the left side of the screen, you can find online calculators that convert one currency into another and compare the values of hundreds of currencies. You can also download long-term exchange rate data by using the FXHistory link.

- **Political risk:** An emerging nation may be a safe and stable place to invest, until a new regime is voted into power. Practically overnight, a nation can go from being a welcoming place for outside investors to being both hostile and destabilised. The risk of civil unrest and war can also greatly affect the value of your investment.

- **Regulatory risk:** Some foreign countries don't have the same level of regulatory and financial oversight over companies doing business in their borders that Australia does. Accounting rules, for example, may be more lax in some countries, which might increase the chances of fraud.

Part V
The Part of Tens

Glenn Lumsden

'… and that signals the end of today's trading.'

In this part ...

No *For Dummies* book would be complete without a Part of Tens. This part is the place for you to find some of the information readers look for most when they dabble with online investing. Here we address ways to avoid the most common mistakes made by online investors and also highlight techniques to protect your financial and personal information online. Security is critical for online investors, who are passing very sensitive data over the (very public) internet.

Chapter 19

Ten Top Mistakes Made by Online Investors

. . . .

In This Chapter

▶ Finding out about common mistakes online investors make

▶ Avoiding the mistakes that can eat into your returns

▶ Getting answers to questions before you make a mistake

▶ Understanding that it's okay to make a mistake once

. . . .

*W*hen people tell us they're afraid to start investing online, most of the time it's the fear of making a mistake that's holding them back. With its formulas, charts and jargon, investing online can seem scary and intimidating. For some investors, the thought of managing their money by themselves is overwhelming. The fear of making a mistake and losing hard-earned money is too much to bear.

Calming these fears is what this chapter is all about. Most of the mistakes investors make can be neatly placed into ten categories, each of which we explain in this chapter. By reading about the common mistakes other online investors make, you'll probably think twice before committing them yourself. We discuss the ten most common mistakes, explain why they're made and show you how to avoid them.

Buying and Selling Too Frequently

One of the greatest things about online investing is that it gives investors the power to buy and sell stocks whenever they want. Unfortunately, though, some investors turn this 24/7 access to their portfolios and stock trading into a liability.

Don't get us wrong; it's great that investors can check their portfolios whenever they want instead of calling a broker or waiting for a printed brokerage statement to arrive in the mail. It's just that constant access turns some investors into

- **Obsessive portfolio checkers.** These investors are constantly logging on to their online brokerage accounts and checking the value of their portfolios. And we mean constantly — often several times a day. This is a problem because it makes investors get overly concerned about the short-term swings in their stocks.

  If the market falls 1 per cent one day, these investors measure how much money they lost and start thinking about all the things they could have bought if they'd just sold the day before. Clearly, no-one can have the foresight to sell ahead of a 1 per cent downdraft, much less a 10 per cent correction. But these obsessive investors start to take every $1 move in their portfolio personally.

  Checking your portfolio's value online is fine, unless it starts to affect your judgement. If you find you're telling yourself you should have sold or bought because the market is up or down in a given day, you may be missing the point of investing.

- **Investors with itchy trigger-fingers.** These investors are so antsy that they can't help but trade. They buy and sell stocks in a flash because, well, because they can. Trigger-fingered investors also seem to get a rush out of trading online, much like someone may get when playing a poker machine.

  The trouble, though, is that these investors are hurting themselves more than helping. Not only will they end up paying more in taxes than they should if they do somehow manage to make a profit, but they're setting themselves up for losses as they dump stocks they can't remember why they bought in the first place. Without an asset-allocation plan in place, these investors are just haphazardly buying stocks and have no idea what their plan is. You can find out how to determine the perfect asset allocation for you in Chapter 7.

Letting Losers Run and Cutting Winners Short

Human nature, in some respects, is your worst enemy when investing online. Humans react in particular ways when faced with certain circumstances, but those reactions can work against you in investing. Two of those elements of human nature are defending bad decisions too long and cashing in on good decisions too early.

If you've ever been to the races, you've seen this before — just before the last race, gamblers who haven't won all day preparing a final plunge hoping to 'win it all back'. The same thing, sadly, happens with some investors. Investors who buy an individual stock that collapses often hang on to it, figuring that 'it will come back' because 'it's a good company'.

When you're buying individual stocks, cutting your losses is critical. Pick a percentage you're willing to risk and stick with it. You can use stop-loss orders or protective puts, both described in Chapter 4.

Other investors make the opposite mistake, by cashing in winning stocks too soon. Say your asset allocation tells you to put 20 per cent of your stocks in emerging markets, so you buy an emerging-market index fund. If emerging markets soar in the following few weeks, but your emerging-market index fund still accounts for 20 per cent or less of your portfolio, you should resist the temptation to sell it all to lock in your gains. Instead, you should stick with your asset allocation. To understand how asset allocations can boost your returns and cut your risk, refer to Chapter 7.

The rule of cutting losses short applies to individual stocks. If you don't think you'll have the courage to sell individual stocks when they sink, you should instead invest in an index fund or exchange-traded fund (ETF) that follows a broad stock market index, such as the S&P/ASX 200. These investments are already diversified and less risky than individual stocks, so you don't have to worry so much about a 40 per cent or greater decline.

Focusing on the Per-Share Price of the Stock

The fact that one stock is $2 a share and another is $500 a share tells you absolutely nothing about either stock. The $2-a-share stock may actually be more expensive than the $500-a-share stock because it either doesn't grow as rapidly, doesn't earn as much relative to its stock price or is riskier.

A stock's per-share price is meaningful only if you compare it with something else. Typically, investors multiply the stock price by the stock's number of shares outstanding to get the company's *market value*, or *market capitalisation*. A stock's market value tells you whether a stock is small, medium or large, and gives you a good idea of its valuation.

Don't be fooled into thinking it's better to own 1,000 shares of a $2 stock than owning 100 shares of a $20 stock. What really matters is the company's valuation and market value. Think of it this way: What's better, buying one reliable car for $8,000 or ten unreliable and broken-down $800 cars?

Failing to Track Risk and Return

For some reason, prudence vanishes when it comes to online investing. Many online investors, perhaps because it takes some effort and practice, don't take the time to see how much risk they're taking on to get the reward they're expecting from stocks they buy.

The biggest danger of investing without knowing your risk and return is that you risk not knowing whether you're doing more harm than good to your portfolio. You might be spending a great deal of time and effort buying individual stocks, thinking the effort is worthwhile, but it may turn out you'd be better off buying and holding index funds. Instead of burning hours looking at stock charts, you may be better off spending the time with your family, on hobbies or at work.

Chapter 6 shows you the techniques of measuring your portfolio. You can find out how to calculate the returns and risks yourself or check out websites that will do it for you.

Taking Advice from the Wrong People

Not getting stock tips is almost impossible. Turn on the TV. Talk to people sitting next to you on a plane. Chat with other browsers in the financial section of the bookstore. Connect with other investors online. You'll constantly encounter people who are convinced such-and-such a stock is going to take off and that you need to buy in now. Some of our readers have told us they've bought shares of retailers because employees told them to.

Here's our advice: Unless Warren Buffett is the guy sitting next to you on the plane, you're better off politely nodding and wiping your memory clean of all the investing advice you get. Stick with your asset-allocation plan.

Trying to Make Too Much Money Too Quickly

The reason you invest is to make money. But, as an investor, you need to appreciate that wealth is built over time as companies you've invested in expand their revenue and earnings. Generally speaking, stocks return about 10 per cent a year. You can boost that 10 per cent a bit to 13 per cent or so with smart asset allocation and exposure to riskier types of stocks like emerging markets and small companies.

Some investors, though, just aren't satisfied with that. They chase after brand-new IPOs, pile into stocks that have been the market's leaders and load up on penny stocks. These investors are typically the ones who get sucked into 'get-rich-quick' emails, stock conferences and other dubious stock-promotion schemes that make only their promoters rich.

Sometimes things work out okay for these speculators, and they may buy shares of the right stock at the right time. But, more often than not, these speculators suffer as the stocks whip around more than they expected. The volatility proves too much to bear, and the speculators buy and sell stocks at the wrong times. Before they know it, speculators are down 30 per cent or more.

If you limit your investment to a small amount, there's no harm. But, for the bulk of your portfolio, you'll find much better success over the long term if you read Chapters 6 and 7 to find out how to track your risk and return.

Letting Emotions Take Over

It's happened to you before: You've fallen in love. No, we're not talking about your spouse or significant other. We're talking about your favourite stock. Everyone has had one. The stock you fall in love with is the one that you happened to buy at just the right time and have never lost money on. It may be the one that soars and always shows up on the 'Top Performers' lists printed by magazines and websites. It's easy to be proud of a stock, just like parents who see their kid's name in the paper for their sporting prowess.

Sometimes the opposite happens too. Say your asset allocation calls for you to own large-company stocks, you invest in them and they do nothing. There you are, you own shares of big companies and watch your portfolio go sideways while your friends brag about the tiny upstarts and penny stocks they make a fortune on.

Periods of self-doubt and second-guessing account for many investors' worst decisions. These investors may be so blinded by their enduring affection for a stock they that proudly ride it down lower and lower. It's funny, but the love for the stock wears pretty thin by the time the stock is down 50 per cent or more. What's the answer to this? Unless you're a robot or computer, you're stuck with your emotions. But you can stop these emotions from meddling with your portfolio by sticking with your asset-allocation plan. Yes, we know this asset-allocation stuff is getting repetitive but, trust us, it will protect you from yourself.

Emotions can burn you badly with investments that just keep going down. It's easy to get so fed up with certain stocks that you can't bear to keep buying more. You curse your asset allocation for ruining your portfolio. You might get so disgusted with stocks that you start to enquire about term deposits from the bank.

If you let your greed for huge returns and fear of losses run your investment decisions, you can practically guarantee you'll buy and sell at the wrong time.

If you find that you're an emotional investor and take the market's movements too close to heart, you're probably a good candidate to invest in passive index managed funds and exchange-traded funds. You can just buy these investments and let them ride, removing the temptation to tinker with your portfolio and almost guaranteeing you better results.

Looking to Blame Someone Else for Your Losses

No-one likes to lose money on stocks. And everyone loses money on stocks from time to time. It's how you react to the losses that makes the difference. Some investors go on a witch hunt and start trying to track down anyone who may have mentioned a stock as a good buy, ranging from publications, websites, friends, financial advisers or even company executives.

Certainly, cases of fraud, in the mould of Enron and HIH, exist. These cases are regrettable because even investors who attempted to do their homework by studying the company's financials were misled. But, if you just lost money because you bought a stock at the wrong time or overestimated the company's profit potential, you can only look to yourself. It's best to analyse what you did right and what you did wrong, and learn from it, as opposed to playing an unproductive blame game.

Ignoring Tax Considerations

Come tax time, it's amazing the lengths taxpayers go to cut their tax bill by just a few bucks. Some go as far as to get married or have a child to pay less tax. But many of these same investors ignore or aren't aware of ways of investing that will save them thousands on taxes.

The tax man offers extremely generous tax breaks for investors, if you just know how to take advantage of them. Tax breaks investors should never pass up on include:

- ✔ **Lower tax rates for long-term capital gains:** If you wait more than a year before selling winning stocks, you'll be much further ahead than investors who trade with no regard to taxes. By holding on to stocks for longer than a year, you usually qualify for long-term capital gains tax, which is usually half what you'll pay if you sell stocks in a year or less.

- ✔ **Major tax breaks on superannuation:** With only 15 per cent tax payable on superannuation investments you'd have to be crazy to ignore the huge opportunity this presents you with. By using the power of compounding returns, making additional contributions to your super via salary sacrifice is one of the best things you could ever do.

Dwelling on Mistakes Too Long

It might sound funny to tell you to not think about investing mistakes in a chapter dedicated to mistakes, but it's important to not let a mistake in the past stop you from making progress in the future. So, you bought a stock and rode it down too long before selling it. Don't linger on the mistake. Just don't do it again and, over time, you'll obtain the success in investing you're shooting for.

Chapter 20

Ten Ways to Protect Your Investments and Identity Online

In This Chapter

▶ Finding out about common ways investors are conned online

▶ Reducing your chance of being defrauded

▶ Using the internet securely to research investments and brokers

▶ Determining where you can complain if you've been defrauded

*P*romising a big return to investors is kind of like waving red meat in front of a salivating tiger. Even educated investors can't help but bite when offered what seems to be a plausible chance at winning big-time returns. Investors' innate craving for that big score makes them easy targets for less-than-honest financial snake oil salesmen.

We're always amazed at how people who are usually so careful about their money in everyday life can let their guard down then it comes to investing. The same people who shop at ALDI to save a few bucks may readily hand over their life's savings to a stranger with dubious qualifications selling questionable investments.

It's up to you to do your homework when checking into any investments. Online tools make it easier than ever to sniff out unscrupulous people hawking investment products. Unfortunately, though, the internet is also a boon for the bad guys. Email lets fraudsters reach millions of users with the click of a button. Fraudsters can also glean basic information about you online, perhaps from your Facebook profile, and craft a pitch that seems more realistic and personable. Keeping these things in mind, this chapter points out some of the main types of investment frauds, and shows you how to dodge them.

Beware of Pyramid Schemes

When it comes to investment frauds, *pyramid schemes* are among the greatest hits. Organisers behind pyramid schemes try to convince investors to contribute money and tempt them with promises of a giant payout. That sounds like playing the lottery, we know. But what makes pyramid schemes so insidious is that they're based on a sham that eventually collapses.

Generally, pyramid schemes work like this: Six fraudsters send out emails to as many people as they can, each hoping to get six additional 'investors'. These initial promoters convince investors to sign up by telling them that, if they contribute money, they'll get a 100 per cent or greater return in just 90 days. If the six initial promoters are successful in lining up other participants, they pocket the money from the new investors. But that's just the tip of the pyramid, so to speak. The 36 just-recruited investors are then instructed to get six more investors each, which brings the total number of investors in the scheme to 216. The scheme then continues and, each time more investors are brought in, the previous investors get their payout.

There's just one big problem: The pyramid collapses under its own weight. After 13 rounds of this pyramid scheme, for example, more than 13 billion people are required to keep it going. That's impossible because it exceeds the world's population. So, unless you think you can find six suckers on Mars or Jupiter to buy your stake of a pyramid scheme, you could end up losing your investment. For more information on pyramid schemes, visit ASIC's consumer affairs website at www.fido.gov.au and, from the Scams & Warnings dropdown menu, select Typical Scams and click on Pyramid Schemes.

A close relative of the pyramid scheme is the airplane scheme. The pitch involves filling a 'virtual plane' with 15 passengers, with the 'seats' ranging from economy class to the pilot's seat. Tickets are upwards of $100 each and, by recruiting more players, the first member achieves pilot status. Don't be fooled; this is just another version of the pyramid scheme. The airplane scheme is one flight you should try to miss!

Steer Clear of Ponzi Schemes

Ponzi schemes are some of the oldest frauds in the book. *Ponzi schemes* are a type of pyramid scheme with one key difference: All the money the 'investors' contribute goes to one person — the organiser of the fraud.

Ponzi schemes are pretty simple. The organiser sends out emails offering investors fabulous returns in a very short period. After the initial investors eagerly sign up, the Ponzi promoter takes a cut and then seeks a second round of investors. When the money comes in from the second round of investors, the Ponzi operator takes another cut but also returns a slice of the money to the first round of investors. Clearly, the first investors are ecstatic and eager to tell others about their great investment. Those testimonials play right into the Ponzi operator's hand, who keeps repeating the process until it falls apart.

Avoid Tout Sheets and Know Who You're Taking Advice From

There's no shortage of investment and stock-picking newsletters that claim to have the inside track on the stocks you need to buy now. But some of these newsletters, known in the trade as *tout sheets*, have nefarious intentions. Tout sheets are investment newsletters distributed for the sole purpose of hyping stocks with exaggerated or false information to stir up investors' interest. Tout sheets have proliferated due to the internet, which makes distributing and promoting such things a cinch. (You can read more about investment newsletters in general in Chapters 5 and 13.)

Above all, you need to be perfectly sure an online newsletter is above board. Whenever considering subscribing to a newsletter or following its suggestions, you want to be 100 per cent clear on whether the newsletter writer is paid by the companies to be a tout. *Touts* are hired by companies or shady brokerage firms to stoke interest in stocks by putting out glowing reports on the company based on exaggeration or lies. If the tout is successful in attracting investors and driving up the stock price, the company's executives and brokerage firm can then sell and pocket the quick profit.

For more advice about newsletters, visit ASIC's consumer affairs website at www.fido.gov.au. From the About Financial Products dropdown menu, select Shares and click on Buying and Selling Shares. Then, under Ways to Buy and Sell Shares, click on Share Investment Newsletters. This resource contains a number of other tips that can be useful for evaluating a newsletter's worth and a link to a database where you can check its financial licence.

Don't Fall for Investment Spam Emails

Open your email and you're likely to find all sorts of offers. You'll see emails for prescription drugs, ways to satisfy your partner and hot tips on stocks about to take off.

Generally speaking, *spam*, or *unsolicited bulk emails (UBEs)*, are all very similar. The emails masquerade as being legitimate reports from stock research firms or investors in the know purporting to be passing along their tips out of generosity. The messages will talk about some major development that will move the stock by a huge amount in a short time. And the emails generally pitch penny dreadfuls.

If you get such spam, don't even read it. Trash that rotten spam immediately. They're almost always *pump-and-dump* schemes. They work like this: The fraudsters first pick a few lightly traded stocks and buy them up. After the promotional email goes out, the fraudsters wait for gullible investors to buy shares and drive the stock price up. That's the *pump* part of pump and dump. Next, these investors sell their shares. That's the *dump*.

Don't think for a moment you can profit from these spam emails. Spam Stock Tracker (www.spamstocktracker.com) has tracked how investors would have done if they'd bought the stocks recommended through spam emails. The study found in just a year and a half, investors who bought the stocks suggested in the spams would have lost more than 90 per cent of their money.

Don't fall for the emails from supposed Nigerian nationals hoping to transfer cash to Australia, either. They're scams called *advance fee frauds*, or *4-1-9 frauds*, after that section of the Nigerian penal code. Don't participate in these.

Protect Your Identity

Communicating online can be fun. It's easy to find other people out there with similar interests and ideas, thanks to the wonder of social networking. But it pays to be careful too. Identity theft is a growing problem in Australia and around the world.

We show you how to keep your computer secure in Chapter 2 and, in Chapter 5, we run through some simple methods available to reduce the risk of identity theft when using social-networking websites. Here are some other valuable online resources for anyone who communicates or transacts online:

- ✔ **Stay Smart Online** (www.staysmartonline.gov.au) is a government initiative that contains great basic information about how to secure your computer and take precautions when you make transactions online. It also contains a glossary of terms and a collection of useful links.

- ✔ **Protect Your Financial Identity** (www.protectfinancialid.org.au) is all about protecting yourself from identify theft and was produced in conjunction with the Australian Bankers' Association. It provides a selection of great factsheets that cover every topic from what to do if you suspect your identity has been stolen to checking your credit file. A great resource worth bookmarking.

- ✔ **NetAlert** (www.netalert.gov.au) is another site produced by the Australian government, but this one is aimed at providing families with advice for safe web surfing. Importantly, it also contains great advice on the privacy issues surrounding blogs and social-networking sites.

Familiarise Yourself with the Fingerprints of a Scam

There are only so many ways to rob a bank. Face it, most of the scams that fraudsters use online and off generally fall into just a few categories, most of which are variants of pyramid or Ponzi schemes. There are twists, such as *affinity frauds*, where the scammers infiltrate a group of investors of a similar age, race or hobby, gain the trust of the group and then use the group members to promote the scheme to each other.

Still, a few common traits should set off alarm bells in your head:

- ✔ **Promises of guaranteed returns that seem abnormally large:** By reading Chapter 1, you know that stocks have returned roughly 12 per cent average annual returns. If someone tells you he can get you a return of greater than 12 per cent a year, you know the investment is riskier than stocks. So, if the promoter says the returns are guaranteed or risk-free, you know something isn't right.

✔ **Pressure to act right now:** Perpetrators of frauds know they have to get your chequebook open now, or you may get cold feet and start thinking about the risks. If you're told you have to invest now or you'll miss out, you're better off missing out on the 'opportunity'.

✔ **No documentation on paper:** Bad guys hate paper trails and try their best to avoid documenting anything. If you can't print out the information about an investment, you shouldn't invest in it. Proper investment proposals should be registered with regulators and come with a prospectus, an annual report and other financial statements.

Learn to Be an Online Sleuth

Scammers often reinvent themselves and try different scams until they get caught. If you're being pitched an investment or seminar, try to find out whether the person or company has been in trouble before. Get as much information as you can about the person and try this list of suggestions:

✔ **Google** (www.google.com.au) has got to be one of the best inventions ever, don't you think? Running the names of people and companies through Google and Google News is a great way to find more information about a company.

✔ **Not Good Enough** (www.notgoodenough.org) is a consumer rights website where consumers vent about being wronged, and it contains a small amount of content about financial products too. Another good site to bookmark.

✔ **ASIC's Banned & Disqualified Persons** (www.search.asic.gov.au/ban.html) contains a searchable database of individuals ASIC has banned and disqualified from running companies or giving financial advice. If you smell something fishy, then here is a good place to start checking.

✔ **ASIC's National Names Index** (www.search.asic.gov.au/gns001.html) contains a searchable database of all the registered company names in Australia, as well as those that have been deregistered for impropriety. A must-visit destination for any budding online sleuth.

Know How to Complain If You Suspect a Fraud

Being taken in by a fraud may be embarrassing. But, if you feel that you've been had, letting regulators know right away is critical. The sooner you can tip off the authorities, the greater the chance the fraudster can be nailed and the better the chance of recovering money.

Once again, ASIC's consumer affairs website, FIDO, is the best place to make yourself heard. Visit www.fido.gov.au and, from the Scams & Warnings dropdown menu, select Reporting a Scam for phone numbers, email addresses and forms.

Make Sure Your Computer Is Locked Down

You should always be concerned with computer security. Make sure you have the proper software and other safeguards installed to protect your computer from viruses and hackers. You have many options, including some offered by the online brokers themselves. When you're online using a public wireless network service, such as those in Starbucks coffeehouses, you should be especially careful. You can read more about ways to lock down your computer in Chapter 2.

But online criminals also use other low-tech methods to dupe investors. The most common trick used is *phishing*, pronounced 'fishing'. In phishing scams, the fraudster sends out millions of emails purporting to be from a bank (say Westpac), a store (like Harvey Norman), a government agency (perhaps the ATO) or an online service (like PayPal or eBay). These emails are carefully crafted to appear official and generally ask the recipients to click a link to confirm or update personal information.

Here are a couple ways to protect yourself from these scams:

✔ **Log in routinely:** Log in directly to your bank, online broker, PayPal and other important accounts and routinely check the messages section. Generally, when these companies want to reach you, they leave a message for you on the site.

✔ **Never click links in emails:** If you get an email claiming to be from your online brokerage, assume it's a fraud. Don't click the link in the email that claims to direct you to the website. Instead, manually enter the site's address into your browser or click the favourite or bookmark that you set up for the site.

✔ **Hover your pointer over the link:** If you want to know whether the email is phishing for information, put your cursor over the link in the email. Do *not* click the link, but look in the lower-left corner of the screen. You see the address the link wants to take you to. If it's not the complete address of the site it purports to be, you know instantly it's a fraud.

Be Aware of Online Sources for More Information

Scams are constantly evolving. It's up to you to be constantly vigilant and be aware the internet is a perfect environment for people trying to fool you and take your money. That doesn't mean you should unplug your computer and give up on online investing. It's just that being aware of the potential risks is up to you.

Internet sources can help online investors understand how to protect themselves, including:

✔ **SCAMwatch** (www.scamwatch.gov.au) explains common examples of online and offline fraud and explains why they work. It also contains some great tips on making yourself 'scamproof'. If you've ever been scammed before, you'll want to visit this site, if just to make sure that it never happens again.

✔ **The Australian Competition and Consumer Commission** (www.accc. gov.au) is the body that promotes fair trade in Australia, which means that when companies engage in misleading conduct the ACCC pulls them up on it. Here you'll find rulings on everything from blue-chip companies to dodgy property developers. A comprehensive source of information that is constantly updated.

✔ **Consumer affairs departments** are part of each state government. To find the online presence of the consumer affairs agency in your state or territory, use a search engine such as Google and just enter the name of your state or territory followed by the words **consumer affairs** and you should have it. State-based bureaus like these are useful because, often, frauds like affinity scams are localised. These bodies can be very effective at informing and warning community members when they strike.

As part of the first generation of investors who can completely control their finances with the aid of a computer and internet connection, most of all you'll need to remember not to be too hard on yourself. Throughout your investing lifetime you can expect to have wins and losses, but, if you realise that you'll learn much more from your losses than you ever will from your wins, the losses may become a bit easier to take. Investing is a lot like sports or studying, in the sense that the more preparation you do, the luckier you get. Only, you now know it's not just luck, but don't tell anyone just yet.

Index

• D •

• E •

FOR DUMMIES®

Business & Investment

Small Business FOR DUMMIES

1-74031-109-4
$39.95

Business Plans FOR DUMMIES

1-74031-124-8
$39.95

Investing for Australians ALL-IN-ONE FOR DUMMIES

0-7314-0838-1
$54.95

Superannuation FOR DUMMIES

0-7314-0715-6
$39.95

Buying & Selling Your Home FOR DUMMIES

1-74031-166-3
$39.95

Investing in Real Estate FOR DUMMIES

0-7314-0724-5
$39.95

Share Investing FOR DUMMIES

1-74031-146-9
$39.95

Charting FOR DUMMIES

0-7314-0710-5
$39.95

Leadership FOR DUMMIES

0-7314-0787-3
$39.95

Freelancing for Australians FOR DUMMIES

0-7314-0762-8
$39.95

Australian Resumes FOR DUMMIES

1-74031-091-8
$39.95

Sorting Out Your Finances FOR DUMMIES

0-7314-0746-6
$29.95

FOR DUMMIES®

Reference

Work / Life Balance
0-7314-0723-7
$34.95

World Poverty
0-7314-0699-0
$34.95

Sustainable Living
1-74031-157-4
$39.95

Wedding Planning
0-7314-0721-0
$34.95

Gardening
1-74031-007-1
$39.95

Australia's Dangerous Creatures
0-7314-0722-9
$29.95

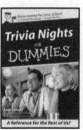

Trivia Nights
0-7314-0594-3
$24.95

English Grammar
0-7314-0752-0
$34.95

Technology

The Internet
0-7314-0985-X
$39.95

QuickBooks QB
0-7314-0761-X
$39.95

MYOB Software
0-7314-0941-8
$39.95

eBay
1-74031-159-0
$39.95

FOR DUMMIES®

Health & Fitness

Breast Cancer FOR DUMMIES

A Reference for the Rest of Us!

1-74031-143-4
$39.95

Menopause FOR DUMMIES

A Reference for the Rest of Us!

1-74031-140-X
$39.95

Food & Nutrition FOR DUMMIES

A Reference for the Rest of Us!

0-7314-0596-X
$34.95

Diabetes FOR DUMMIES

A Reference for the Rest of Us!

1-74031-094-2
$39.95

Fitness FOR DUMMIES

A Reference for the Rest of Us!

1-74031-009-8
$39.95

Weight Training FOR DUMMIES

A Reference for the Rest of Us!

1-74031-044-6
$39.95

Yoga FOR DUMMIES

A Reference for the Rest of Us!

1-74031-059-4
$39.95

Pilates FOR DUMMIES

A Reference for the Rest of Us!

1-74031-074-8
$39.95

Golf FOR DUMMIES

A Reference for the Rest of Us!

1-74031-011-X
$39.95

Cricket FOR DUMMIES

A Reference for the Rest of Us!

1-74031-173-6
$39.95

Aussie Rules FOR DUMMIES

A Reference for the Rest of Us!

0-7314-0595-1
$34.95

Sailing FOR DUMMIES

A Reference for the Rest of Us!

0-7314-0644-3
$39.95

Printed in Australia
14 Jul 2021
766613